Enterprise Solution Patterns Using Microsoft .NET

Version 2.0

patterns & practices

David Trowbridge, Microsoft Prescriptive Architecture Guidance

Dave Mancini, Microsoft Core Infrastructure Solutions

Dave Quick, Microsoft Core Infrastructure Solutions

Gregor Hohpe, ThoughtWorks, Inc.

James Newkirk, ThoughtWorks, Inc.

David Lavigne, SBI and Company

Contents

Chapter 4

Deployment Patterns 147

Chapter 6

Services Patterns   265

Foreword

This is a collection of patterns that will help you use Microsoft .NET, which contains many objects that follow patterns we've found useful. These objects are brought to life by the common language runtime which makes for strongly-patterned objects. An easy way to think about this is that the runtime takes care of so many aspects of an object that just the pattern parts are left. Patterns were important before the common language runtime, but now they are even more important.

You will find here a collection of patterns that you will see in most every transaction-processing Web application. These sorts of applications are really important to enterprise developers who are important to this book's authors. This is an important focus in the here and now. Of all the pattern books that could have been written about .NET, this is the most likely to be important to you today. Thank you, authors.

I could go on about Web applications but I wanted to point out an even more interesting thing about this collection. Whenever we pull patterns together our choices say something important about how we work. Our philosophy of work runs through our selections. For example, in the *Design Patterns* book, [Gamma, et. al, Addison-Wesley], the philosophy was to make programs flexible. This is important, of course, and some of those patterns are included here. But there are two other philosophies present in this volume worth mentioning.

One philosophy is that in a continuously evolving environment like the enterprise, every complexity has a cost. You'll find a variety of patterns here that at first seem contradictory. That's because the authors know that successful enterprise applications start simple and grow over time. Something simple works for a while then it needs to be replaced. You'll find patterns here for both the simple and its replacement. This isn't the same as doing it wrong and then making it right. Both patterns are right, just not at the same time on a given project.

Another philosophy that runs through these patterns is that different people in the enterprise use different patterns for different purposes. Some patterns are more about the user experience than anything else. We can say that these patterns, and the people that apply them, are working in service of the user. The more these folks understand their users, the better they will be able to apply these patterns and the better their programs will be for their effort. Contrast this to classic concerns of the enterprise: efficiency, security, reliability, and so on. This collection includes patterns about these problems, too. When you apply them you will be working in service of the enterprise. It is also likely that you personally won't apply all the patterns in this book. That doesn't mean that you can't read them and understand more about how at least some of your colleagues think.

Many of the patterns are backed up by specific objects already available in .NET. For these, you will find implementations that tell you how to use these objects rather than telling you how to make these objects from scratch. Traditionally, implementation examples have been included as just one section of a pattern. These are just examples meant to be understood and emulated. The implementation "patterns" included in this volume are much more. They describe the practical experience the authors have had with using specific capabilities of .NET and, as such, amount to their best advice on how to proceed.

When you find a pattern that you need and follow it to the implementation in .NET, you are using this volume as an index into the .NET libraries. The authors have organized all the patterns on a grid that categorizes the patterns according to levels of abstraction and viewpoints. Use this grid to find patterns that should be familiar. From there, you can find .NET capabilities that apply to the work you already do. You can also look around at patterns in neighboring parts of the grid. If these are familiar, move a little further. Soon you'll find the unfamiliar and can start benefiting from the experience of others. This works even if you know more about .NET than you do about patterns. Find the patterns that talk about sections of .NET that you use, find them on the grid, and then look around.

This work is very much about helping you use the technology built into .NET. There is a temptation to enumerate the features of .NET in a work like this. The authors have worked hard to avoid this. When they did slip into a little bit of proud boasting, the reviewers, myself included, insisted that the patterns be rewritten to be the simplest advice you can use.

I'll close by mentioning two more ways this work is important. The pattern community has invested a decade finding, writing, and reviewing patterns in what would have to be called an academic tradition of impartiality. This work is different. It is clearly in the sponsor's interest to have .NET well understood and this volume has that goal. However, that the sponsor would invest effort writing patterns is their acknowledgment that the decade of work has merit. The pattern community should be proud and should respond by reading, reviewing, debating, and enlarging this work.

Finally, enterprise developers and administrators should study these and other patterns not just because they offer advice that can be applied immediately, but because they provide a vocabulary to talk about intellectual property independent of that property. Consider this work a first step in a new conversation with a company that wants to succeed by serving you. Your participation in a public dialog represents a sweet-spot for interacting with a vendor that lies somewhere between focus groups and the traditional code release cycle. It is a new way for a big corporation to listen.

Ward Cunningham of Cunningham & Cunningham, Inc.

January, 2003

Preface

Welcome to *Enterprise Solution Patterns Using Microsoft .NET*. This guide briefly introduces patterns and describes a new organizational approach that categorizes them according to various viewpoints and relationships. The guide then presents 32 patterns that span several of these viewpoints, and explains how they can be integrated into an enterprise solution.

Increasingly, software design professionals are using patterns to efficiently share the important architectural tradeoffs and design decisions they make while architecting and building enterprise solutions. Christopher Alexander first used patterns to describe architecture and design in his book, *The Timeless Way of Building*; however, his patterns were for towns, buildings, and rooms. Software design professionals soon recognized the value of patterns as a language for sharing design experiences.

Over the past decade, the burgeoning patterns community has discovered patterns in many areas of system architecture and software development. This book embraces the continuing work of the patterns community and extends it by showing how to apply patterns to building software-intensive systems that use Microsoft® .NET. Early on, customer, partner, and internal feedback indicated that a single book should revisit established patterns as well as Microsoft-specific patterns. Therefore, that is what this book does.

The book includes established architecture and design patterns that are platform independent, and augments them with implementation patterns that apply specifically to Microsoft .NET. Early feedback from .NET developers and system architects has confirmed that patterns are invaluable tools for sharing expertise in .NET. Patterns give developers and architects a common language to help bridge the gap between their two disciplines. The authors hope they prove useful to you and that you will contribute to the growing patterns community for .NET. There is much more work to be done.

Who Should Read This Book

Most readers of this book should fall into one of three categories:

- Architects, designers, and developers who are new to patterns
- Architects and designers who already use patterns to build enterprise solutions
- System architects and system engineers who architect or design systems infrastructure

For those in the first group, the first two chapters are very important to understanding why and how you should use patterns. These chapters are essential in understanding the last four chapters, which collectively form a pattern catalog. You are likely to discover that you have implemented some of these patterns before without knowing that they were patterns.

Readers in the second group are familiar with most of the content in Chapter 1, "Patterns for Building Enterprise Solutions." Chapter 2, "Organizing Patterns," introduces new material on how Microsoft is organizing its pattern repository. Most of the patterns in Chapters 3 through 7 will be familiar to you; however, the implementation examples provided should help you apply them to .NET.

The last group should read the first two chapters and pay special attention to Chapter 4, "Deployment Patterns" and Chapter 7, "Performance and Reliability Patterns." These chapters focus on the patterns that are directly applicable to the infrastructure.

How This Book Is Organized

Chapter 1, "Patterns for Building Enterprise Solutions," introduces the notion of a pattern, explains how a pattern documents simple, proven mechanisms, and shows how collections of patterns provide a common language for developers and architects. To illustrate these concepts, this chapter applies abbreviated versions of actual patterns to real-life development situations.

Chapter 2, "Organizing Patterns," explains how patterns emerge at different levels of abstraction and across a variety of domains. This chapter explores pattern levels in detail and outlines an organizing frame that helps you find relevant patterns quickly. The chapter then demonstrates how patterns provide a vocabulary to efficiently describe complex solutions without sacrificing detail.

Chapters 3 through 6 present a catalog of 27 patterns, which are grouped into clusters. Each chapter starts by describing how the patterns in a particular cluster are related and then gives direction on when to use the patterns. For implementation patterns, code examples are written in C# and are for example purposes only. The example code is not meant to be used in production.

Chapter 3, "Web Presentation Patterns," describes design and implementation patterns related to constructing dynamic Web applications. Depending on the size and the complexity of the application, different design tradeoffs have to be made. The Web Presentation patterns cluster offers a number of pattern alternatives that illustrate the varied types of applications and their resulting tradeoffs.

Chapter 4, "Deployment Patterns," helps reduce the tension between application development and system infrastructure teams by offering guidance on how to optimally structure your applications and technical infrastructure to efficiently fulfill your solution requirements. The patterns discuss such topics as organizing your application into logical layers, refining layers to provide and consume services, organizing hardware into physical tiers, and allocating processes to processors with a deployment plan.

Chapter 5, "Distributed Systems Patterns," introduces concepts relevant to both the Distributed Systems and Services patterns clusters, including the distinction between interface-based and service-based collaboration and the concept of near versus far links. Distributed Systems patterns, as defined here, focus on instance-based collaboration and near links.

Chapter 6, "Services Patterns," briefly revisits collaboration concepts introduced in the previous chapter before presenting patterns that focus on collaboration between applications and external services. In contrast with Distributed Systems, Services patterns are primarily concerned with systems connected by far links using service-based collaboration.

Chapter 7, "Performance and Reliability Patterns," discusses how enterprise solutions must reliably meet the needs of an unpredictable number of users, and often must operate 24 hours a day, seven days a week. Although there are many ways to increase performance and improve reliability, this patterns cluster focuses how to combine multiple systems that serve any number of applications or users for greater scalability and improved availability.

Appendix A, "Pattlets," presents a list of patterns that this guide mentions, but that it does not discuss in detail. These patterns are named *pattlets* to distinguish them from the rest of the patterns in the catalog. For more information about why pattlets are used, see Chapter 2, "Organizing Patterns."

Documentation Conventions

This guide uses the following style conventions and terminology.

Table 1: Style Conventions Table

Element	Meaning
Bold font	Objects, classes, methods, predefined functions, and events.
Italic font	Names of patterns and pattlets referenced in this guide. New terminology also appears in italic on first use.
`Monospace font`	Code examples.
Note	Alerts you to supplementary information. Community

Community

The patterns in this guide are part of a new Patterns community on GotDotNet. GotDotNet is a Microsoft .NET Framework Community Web site that uses workspaces in an online collaborative development environment where .NET developers can create, host, and manage projects throughout the project life cycle. You can also use this Patterns community to post questions, provide feedback, or connect with other users for sharing ideas.

Access to the Patterns community is available from the following Web site:

http://gotdotnet.com/team/architecture/patterns

Feedback and Support

The authors would appreciate your feedback on this material. In particular, they would be grateful for any guidance on the following topics:

- Is the information that is presented in this guide useful for you?
- Is this information presented in the correct sequence and with the appropriate level of detail?
- Are the chapters readable and interesting?
- Overall, how do you rate the material?

Send your feedback to the following e-mail address: pnppatfb@microsoft.com. Please be aware that this is not a technical support alias; to obtain technical support for Microsoft products and technologies, visit http://support.microsoft.com.

The patterns documented here are designed to jump-start the architecture and design of enterprise applications. Patterns are simple mechanisms that are meant to be applied to the problem at hand and are usually combined with other patterns. They are not meant to be plugged into an application. Example code is provided "as is" and is not intended for production use. It is only intended to illustrate the pattern, and therefore does not include extra code such as exception handling, logging, security, and validation. Although this deliverable has undergone testing and review by industry luminaries, it is not supported like a traditional Microsoft product.

Acknowledgments

Many thanks to the following advisors who provided invaluable assistance:

- Ward Cunningham, Cunningham & Cunningham, Inc.
- Martin Fowler, ThoughtWorks, Inc.
- Ralph Johnson, University of Illinois at Urbana-Champaign
- Robert C. Martin, Object Mentor

Thanks also to the many contributors who assisted us in the production of this book, in particular:

- Mohammad Al-Sabt, Microsoft Prescriptive Architecture Guidance
- Chris Colleran, Colleran.net, LLC
- Matt Evans, Microsoft Prescriptive Architecture Guidance
- Xiao Guo, ThoughtWorks, Inc.
- Steve Kirk, MSDN
- Rick McUmber, RDA
- Vijay Srinivasan, Satyam Computer Services
- Jonathan Wanagel, Microsoft Prescriptive Architecture Guidance

Finally, thanks to the companies that agreed to participate in our user experience test:

- Atmedica USA, LLC, a MediMedia USA company
- Safeco Insurance Company
- SBI and Company
- ThoughtWorks, Inc.

1

Patterns for Building Enterprise Solutions

"A complex system that works is invariably found to have evolved from a simple system that worked…A complex system designed from scratch never works and cannot be patched up to make it work. You have to start over with a working simple system." — John Gall in *Systemantics: How Systems Really Work and How They Fail*

Enterprise class business solutions, the kind that companies bet their business on, are often extremely complex and must perform well against high expectations. Not only must they be highly available and scalable in the face of unpredictable usage, they must also be malleable and predictable in response to rapidly changing business requirements.

The best solutions are those composed of a set of smaller, simple mechanisms that solve simple problems reliably and effectively. During the process of building larger and more complex systems, these simple mechanisms combine to evolve the larger system.

Knowledge of these simple mechanisms does not come easy. It usually resides in the minds of experienced developers and architects and is an important part of the tacit knowledge they bring to projects.

This guide captures the knowledge of seasoned developers and presents it in the form of a patterns catalog. Each pattern contains a simple, proven mechanism that solves a small problem effectively. Although you can understand and apply each pattern individually, you often combine these patterns to build complex systems.

Patterns are useful to developers and architects because they:

- Document simple mechanisms that work.
- Provide a common vocabulary and taxonomy for developers and architects.
- Enable solutions to be described concisely as combinations of patterns.
- Enable reuse of architecture, design, and implementation decisions.

This chapter introduces the notion of a pattern, explains how a pattern documents simple, proven mechanisms, and shows how collections of patterns provide a common language for developers and architects. To illustrate these concepts, this chapter applies abbreviated versions of actual patterns to real-life development situations.

Patterns Document Simple Mechanisms

A pattern describes a recurring problem that occurs in a given context and, based on a set of guiding forces, recommends a solution. The solution is usually a simple mechanism, a collaboration between two or more classes, objects, services, processes, threads, components, or nodes that work together to resolve the problem identified in the pattern.

Note: Although the underlying mechanisms described in these patterns are conceptually simple, in practice their implementation can become quite complex. The implementation requires skill and judgment to tailor general patterns to fit specific circumstances. In addition, the pattern examples in this chapter are highly abbreviated for the purpose of introduction; the actual patterns in subsequent chapters are much more detailed.

Consider the following example:

You are building a quote application, which contains a class that is responsible for managing all of the quotes in the system. It is important that all quotes interact with one and only one instance of this class. How do you structure your design so that only one instance of this class is accessible within the application?

A simple solution to this problem is to create a **QuoteManager** class with a private constructor so that no other class can instantiate it. This class contains a static instance of **QuoteManager** that is returned with a static method named **GetInstance()**. The code looks something like this:

```
public class QuoteManager
{
    //NOTE: For single threaded applications only
    private static QuoteManager _Instance = null;
    private QuoteManager() {}
    public static QuoteManager GetInstance()
    {
        if (_Instance==null)
        {
            _Instance = new QuoteManager ();
        }
        return _Instance;
    }

    //... functions provided by QuoteManager
}
```

It is likely that you have solved problems like this in a similar manner, as many other developers have. In fact, pattern writers on the lookout for recurring problems and solutions have observed this kind of implementation frequently, distilled the common solution, and documented the problem-solution pair as the *Singleton* pattern [Gamma95].

Patterns as Problem-Solution Pairs

Notice that the *Singleton* pattern does not mention a **Quote** or **QuoteManager** class. Instead, the pattern looks something like the following abbreviated example.

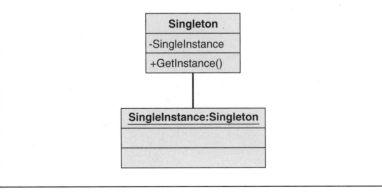

Singleton

Context

Control access to a class by controlling its instantiation process

Problem

An application contains a certain type of data that needs to be globally accessed and maintained. At the same time, this type of data is often unique in the system. How do you provide an accessible interface to a class, but control the number of instances within the system?

Solution

The class itself is responsible for creating a single instance and providing global access to that instance. Create a class that contains a static instance of the Singleton that is returned with a static method named getinstance().

Figure 1.1
Singleton pattern, abbreviated

Comparing the abbreviated pattern example in Figure 1.1 with the **QuoteManager** source code illustrates the difference between the pattern, which is a generalized problem-solution pair, and the application of the pattern, which is a very specific solution to a very specific problem. The solution, at a pattern level, is a simple, yet elegant, collaboration between several classes. The general collaboration in the pattern applies specifically to the **QuoteManager** class, which provides the mechanism that controls instantiations in the quote application. Clearly, you can apply the same pattern to countless applications by modifying the pattern slightly to suit specific local requirements.

Written patterns provide an effective way to document simple and proven mechanisms. Patterns are written in a specific format, which is useful as a container for complex ideas. These patterns exist in the minds of developers, and their code, long before they are documented and given pattern names. At some point, pattern writers discover these patterns from actual implementations and generalize them so they can be applied to other applications.

Although pattern writers usually provide implementation code examples within these generalized patterns, it is important to understand that there are many other correct ways to implement these patterns. The key here is to understand the guidance within the pattern and then customize it to your particular situation. For example, if you are familiar with the *Singleton* pattern, you probably noticed that the code example is based on the [Gamma95] implementation. This implementation is used here because it is the most popular example and requires the least explanation for the purposes of this introduction to patterns. However, an implementation of *Singleton* optimized for the C# language would look quite different, and while these two implementations differ significantly, both would be correct.

Patterns at Different Levels

Patterns exist at many different levels of abstraction. Consider another example, this time at a higher level of abstraction than the level of source code:

> You are designing a Web-based quote application containing a great deal of business and presentation logic, which, in turn, depends on numerous platform software components to provide a suitable execution environment. How do you organize your system at a high level to be flexible, loosely coupled, and yet highly cohesive?

One solution to this problem involves organizing your system into a series of layers, with each layer containing elements at roughly the same level of abstraction. You then identify the dependencies in each layer and decide on either a strict or a relaxed layering strategy. Next, you decide if you are going to create a custom layering scheme or adopt a layering scheme previously documented by others. In this case, let's say you decide to use a well-known layering strategy: one layer each for presentation, business logic, and data access. Figure 1.2 shows how your layering scheme might look.

Quote Presentation Layer

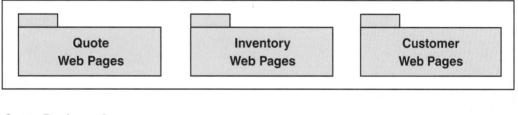

Quote Business Layer

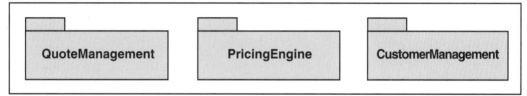

Quote Data Access Layer

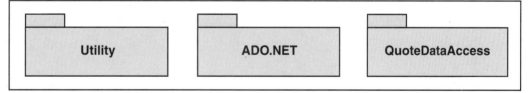

Figure 1.2
Quote application layers

If you always design systems this way, then you employ this pattern already, independent of any generalized pattern. Even so, there are many reasons why you might want to understand the patterns that underpin this design approach. You may be curious about why systems frequently are built this way, or you may be looking for more optimal approaches to problems that this pattern does not quite resolve. In either case, it is worth examining the patterns and mechanisms at work here.

Using layers as a high-level organizing approach is a well-established pattern described in the *Layers* pattern [Buschmann96]. Figure 1.3 shows an abbreviated version of this pattern.

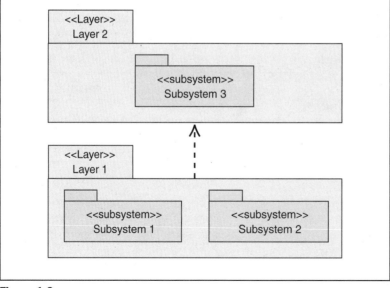

Layers

Context

You are working with a large, complex system and you want to manage complexity by decomposition

Problem

How do you structure an application to support such operational requirements as maintainability, reusability, extensibility, scalability, robustness, and security?

Solution

Compose the solution into a set of layers. Each layer should be cohesive and at roughly the same level of abstraction. Each layer should be loosely coupled to the layers underneath ….

Figure 1.3
Layers pattern, abbreviated

This simple strategy for organizing applications helps to solve two challenges in software development: the management of dependencies and the need for exchangeable components. Building applications without a well-considered strategy for dependency management leads to brittle and fragile components, which are difficult and expensive to maintain, extend, and substitute.

The mechanisms at work inside the *Layers* pattern are more subtle than those of the *Singleton*. For *Layers*, the first collaboration is at design time between classes, because the layered organization localizes the effects of source code changes and prevents the changes from rippling throughout the entire system. The second collaboration is at runtime, when relatively independent components within a layer become exchangeable with other components, again isolating the rest of the system from impact.

Although the *Layers* pattern is general enough to apply to areas such as network protocols, platform software, and virtual machines, it does not resolve certain specific forces that are present in enterprise-class business solutions. For example, in addition to managing complexity by decomposition (the essential problem solved by *Layers*), business solution developers also need to organize for effective reuse of business logic and conserve valuable connections to expensive resources such as databases. One way to solve this problem is by using the *Three-Layered Application* pattern. Figure 1.4 on the next page shows the abbreviated description of this pattern.

Three-Layered Application

Context

You are building a business solution using layers to organize your application

Problem

How do you organize your application to reuse business logic, provide deployment flexibility and conserve valuable resource connections?

Solution

Create three layers: presentation, business logic (domain), and data access. Place all components responsible for the view in the presentation layer. Encapsulate all business logic in domain layer components that implement well-known component interfaces. Locate all database-related code, including database client access and utility components, in the data access layer. Require the data access layer to be responsible for connection pooling when accessing resources. Make sure you eliminate the dependencies between data access components and business layer components. Either eliminate dependencies between the business layer and the presentation layer or manage the dependencies here using the *Observer* pattern.

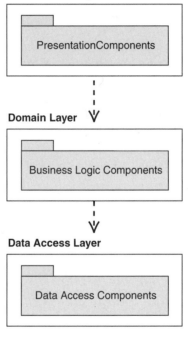

Presentation Layer

PresentationComponents

Domain Layer

Business Logic Components

Data Access Layer

Data Access Components

Figure 1.4

Three-Layered Application, abbreviated

Again, there is a difference between the pattern (*Three-Layered Application*) and the application of the pattern (quote application layering model). The pattern is a generalized problem-solution pair on the topic of application organization. In contrast, the application of the pattern solves a very specific problem by creating specific layers, each layer resolving very specific requirements.

Simple Refinement

Notice that *Three-Layered Application* is really a simple refinement of *Layers*; the context, forces, and solution identified in *Layers* still apply to *Three-Layered Application*, but not the other way around. That is, the *Layers* pattern constrains *Three-Layered Application*, and the *Three-Layered Application* pattern refines the *Layers* pattern. This pattern relationship is useful to manage complexity. After you understand one pattern, you must only understand the incremental differences between the initial pattern and patterns that refine it. Another example, this time in the area of Web services, should help to illustrate the concept of refinement:

You built a quote application for a successful enterprise that is rapidly expanding. Now you want to extend the application by exposing your quote engine to business partners and integrating additional partner services (such as shipping) into the quote application. How do you structure your business application to provide and consume services?

One solution to this problem is to extend *Three-Layered Application* by adding additional service-related responsibilities to each layer. The business layer adds the responsibility for providing a simplified set of operations to client applications through *Service Interfaces*. The responsibilities of the data access layer broaden beyond database and host integration to include communication with other service providers. This additional functionality in the data access layer is encapsulated in *Service Gateway* components, which are responsible for connecting to services (both synchronously and asynchronously), managing basic conversational state with the service, and notifying business process components of significant service-related events.

The *Three-Layered Services Application* (Figure 1.5, on the next page) captures this problem-solution pair.

Three-Layered Services Application

Context

You are building a business solution that uses presentation, business, and data access layers to organize your application. You want to expose some of the core functionality of your application as services that other applications can consume and enable your application to consume other services.

Problem

How do you organize your application to provide and consume granular data and logical elements from highly variable sources?

Solution

Decompose your application logic into a collaborating set of services that provide parts of the overall system functionality. Next, in the domain layer, identify a Service Interface for each service that is independent of the underlying implementation. Finally, extend the data access layer to use Service Gateways to communicate with other service providers. If application navigation logic is sufficiently complex, consider user interface process components as part of the presentation layer to encapsulate and reuse this logic.

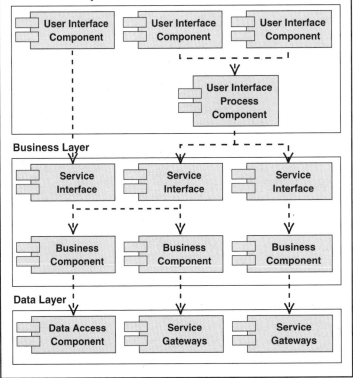

Figure 1.5

Three-Layered Services Application, abbreviated

Applying the *Three-Layered Services Application* pattern to the quote application example results in the following model.

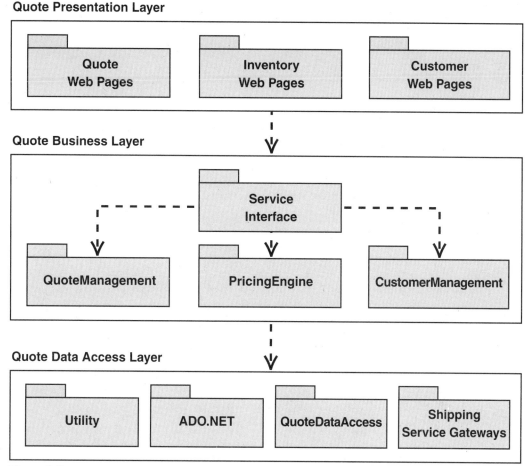

Quote Presentation Layer

Quote Business Layer

Quote Data Access Layer

Figure 1.6
Three-Layered Services Application applied to the quote application

Notice the relationships between these patterns (see Figure 1.7, on the next page). *Layers* introduces a fundamental strategy for organizing a software application. *Three-Layered Application* refines this idea and constrains it to business systems that require business logic reuse, flexible deployment, and efficient use of connections. *Three-Layered Services Application* refines *Three-Layered Application* and extends the design to provide and consume granular elements of data and logic from highly variable sources.

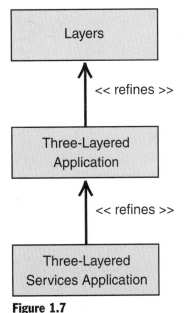

Figure 1.7
Refinement of related patterns

Adding additional types of components to specific layers is not the only way to manage this growing complexity. As complexity warrants, designers often create additional layers within the application to handle this responsibility. For example, some designers move *Service Interfaces* into a separate layer. Other designers separate the business layer into a domain layer and an application layer. In any case, you sometimes see these three layers expanded to four, five, or even six layers as designers use this pattern in response to complex requirements. Conversely, the *Layers* pattern was also used in the relatively simpler days of client-server applications, when two-layered applications were the standard.

When grouped together, these *Layers* variations form a cluster of patterns (see Figure 1.8) that visually represents common approaches to application layering. Clustering, used in this context, simply means a logical grouping of some set of similar patterns. This notion of a cluster is quite useful for expanding the view of patterns to encompass an entire solution, and for identifying clusters of patterns that address similar concerns in the solution space. Chapter 2, "Organizing Patterns," discusses clusters in more detail.

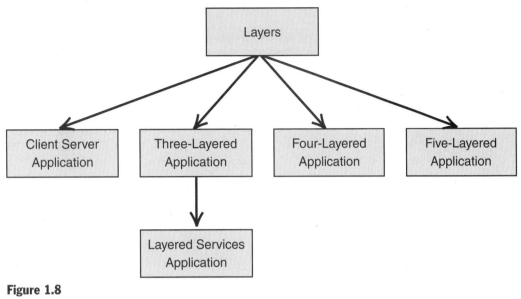

Figure 1.8
A cluster of patterns

Common Vocabulary

While considering the *Singleton, Layers, Three-Layered Application*, and *Layered Services Application* patterns, you probably noticed that patterns also provide a powerful vocabulary for communicating software architecture and design ideas. Understanding a pattern not only communicates the knowledge and experience embedded within the pattern but also provides a unique, and hopefully evocative, name that serves as shorthand for evaluating and describing software design choices.

For example, when designing an application a developer might say, "I think the pricing engine should be implemented as a *Singleton* and exposed through a *Service Interface.*" If another developer understands these patterns, he or she would have a very detailed idea of the design implications under discussion. If the developer did not understand the patterns, he or she could look them up in a catalog and learn the mechanisms, and perhaps even learn some additional patterns along the way.

Patterns have a natural taxonomy. If you look at enough patterns and their relationships, you begin to see sets of ordered groups and categories at different levels of abstraction. For example, the *Singleton* pattern example was at a lower level of abstraction than the *Layers* pattern, but the *Layers* pattern had a set of related patterns that refined it in one way or another. Chapter 2 further expands and refines this taxonomy.

Over time, developers discover and describe new patterns, thus extending the community body of knowledge in this area. In addition, as you start to understand patterns and the relationships between patterns, you can describe entire solutions in terms of patterns.

Concise Solution Description

In this guide, the term solution has two very distinct meanings: first, to indicate part of a pattern itself, as in a problem-solution pair contained within a context; second, to indicate a business solution. When the term *business solution* is used, it refers to a software-intensive system that is designed to meet a specific set of functional and operational business requirements. A software-intensive system implies that you are not just concerned with software; you must deploy this software onto hardware processing nodes to provide a holistic technology solution. Further, the software under consideration includes both custom-developed software and purchased software infrastructure and platform components, all of which you integrate together.

Summary

This chapter introduced the concept of a pattern, explained how patterns document simple, proven mechanisms, and showed how patterns provide a common language for developers and architects. Chapter 2 explains how to organize your thinking about patterns, and how to use patterns to describe entire solutions concisely.

2

Organizing Patterns

> "Each pattern then depends both on the smaller patterns it contains, and on the larger patterns within which it is contained." — Christopher Alexander in *The Timeless Way of Building*

An innovation in one area of technology often fuels a breakthrough in another area. Radar technology turned into a cooking device: the microwave oven. The Internet itself was originally designed as a military communications network with resilience against single points of attack and has since turned into the world's largest repository of knowledge. Similarly, patterns, originally applied to building and town architecture, were quickly embraced by the software development community as a means to describe complex software systems.

Today there are dozens of patterns related to software with more emerging daily. This abundance of patterns creates a new set of challenges. How can a developer identify those patterns that are most relevant to the task at hand? Is the collection of patterns sufficient to describe complete solutions?

This chapter answers some of these questions by demonstrating how to:

- Identify relationships between patterns.
- Group patterns into clusters.
- Identify patterns at various levels of abstraction.
- Apply patterns to multiple aspects of a solution.
- Organize patterns into a frame.
- Use patterns to describe solutions concisely.

Pattern of Patterns

One reason the object-oriented programming community embraced patterns so emphatically is because patterns describe relationships. The base element of object-oriented programming is a class. However, a single class is not very meaningful apart from its relationship to other classes that make up the solution. Each pattern typically describes a cluster of classes, highlighting the relationships and interactions between them. Thus, patterns turn the sea of classes into a much more manageable collection of patterns.

Now that the number of available patterns easily exceeds the number of classes in an average application, you may suddenly find yourself in a sea of patterns. How can you make sense out of all these patterns? Again, the relationships between items appear to be the key. It is easy to see that some patterns are closely related to other patterns. For example, some patterns are refinements of others. *Three-Tiered Distribution* is a specific application of the concept of *Tiered Distribution. Observer* is frequently used to implement a part of the *Model-View-Controller* pattern. *Page Controller* describes the controller portion of *Model-View-Controller* in more detail. *Implementing Page Controller in ASP.NET* is an implementation of the *Page Controller* pattern using Microsoft® ASP.NET.

To begin organizing patterns according to relationship, visualize a set of patterns as small circles (see Figure 2.1):

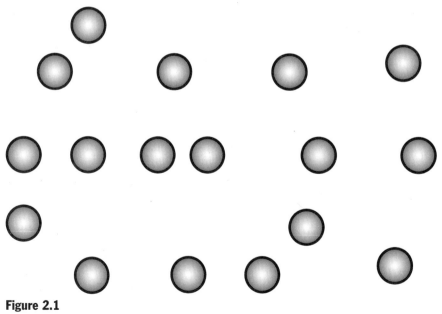

Figure 2.1
A set of patterns

If you draw a line between each pair of patterns that share some relationship, you get a picture like this:

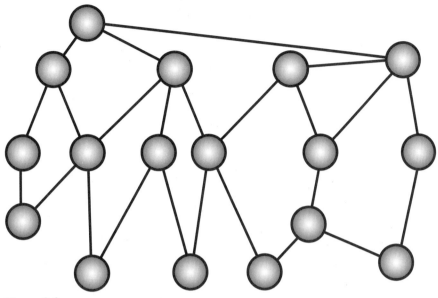

Figure 2.2
Pattern relationships represented as lines

The somewhat random collection of circles becomes a connected web of patterns. When you look at a pattern, you can now identify closely related patterns and review those as well. You can also identify "neighborhoods" of closely related patterns and see how they are related to other, more remote patterns.

Pattern Clusters

Charting the relationships between patterns helps you navigate from one pattern to a set of related patterns. However, it does not yet tell you where to start. If you are building a Web application, should you read the *Model-View-Controller* pattern first or should you look at *Page Cache* instead? Should you look at a *Broker* as well?

Pattern *clusters* are groupings of patterns that relate to a specific subject area. For example, you can start with the Web Presentation cluster to find the patterns that are relevant to creating the front end of a Web application. Likewise, the Distributed Systems cluster contains patterns that are helpful in communicating with remote objects. Dividing the collection of patterns into clusters enables you to examine a group of patterns together. Although the pattern graph shows that two patterns are related, the cluster overview describes, in much more detail, how to combine the patterns to build actual solutions. Each cluster takes the reader on a guided tour through all the patterns within the cluster. Taking some inspiration from Christopher Alexander's world of town and building architecture, you can draw an analogy between a cluster and a city neighborhood. To stretch this analogy a little bit further, you can consider the cluster overview a neighborhood tour offered by the local tourism office.

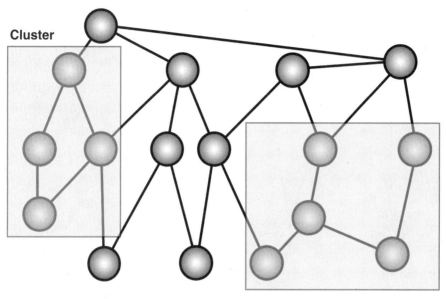

Figure 2.3
Pattern clusters

This initial release of *Enterprise Solution Patterns Using Microsoft .NET* (ESP) identifies the five clusters shown in Table 2.1.

Table 2.1: Enterprise Solution Patterns Clusters

Cluster	Problem
Web Presentation	How do you create dynamic Web applications?
Deployment	How do you divide an application into layers and then deploy them onto a multi-tiered hardware infrastructure?
Distributed Systems	How do you communicate with objects that reside in different processes or different computers?
Performance and Reliability	How do you create a systems infrastructure that can meet critical operational requirements?
Services	How do you access services provided by other applications? How do you expose your application functionality as services to other applications?

Chapters 3 through 7 describe these clusters in detail.

Different Levels of Abstraction

Dividing patterns into clusters makes them more manageable. If you are building the front end of a Web application, start with the Web Presentation cluster, take the quick tour, and see what other patterns are related to this cluster. Keep in mind, though, that different people may be interested in different aspects of building a Web application, depending on the role they are playing or the stage of the project. A developer may be most interested in the most efficient implementation of the *Page Controller* pattern on the Microsoft .NET Framework, while an architect may be more interested in deciding whether to use a three-tiered or a four-tiered application architecture.

Level of abstraction, therefore, is a useful way to categorize patterns so that different user groups can find the patterns that correspond most closely to their area of interest. Dividing the patterns from general to more specific detail also helps you decide which patterns to consider first. You may want to think about how many tiers your application should have before you consider the intricacies of ASP.NET caching directives described in the *Implementing Page Cache with ASP.NET* pattern.

One way categorize the patterns is to divide the pattern graph into the three levels shown in Figure 2.4.

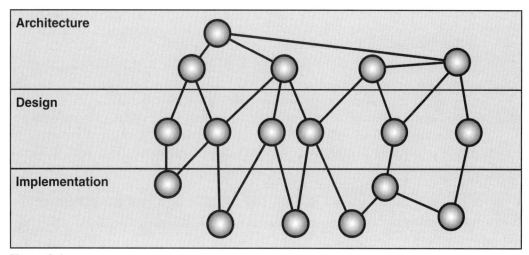

Figure 2.4
Levels of abstraction

This division largely coincides with the terminology used in some of the most influential books about software patterns.

Architecture Patterns

"An architectural pattern expresses a fundamental structural organization schema for software systems. It provides a set of predefined subsystems, specifies their responsibilities, and includes rules and guidelines for organizing the relationships between them." [Buschmann96]

ESP follows the Buschmann, et al. definition of architecture patterns. These patterns describe how to structure an application at the highest level. For example, the *Layered Application* pattern is an architecture pattern.

Design Patterns

"A design pattern provides a scheme for refining the subsystems or components of a software system, or the relationships between them. It describes a commonly recurring structure of communicating components that solves a general design problem within a particular context." [Gamma95]

Design patterns provide the next level of refinement, as described in the seminal work by Gamma, et al. Many of the iconic patterns, such as *Model-View-Controller* or *Singleton*, are in this layer.

Implementation Patterns

The patterns community refers to more detailed, programming-language-specific patterns as *idioms*. This definition works well for software patterns. However, the scope of this guide is not just software, but software-intensive systems, including the deployment of the software onto hardware processing nodes to provide a holistic business solution. Therefore, ESP modifies the definition of an idiom given in *Pattern-Oriented Software Architecture (POSA)* [Buschmann96] to reflect the broader scope and relabels these patterns as *implementation patterns*:

An implementation pattern is a low-level pattern specific to a particular platform. An implementation pattern describes how to implement particular aspects of components or the relationships between them, using the features of a given platform.

The ESP implementation patterns demonstrate how to implement design concepts using the.NET Framework. In some cases, the framework already incorporates the bulk of the work, making the developer's task easier.

Note: Even though *POSA* [Buschmann96] defines idioms as patterns and *The Timeless Way of Building* [Alexander79] includes implementation patterns in his original pattern work, there is a debate among some members of the pattern community as to whether implementation patterns are true patterns. Regardless of how they can be classified, they are very helpful when thinking about patterns, and are therefore included in this guide.

Dividing the collection of patterns into three levels of abstraction makes it easier for different user groups to identify patterns that relate to their fields of interest and expertise. The resulting model flows from high-level organization, through progressive refinement of subsystems and components, down to the implementation of these patterns using platform-specific technology.

Viewpoints

Although the levels of abstractions help to address different user groups, they do not reflect the fact that a software solution encompasses much more than code components. A holistic view of building an enterprise solution includes custom-developed software, platform software, hardware infrastructure, and the deployment of software onto hardware. Because of the stark differences between these areas, it makes sense to align the patterns with this nomenclature.

Keep in mind that these four areas describe different viewpoints of the same solution. Therefore, unlike the levels of refinement, these viewpoints do not describe a hierarchy, but simply provide four different ways of looking at the same thing. You can compare these viewpoints to different types of maps. One map of a region may depict traffic networks such as roads and freeways, while another map of the same area shows the topography. Still another map may show state and county borders. Each map has its own vocabulary. For example, lines in the topographical map represent elevations, while lines in the traffic map represent streets. Nevertheless, all maps describe the same subject: a specific geographic region.

Each viewpoint itself can also focus on different levels of abstraction. Therefore, ESP depicts the following viewpoints as vertical slices across the pattern graph: database, application, and infrastructure. There is often a significant gap between the application and infrastructure viewpoints. Concepts, abstractions, and skill sets are sufficiently different to warrant the insertion of a buffer between the two that helps to bridge the divide. This viewpoint is called the deployment viewpoint.

This line of reasoning results in the four viewpoints shown in Table 2.2.

Table 2.2: Enterprise Solution Patterns Viewpoints

Viewpoint	Description
Database	The database view describes the persistent layer of the application. This view looks at such things as logical and physical schemas, database tables, relationships, and transactions.
Application	The application view focuses on the executable aspect of the solution. It includes such things as domain models, class diagrams, assemblies, and processes.
Deployment	The deployment view explicitly maps application concerns to infrastructure concerns (for example, processes to processors).
Infrastructure	The infrastructure view incorporates all of the hardware and networking equipment that is required to run the solution.

Figure 2.5 overlays these viewpoints as vertical lines over the pattern graph and the levels of abstraction.

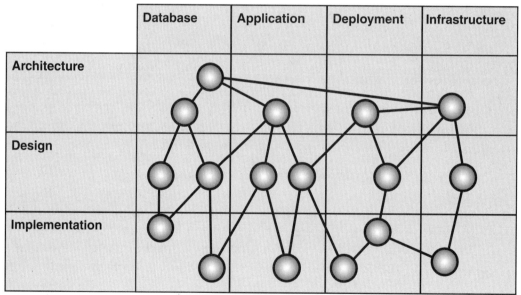

Figure 2.5
Adding viewpoints

For the sake of simplicity, Figure 2.5 does not show the cluster boundaries. However, the clusters, the layers of abstraction, and the viewpoints exist in parallel. They represent different ways to access the same set of patterns.

The Pattern Frame

The combination of three levels of refinement on the vertical axis and the four viewpoints on the horizontal axis results in a grid-like organization of the pattern graph. This arrangement, called the *Pattern Frame*, is shown in Figure 2.6.

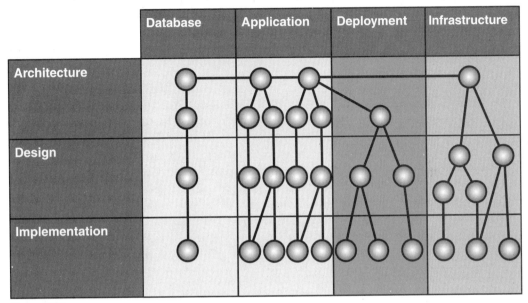

Figure 2.6
The Pattern Frame

The Pattern Frame is included with each individual pattern description as a point of reference and as a navigational aid.

Constraints

The Pattern Frame organizes the collection of patterns into meaningful subcategories. For example, you can now focus on the design patterns of the Database view or on the implementation patterns of the Application view.

However, software takes many forms. Today, software operates embedded systems such as pacemakers and telecommunications equipment, real-time systems such as antilock brakes, or in data warehousing systems constructed to analyze consumer buying behavior. Trying to address patterns related to all these flavors of software solutions would quickly enlarge the scope of any single book or pattern repository. ESP, therefore, constrains the patterns to enterprise business solutions. Because this term is somewhat nebulous, ESP identifies a small set of specific top-level architectural patterns, or root patterns, within the pattern graph. All other patterns in this collection adhere to the following constraints:

- Online transaction processing (OLTP)
- Object-oriented
- Layered application
- Tiered distribution systems

OLTP systems are database subsystems that manage the processing of transactions. These subsystems ensure that each transaction is atomic, consistent, isolated, and durable (the so-called ACID properties). In practice, these applications often manipulate one or more relational databases that maintain the business state of the enterprise. In other words, these are the databases that keep track of the customers, orders, accounting, and so on. By identifying OLTP as a top-level constraint in the Pattern Frame, ESP excludes online analytical processing (OLAP) or simple flat file systems that do not support transactions. The *online* aspect of OLTP implies that these systems are reading or updating the database immediately in response to a change in business state, which excludes offline batch processing from consideration.

From the application viewpoint, the Pattern Frame is constrained by two patterns: *Object-Oriented Application* and *Layered Application*. Most, if not all, of the application viewpoint patterns depend on object-oriented concepts such as encapsulation, polymorphism, and inheritance to successfully resolve their forces. Therefore, the Pattern Frame addresses only object-oriented applications and specifically does not address procedural applications.

Interesting enterprise applications are usually composed of a large number of objects and services that must collaborate to provide something of value to the business. To manage these collaborations, there must exist some high-level organization of the system. Most enterprise class systems use a layered approach to manage this complexity. As a result, the Pattern Frame addresses only applications that are designed as a set of layers and specifically excludes monolithic applications with little or no internal structure.

From the infrastructure viewpoint, the model is constrained to a hardware infrastructure that supports distributing an application over a number of servers arranged into tiers. The tiered approach is commonly used for enterprise applications, because it has a relatively low startup cost and it supports a scaling out strategy where inexpensive servers can be added to the infrastructure to add incremental capability. Excluded from the model are solutions based on deploying applications to a single mainframe or large multiprocessor computer.

The deployment perspective is concerned with bridging the gap across the applications and infrastructure viewpoints. As a consequence, it does not have any constraints of its own, but operates within the constraints set by the application and infrastructure viewpoints. In other words, the highest-level deployment pattern is about mapping layered applications to a tiered distribution infrastructure and does not impose any additional constraints of its own.

Taken as a group, these four high-level constraints, or root constraints, help to narrow the patterns that are in scope for the remainder of this guide. Figure 2.7 shows the root constraints along the top of the Pattern Frame.

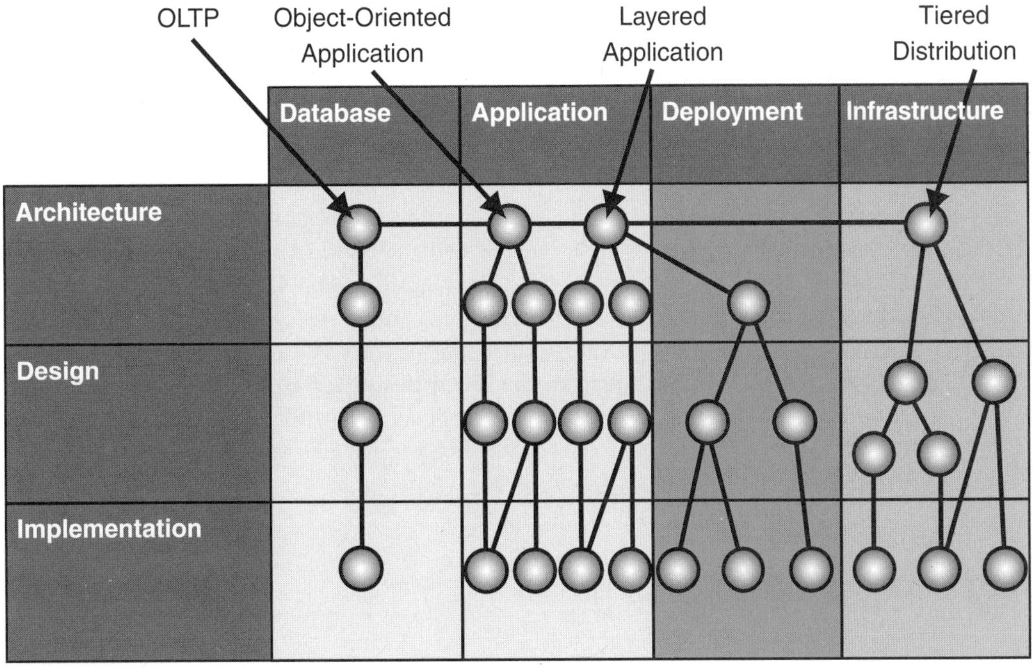

Figure 2.7
Root constraints of the Pattern Frame

Reducing the scope of the Pattern Frame makes it possible to focus on specific patterns and the relationships between them in more relevant detail.

Pattlets

The use of root constraints reduces the number of patterns to a manageable order of magnitude. Nevertheless, elaborating on all patterns in the grid takes a significant amount of effort. Developing all patterns in isolation and then publishing "the ultimate patterns guide" would counteract many benefits realized by the patterns communities. Patterns need to evolve as the collective understanding of them evolves. Patterns are not created by a single author, but are harvested from actual use in the software development community. Recognizing the evolutionary nature of patterns, the authors of this guide have published the subset of patterns included here to obtain feedback and start building a community.

Deferring patterns until later, however, leaves holes in the pattern graph, which could result in related patterns suddenly becoming disconnected. To preserve the integrity of the relationships inside the pattern graph, this guide includes the patterns that were not included in the first release as *pattlets*. Pattlets are actual patterns that have not yet been documented in detail. A pattlet describes a solution to a problem, but does not contain a detailed description of the context, problem, or forces that may impact the solution.

The concept of pattlets is also useful for referencing prior pattern works. The patterns community has been discovering and documenting software patterns for over a decade. It would be foolish to try to replicate these efforts. It would also be foolish, however, to require readers to purchase several other books as context for these patterns. Therefore, this guide includes a pattlet whenever it references a pattern that is described in an existing book about patterns. The pattlet includes the reference to the original work for those readers who would like to look at the complete pattern in more detail.

For a detailed list of all pattlets, see Appendix A.

Pattern Language for Solutions

The constrained Pattern Frame and the patterns it contains provide enough data points to begin using patterns to describe entire solutions. In fact, the quoting example from Chapter 1 can be described in terms of patterns. Recall that the requirements specified a Web-based quote application. Someone describing the architecture of the solution might say something like this:

> Let's start by looking at the quote application at the architecture level of abstraction. From the application viewpoint, the quote application is an *Object-Oriented Application* that is logically structured as a *Three-Layered Services Application*. From the database viewpoint, the application is based on the *OLTP* processing model. From the infrastructure viewpoint, the hardware and network architecture are based on *Four-Tiered Distribution*, which calls for separate physical tiers for Web

server and application server functionality. And finally, from the deployment viewpoint, the team has created a *Deployment Plan* to map components to servers, based on a Complex Web Application.

This concisely describes the architecture of the solution across all four of the viewpoints to anyone familiar with the referenced patterns. Continuing down one level of abstraction, you can see how someone might describe the design of the system:

From the application viewpoint, let's consider each layer of our *Three-Layered Services Application* separately.

The presentation layer is structured around a Web presentation framework based on *Model-View-Controller (MVC)*. Although *MVC* provides a level of separation between business and presentation logic, each page contains a great deal of common logic. To eliminate this redundancy, we use a *Page Controller* to render common headers and footers and set a friendly display name for the user.

The business layer holds the Customer, Quote, Order, Line Item, and Inventory domain objects. The domain objects are realized using *Table Module [Fowler03]* because speed of development is a key requirement. The Complex Web Application *Deployment Model* calls for separate Web and application tiers. Therefore, the two tiers communicate through a *Broker*. Business entities, acting in the role of *Data Transfer Objects [Fowler03]*, are used to encapsulate the information traveling between the two tiers.

The data layer uses a *Data Table Gateway [Fowler03]* to access the *OLTP* database subsystem and a number of data access components to support the persistence requirements of the domain objects.

From the infrastructure viewpoint: to meet the operational requirements of the business, we build on the basic *Four-Tiered Distribution* model by adding *Load Balanced Cluster* and *Failover Cluster*. Responding to a requirement calling for a high level of concurrent users, we added load balancing to our Web tier. To meet availability requirements, we added clustering to our database tier.

The description could continue on to describe the data and deployment viewpoints at the same level of abstraction. To continue, instead, down one more level of abstraction, you can see how someone might describe the implementation of the solution:

Let's look at the solution from the application viewpoint. The solution is built using Microsoft .NET technology. The presentation layer is based on the Web presentation framework that is built into ASP.NET. ASP.NET simplifies the implementation of *Model-View-Controller* with the built-in code-behind page feature. We use the built-in *Page Controller* mechanism in ASP.NET to implement our presentation logic. The domain objects in the business layer are managed .NET objects. Because the presentation layer and business layer are deployed on separate tiers, we use *Implementing Broker with .NET Remoting Using Server-Activated Objects*. Finally, the data layer is based on the ADO.NET classes within the .NET Framework to provide database access. The *Table Modules* and business entities are constructed using the DataSet component of ADO.NET. The remainder of the Data Access Components are provided by the *Microsoft Application Blocks for .NET* building block.

From the infrastructure viewpoint: Microsoft SQL Server®, running in a failover cluster, is used for the *OLTP* database subsystem. Microsoft Network Load Balancing clusters provide load balancing between Web servers.

All of these conversations make frequent references to patterns. This can be daunting at first, but when you understand the patterns used, you realize that even this brief description gives you a detailed understanding about how the system works. Notice that you gained this understanding without having to wade through reams of documentation or step through endless lines of code. The communication benefits of patterns become clear if you imagine how much more work would be involved in describing the solution without using patterns.

Summary

This chapter demonstrated how patterns provide a vocabulary to efficiently describe complex solutions without sacrificing detail. Effectively, the patterns form a new language with which architects and designers can communicate their thinking.

Because of the large number of patterns involved in building enterprise solutions, it can seem difficult to learn this new language. This guide structures the patterns into smaller, more closely related sets of patterns. This allows you to get started by using a smaller set of patterns, depending on your specific interest or the stage of the project.

This chapter introduced four mechanisms to help you navigate the patterns:

- **Relationships**. Relationships between patterns help you to identify patterns that are closely associated to the pattern you are using (for example, *Page Controller* focuses on the controller aspect of *Model-View-Controller*).

- **Clusters**. Clusters group patterns that belong to a common subject area (for example, Web Presentation).

- **Levels of abstraction**. Levels of abstraction allow you to describe concepts in a manner that is consistent with the level of detail of your discussion (for example, an architectural conversation).

- **Viewpoints**. Viewpoints help you select the vocabulary that is relevant to a team's particular role (for example, the infrastructure team).

These mechanisms are not meant to constrain your thinking, but instead are intended to make looking at complex systems easier. With practice, you will naturally switch between these mechanisms as you switch between roles, subject areas, and levels of detail.

3

Web Presentation Patterns

"An architect's first work is apt to be spare and clean. He knows he doesn't know what he is doing, so he does it carefully and with great restraint. As he designs the first work, frill after frill and embellishment after embellishment occur to him. These get stored away to be used 'next time'…This second system is the most dangerous system a man ever designs…The general tendency is to over-design the second system using all the ideas and frills that were cautiously sidetracked on the first one." — Frederick P. Brooks, Jr. in *The Mythical Man Month*, 1972[1]

The first systems on the Web were simply linked static HTML pages that enabled document sharing between distributed teams. As user adoption increased, dynamic Web pages that responded to user input became common. Early dynamic pages were typically written as Common Gateway Interface (CGI) scripts. These CGI scripts not only contained the business logic for deciding what to display in response to user input, they also generated the presentation HTML. As demand for more complex logic increased, so did the demand for richer and more engaging presentations. This increased complexity strained the CGI programming model.

Soon page-based development (for example, ASP and JSP) emerged. This allowed developers to embed script directly into HTML pages, thus simplifying the programming model. As these embedded script applications became more complex, developers wanted to separate out business logic from presentation logic at the page level. In response, tag libraries with helper objects and code-behind page strategies emerged. Elaborate frameworks appeared, which offered dynamically configurable site navigation and command dispatchers, all at the cost of additional complexity. Given the wide range of Web presentation options now available, how do you choose the appropriate Web presentation design strategy for your application?

---

1. This quotation is intended to emphasize the dangers of adding unnecessary complexity to a system. By using Brooks' original words, the authors of this guide are not advocating his particular choice of pronouns.

Complexity and Redundancy

Unfortunately, there is no single design strategy that is right for all situations. This is due to the competing needs in software design to eliminate excessive redundancy and excessive complexity.

You can start with a simple page that contains embedded script, and soon the business logic is repeated across files, making the system difficult to maintain and extend. You can move this logic into a set of collaborating components to eliminate redundancy, but doing so adds complexity to the solution. Instead, you can start off with a framework that offers tag libraries, dynamic configuration, and command dispatchers, but although this eliminates redundant code, it adds a great deal of complexity to the system, often unnecessarily.

Adding complexity obscures your intentions, making the system more difficult for other developers to understand. The added complexity also makes the system harder to maintain and extend, thereby increasing the total cost of ownership. If this added complexity is carefully considered and reserved for meeting current requirements, it can be worthwhile. Extra complexity is sometimes added based on speculation that it *might* be needed someday, rather than based on current requirements. This can clutter code with unnecessary abstractions that impede understanding and your ability to deliver a working system today.

So, again, how do you wade through the choices to arrive at an appropriate Web presentation design strategy for your application?

First, it is important to understand the key Web application design issues, possible solutions, and the associated tradeoffs. This chapter gives developers a strong head start down that path. In the process, you will become familiar with options, assess tradeoffs, and then pick the least complex solution that meets the application's requirements. Think carefully before choosing a more complex solution that supports possible future change scenarios over a simpler solution that meets today's requirements. Sometimes the extra cost is justified, but quite often it is not.

Patterns Overview

This patterns cluster starts off simply with *Model-View-Controller (MVC)*, a long-standing pattern that has stood the test of time when it comes to separating business logic from presentation logic. Although this pattern is not new [Buschmann96], this collection presents it in a simplified form that is tailored for building business solutions, not for building user interface frameworks for rich clients. The pattern is written first at the design level, and is then mapped to a platform implementation named *Implementing Model-View-Controller in ASP.NET*. Figure 3.1 shows the Web Presentation patterns cluster.

Design

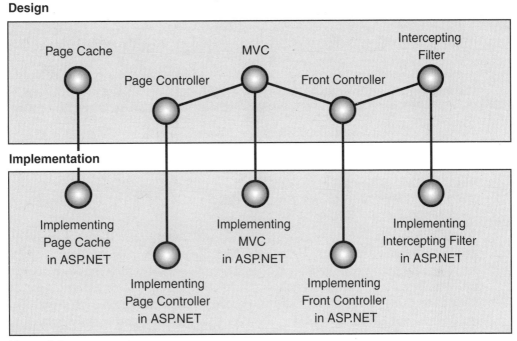

Figure 3.1
Web Presentation patterns cluster

The implementation of *MVC* with Microsoft® ASP.NET starts with an example of a simple system, written on a single page, with application logic embedded in the presentation elements. As complexity grows, the code-behind feature of ASP.NET is used to separate the presentation code (view) from the model-controller code. This works well, until requirements drive you to consider reusing the model code, without the controller, to avoid redundancy within your application. At this point, independent models are created to abstract the business logic, and the code-behind feature is used to adapt the model to the view code. The implementation then finishes off with a discussion about the testing implications of this MVC approach.

So far, the use of the *Model-View-Controller* pattern has focused on the model and the view; the controller plays a relatively minor role. In fact, the controller at work in this pattern is really the implicit controller in ASP.NET. It is responsible for sensing user events (requests and postbacks) and wiring those events to the appropriate system response, which in this case is the events in the code-behind page.

In dynamic Web-based applications, many common tasks are repeated during each page request, such as user authentication, validation, request parameter extraction, and presentation-related database lookups. Left unmanaged, these tasks can quickly lead to unnecessary code duplication. Because these tasks have everything to do with sensing user events and determining the proper system response, the logical place to put this behavior is in the controller.

More Powerful Controllers

The next pattern in this cluster is *Page Controller,* which is a refinement of *Model-View-Controller* and is appropriate for the next level of complexity. This pattern uses a controller at the page scope, accepts input from the page request, invokes the requested actions on the model, and then determines the correct view to use for the resulting page. Duplicate logic, such as validation, is moved into a base controller class.

Implementing Page Controller with ASP.NET illustrates the power of the ASP.NET built-in page controller functionality with a common look-and-feel example. The implementation also uses the *Template Method* [Gamma95] pattern, in conjunction with *Page Controller,* to define the skeleton of an algorithm in an operation, deferring some of those steps to subclasses.

As more complexity is added to the application, eventually the page controller accumulates a great deal of logic in the base class, a problem which is often solved by deepening the page controller inheritance hierarchy. Given enough complexity, both of these factors lead to code that is hard to maintain and extend. Also, certain applications need dynamic configuration of navigation maps, which would potentially span multiple page controllers. When this level of complexity occurs, it is time to consider *Front Controller.*

Front Controller, the next pattern in this catalog, is also a refinement of *Model-View-Controller.* In a front controller, all of the requests are channeled through a single, usually, two-part controller. The first part of the controller is the handler, and the second part is a hierarchy of *Commands* [Gamma95]. The commands themselves are part of the controller and represent specific actions that the controller triggers. After the action has executed, the command chooses which view to use to render the page. Usually, this controller framework is built to use a configuration file that maps requests to actions, and is therefore easy to change after it is built. The tradeoff, of course, is in the level of complexity inherent in this design.

Filters and Caching

The last two patterns in this cluster involve filters and caching.

Intercepting Filter offers a solution to the problem of how to implement common preprocessing and post-processing of the HTTP request. An *Intercepting Filter* is an ideal place to perform common tasks that are not application-specific, such as security checks, logging, compression, encoding, and decoding. Intercepting filters are typically concerned with performing one particular task. If multiple tasks execute against the HTTP request, multiple filters are chained together. *Implementing Intercepting Filter in ASP.NET Using HTTP Module* highlights the ease with which you can implement this pattern in ASP.NET.

Page Cache deals with increasing the scalability and performance of Web applications by keeping a copy of often-used dynamic Web pages that are expensive to create. After the page is initially created, the copy is sent in response to future requests. *Page Cache* also discusses several key cache design factors such as cache refresh, data freshness, and cache granularity. *Implementing Page Cache in ASP.NET Using Absolute Expiration* demonstrates the built-in page cache functionality of ASP.NET.

Web Presentation Patterns

The following table lists the patterns included in the Web Presentation patterns cluster. The patterns are arranged so that later patterns build on earlier patterns. This implies a progression from more general patterns (such as *Model-View-Controller*) to more specific patterns (such as *Intercepting Filter*).

Table 3.1: Web Presentation Patterns

Pattern	Problem	Associated implementations
Model-View-Controller	How do you modularize the user interface functionality of a Web application so that you can easily modify the individual parts?	*Implementing Model-View-Controller in ASP.NET*
Page Controller	How do you best structure the controller for moderately complex Web applications so that you can achieve reuse and flexibility while avoiding code duplication?	*Implementing Page Controller in ASP.NET*
Front Controller	How do you best structure the controller for very complex Web applications so that you can achieve reuse and flexibility while avoiding code duplication?	*Implementing Front Controller in ASP.NET Using HTTP Handler*
Intercepting Filter	How do you implement common pre- and post-processing steps around Web page requests?	*Implementing Intercepting Filter in ASP.NET Using HTTP Module*
Page Cache	How do you improve the response time of dynamically generated Web pages that are requested frequently but consume a large amount of system resources to construct?	*Implementing Page Cache in ASP.NET Using Absolute Expiration*
Observer	How can an object notify other objects of state changes without being dependent on their classes?	*Implementing Observer in .NET*

Model-View-Controller

Context

The purpose of many computer systems is to retrieve data from a data store and display it for the user. After the user changes the data, the system stores the updates in the data store. Because the key flow of information is between the data store and the user interface, you might be inclined to tie these two pieces together to reduce the amount of coding and to improve application performance. However, this seemingly natural approach has some significant problems. One problem is that the user interface tends to change much more frequently than the data storage system. Another problem with coupling the data and user interface pieces is that business applications tend to incorporate business logic that goes far beyond data transmission.

Problem

How do you modularize the user interface functionality of a Web application so that you can easily modify the individual parts?

Forces

The following forces act on a system within this context and must be reconciled as you consider a solution to the problem:

- User interface logic tends to change more frequently than business logic, especially in Web-based applications. For example, new user interface pages may be added, or existing page layouts may be shuffled around. After all, one of the advantages of a Web-based thin-client application is the fact that you can change the user interface at any time without having to redistribute the application. If presentation code and business logic are combined in a single object, you have to modify an object containing business logic every time you change the user interface. This is likely to introduce errors and require the retesting of all business logic after every minimal user interface change.

- In some cases, the application displays the same data in different ways. For example, when an analyst prefers a spreadsheet view of data whereas management prefers a pie chart of the same data. In some rich-client user interfaces, multiple views of the same data are shown at the same time. If the user changes data in one view, the system must update all other views of the data automatically.

- Designing visually appealing and efficient HTML pages generally requires a different skill set than does developing complex business logic. Rarely does a person have both skill sets. Therefore, it is desirable to separate the development effort of these two parts.

- User interface activity generally consists of two parts: presentation and update. The presentation part retrieves data from a data source and formats the data for display. When the user performs an action based on the data, the update part passes control back to the business logic to update the data.

- In Web applications, a single page request combines the processing of the action associated with the link that the user selected with the rendering of the target page. In many cases, the target page may not be directly related to the action. For example, imagine a simple Web application that shows a list of items. The user returns to the main list page after either adding an item to the list or deleting an item from the list. Therefore, the application must render the same page (the list) after executing two quite different commands (adding or deleting)—all within the same HTTP request.

- User interface code tends to be more device-dependent than business logic. If you want to migrate the application from a browser-based application to support personal digital assistants (PDAs) or Web-enabled cell phones, you must replace much of the user interface code, whereas the business logic may be unaffected. A clean separation of these two parts accelerates the migration and minimizes the risk of introducing errors into the business logic.

- Creating automated tests for user interfaces is generally more difficult and time-consuming than for business logic. Therefore, reducing the amount of code that is directly tied to the user interface enhances the testability of the application.

Solution

The *Model-View-Controller (MVC)* pattern separates the modeling of the domain, the presentation, and the actions based on user input into three separate classes [Burbeck92]:

- **Model**. The model manages the behavior and data of the application domain, responds to requests for information about its state (usually from the view), and responds to instructions to change state (usually from the controller).

- **View**. The view manages the display of information.

- **Controller**. The controller interprets the mouse and keyboard inputs from the user, informing the model and/or the view to change as appropriate.

Figure 3.2 depicts the structural relationship between the three objects.

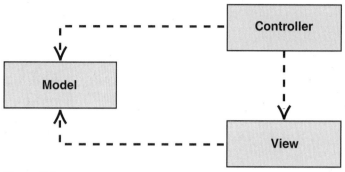

Figure 3.2
MVC class structure

It is important to note that both the view and the controller depend on the model. However, the model depends on neither the view nor the controller. This is one the key benefits of the separation. This separation allows the model to be built and tested independent of the visual presentation. The separation between view and controller is secondary in many rich-client applications, and, in fact, many user interface frameworks implement the roles as one object. In Web applications, on the other hand, the separation between view (the browser) and controller (the server-side components handling the HTTP request) is very well defined.

Model-View-Controller is a fundamental design pattern for the separation of user interface logic from business logic. Unfortunately, the popularity of the pattern has resulted in a number of faulty descriptions. In particular, the term "controller" has been used to mean different things in different contexts. Fortunately, the advent of Web applications has helped resolve some of the ambiguity because the separation between the view and the controller is so apparent.

Variations

In *Application Programming in Smalltalk-80: How to use Model-View-Controller (MVC)* [Burbeck92], Steve Burbeck describes two variations of *MVC*: a passive model and an active model.

The passive model is employed when one controller manipulates the model exclusively. The controller modifies the model and then informs the view that the model has changed and should be refreshed (see Figure 3.3). The model in this scenario is completely independent of the view and the controller, which means that there is no means for the model to report changes in its state. The HTTP protocol is an example of this. There is no simple way in the browser to get asynchronous updates from the server. The browser displays the view and responds to user input, but it does not detect changes in the data on the server. Only when the user explicitly requests a refresh is the server interrogated for changes.

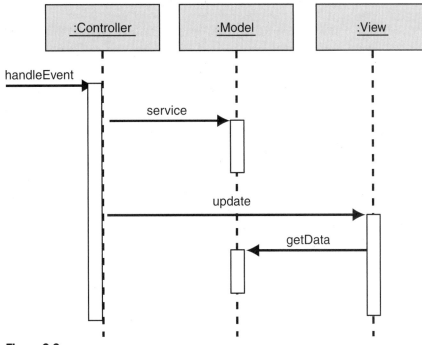

Figure 3.3
Behavior of the passive model

The active model is used when the model changes state without the controller's involvement. This can happen when other sources are changing the data and the changes must be reflected in the views. Consider a stock-ticker display. You receive stock data from an external source and want to update the views (for example, a ticker band and an alert window) when the stock data changes. Because only the model detects changes to its internal state when they occur, the model must notify the views to refresh the display.

However, one of the motivations of using the *MVC* pattern is to make the model independent from of the views. If the model had to notify the views of changes, you would reintroduce the dependency you were looking to avoid. Fortunately, the *Observer* pattern [Gamma95] provides a mechanism to alert other objects of state changes without introducing dependencies on them. The individual views implement the *Observer* interface and register with the model. The model tracks the list of all observers that subscribe to changes. When a model changes, the model iterates through all registered observers and notifies them of the change. This approach is often called "publish-subscribe." The model never requires specific information about any views. In fact, in scenarios where the controller needs to be informed of model changes (for example, to enable or disable menu options), all the controller has to do is implement the *Observer* interface and subscribe to the model changes. In situations where there are many views, it makes sense to define multiple subjects, each of which describes a specific type of model change. Each view can then subscribe only to types of changes that are relevant to the view.

Figure 3.4 shows the structure of the active MVC using *Observer* and how the observer isolates the model from referencing views directly.

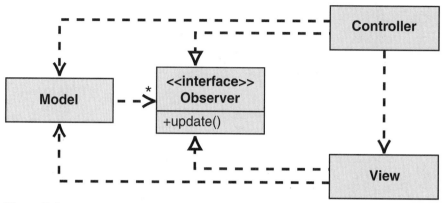

Figure 3.4
Using Observer to decouple the model from the view in the active model

Figure 3.5 illustrates how the *Observer* notifies the views when the model changes. Unfortunately, there is no good way to demonstrate the separation of model and view in a Unified Modeling Language (UML) sequence diagram, because the diagram represents instances of objects rather than classes and interfaces.

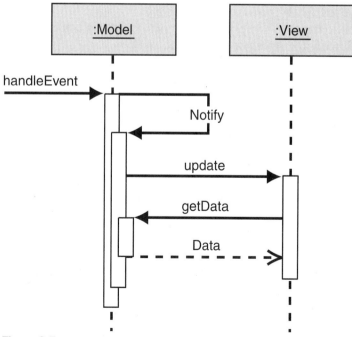

Figure 3.5
Behavior of the active model

Example

See *Implementing Model-View-Controller in ASP.NET.*

Testing Considerations

Testability is greatly enhanced when you employ employing *Model-View-Controller.* Testing components becomes difficult when they are highly interdependent, especially with user interface components. These types of components often require a complex setup just to test a simple function. Worse, when an error occurs, it is hard to isolate the problem to a specific component. This is the reason why separation of concerns is such an important architectural driver. *MVC* separates the concern of storing, displaying, and updating data into three components that can be tested individually.

Apart from the problems posed by interdependencies, user interface frameworks are inherently difficult to test. Testing user interfaces either requires tedious (and error-prone) manual testing or testing scripts that simulate user actions. These scripts tend to be time-consuming to develop and brittle. *MVC* does not eliminate the need for user interface testing, but separating the model from the presentation logic allows the model to be tested independent of the presentation and reduces the number of user interface test cases.

Resulting Context

Architecting the presentation layer around the *MVC* pattern results in the following benefits and liabilities:

Benefits

- **Supports multiple views**. Because the view is separated from the model and there is no direct dependency from the model to the view, the user interface can display multiple views of the same data at the same time. For example, multiple pages in a Web application may use the same model objects. Another example is a Web application that allows the user to change the appearance of the pages. These pages display the same data from the shared model, but show it in a different way.

- **Accommodates change**. User interface requirements tend to change more rapidly than business rules. Users may prefer different colors, fonts, screen layouts, and levels of support for new devices such as cell phones or PDAs. Because the model does not depend on the views, adding new types of views to the system generally does not affect the model. As a result, the scope of change is confined to the view. This pattern lays the foundation for further specializations of this pattern such as *Page Controller* and *Front Controller*.

Liabilities

- **Complexity**. The *MVC* pattern introduces new levels of indirection and therefore increases the complexity of the solution slightly. It also increases the event-driven nature of the user-interface code, which can become more difficult to debug.

- **Cost of frequent updates**. Decoupling the model from the view does not mean that developers of the model can ignore the nature of the views. For example, if the model undergoes frequent changes, it could flood the views with update requests. Some views, such as graphical displays, may take some time to render. As a result, the view may fall behind update requests. Therefore, it is important to keep the view in mind when coding the model. For example, the model could batch multiple updates into a single notification to the view.

Variants

The *Document-View* variant recognizes all three roles of *Model-View-Controller* but merges the controller into the view. The document corresponds to the model role in *MVC*. This variant is present in many existing GUI platforms. An excellent example of *Document-View* is the Microsoft® Foundation Class Library (MFC) in the Microsoft Visual C++® environment. The tradeoff of using this variant is that the view and the controller are more tightly coupled.

Related Patterns

For more information, see the following related patterns:

- *Observer*. This pattern is often mentioned in conjunction with *MVC* due to the need to keep the views and the associated model synchronized.

- *Page Controller* and *Front Controller* describe implementation strategies for the controller portion of the *MVC* pattern.

Acknowledgments

Model-View-Controller began as a framework developed by Trygve Reenskaug for the Smalltalk platform in the late 1970s [Fowler03]. The version you have just read references the following works:

[Burbeck92] Burbeck, Steve. "Application Programming in Smalltalk-80: How to use Model-View-Controller (MVC)." *University of Illinois in Urbana-Champaign (UIUC) Smalltalk Archive*. Available at *http://st-www.cs.uiuc.edu/users/smarch/st-docs/mvc.html*.

[Fowler03] Fowler, Martin. *Patterns of Enterprise Application Architecture*. Addison-Wesley, 2003.

[Gamma95] Gamma, Helm, Johnson, and Vlissides. *Design Patterns: Elements of Reusable Object-Oriented Software*. Addison-Wesley, 1995.

Implementing Model-View-Controller in ASP.NET

Context

You are building a Web application in Microsoft® ASP.NET, and, based on the complexity of your application, you need to separate different aspects of the program to reduce code duplication and to limit the propagation of change.

Implementation Strategy

To explain how to implement the *Model-View-Controller* pattern in ASP.NET and the value provided by separating the model, view, and controller roles in software, the following example refactors a single-page solution, which does not separate all three roles, into a solution that separates the roles. The example application is a single Web page (shown in Figure 3.6) with a drop-down list, which displays recordings that are stored in a database.

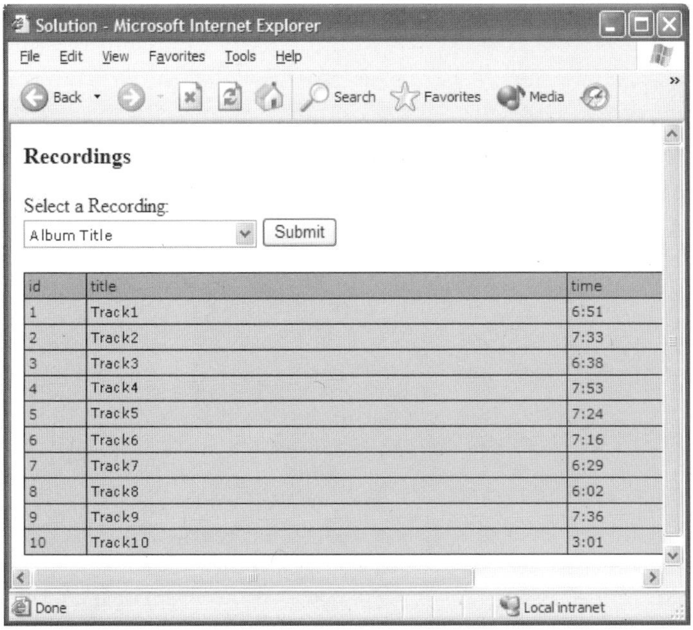

Figure 3.6
Example Web page

The user selects a specific recording from the drop-down list and then clicks the Submit button. The application then retrieves the list of all tracks from this recording from the database and displays the results in a table. All three solutions described in this pattern implement the exact same functionality.

Single ASP.NET Page

There are many ways to implement this page in ASP.NET. The simplest and most straightforward is to put everything in one file called "Solution.aspx," as in the following code example:

```csharp
<%@ Import Namespace="System.Data" %>
<%@ Import Namespace="System.Data.SqlClient" %>
<html>
    <head>
        <title>start</title>
        <script language="c#" runat="server">
            void Page_Load(object sender, System.EventArgs e)
            {
                String selectCmd = "select * from Recording";

                SqlConnection myConnection =
                    new SqlConnection(
                        "server=(local);database=recordings;Trusted_Connection=yes");
                SqlDataAdapter myCommand = new SqlDataAdapter(selectCmd,
                    myConnection);

                DataSet ds = new DataSet();
                myCommand.Fill(ds, "Recording");

                recordingSelect.DataSource = ds;
                recordingSelect.DataTextField = "title";
                recordingSelect.DataValueField = "id";
                recordingSelect.DataBind();
            }

            void SubmitBtn_Click(Object sender, EventArgs e)
            {
                String selectCmd =
                    String.Format(
                    "select * from Track where recordingId = {0} order by id",
                    (string)recordingSelect.SelectedItem.Value);

                SqlConnection myConnection =
                    new SqlConnection(
                        "server=(local);database=recordings;Trusted_Connection=yes");

                SqlDataAdapter myCommand = new SqlDataAdapter(selectCmd,
                    myConnection);

                DataSet ds = new DataSet();
                myCommand.Fill(ds, "Track");

                MyDataGrid.DataSource = ds;
                MyDataGrid.DataBind();
            }
        </script>
    </head>
```

```
<body>
    <form id="start" method="post" runat="server">
        <h3>Recordings</h3>
        Select a Recording:<br />
        <asp:dropdownlist id="recordingSelect" runat="server" />
        <asp:button runat="server" text="Submit" OnClick="SubmitBtn_Click" />
        <p/>
        <asp:datagrid id="MyDataGrid" runat="server" width="700"
              backcolor="#ccccff" bordercolor="black" showfooter="false"
              cellpadding="3" cellspacing="0" font-name="Verdana"
              font-size="8pt" headerstyle-backcolor="#aaaadd"
              enableviewstate="false" />
    </form>
</body>
</html>
```

This file implements all three roles from the pattern but does not separate them into different files or classes. The view role is represented by the HTML-specific rendering code. This page uses an implementation of *Bound Data Control* to display the **DataSet** object that is returned from the database. The model role is implemented in the **Page_Load** and **SubmitBtn_Click** functions. The controller role is not represented directly, but it is implicit in ASP.NET; see *Page Controller*. The page updates when the user makes a request. *Model-View-Controller* describes this as a passive controller. ASP.NET implements the controller role, but the programmer is responsible for connecting the actions to the events to which the controller will respond. In this example, the controller calls the **Page_Load** function before the page loads. The controller calls the **SubmitBtn_Click** function when the user clicks the Submit button.

This page is very straightforward and self-contained. The implementation is useful, and is an excellent starting point when the application is small and does not change very often. You should consider changing this approach, however, if one of more of the following situations occurs in your development effort:

- **You want to increase parallelism and reduce potential for errors**. You may want different people working on the view code and the model code to increase the amount of parallelism and limit the potential for introducing errors. For example, if all of the code is in one page, a developer could change the formatting of the DataGrid and inadvertently change some of the source code that accesses the database. You would not discover this error until the page was viewed again, because the page is not compiled until it is viewed.

- **You want to reuse the database access code on multiple pages**. In this current implementation, there is no way to reuse any of the code in other pages without duplicating it. Duplicate code is difficult to maintain, because if a change occurs in the database code, you have to modify all the pages that access the database.

To address some of these issues, the implementers of ASP.NET introduced the code-behind feature.

Code-Behind Refactoring

The code-behind feature of the Microsoft Visual Studio® .NET development system makes it easy to separate the presentation (view) code from the model-controller code. Each ASP.NET page has a mechanism that allows methods that are called from the page to be implemented in a separate class. This mechanism is facilitated by Visual Studio .NET and it has many advantages, such as Microsoft IntelliSense® technology. When you use the code-behind feature to implement your pages, you can use IntelliSense to show a list of available methods of the objects that you are using in the code behind the page. IntelliSense does not work in .aspx pages.

The following is the same example, this time using the code-behind feature to implement ASP.NET.

View

The presentation code is now in a separate file called Solution.aspx:

```
<%@ Page language="c#" Codebehind="Solution.aspx.cs"
    AutoEventWireup="false" Inherits="Solution" %>
<html>
    <head>
        <title>Solution</title>
    </head>
    <body>
        <form id="Solution" method="post" runat="server">
            <h3>Recordings</h3>
            Select a Recording:<br/>
            <asp:dropdownlist id="recordingSelect" runat="server" />
            <asp:button id="submit" runat="server" text="Submit"
                enableviewstate="False" />
            <p/>
            <asp:datagrid id="MyDataGrid" runat="server" width="700"
                    backcolor="#ccccff" bordercolor="black" showfooter="false"
                    cellpadding="3" cellspacing="0" font-name="Verdana" font-size="8pt"
                    headerstyle-backcolor="#aaaadd" enableviewstate="false" />
        </form>
    </body>
</html>
```

Most of this code is similar to the code used in the first implementation. The main difference is the first line:

```
<%@ Page language="c#" Codebehind="Solution.aspx.cs"
    AutoEventWireup="false" Inherits="Solution" %>
```

This line indicates to the ASP.NET environment that a code-behind class implements methods that are referenced in this page. Because the page is free of any code that accesses the database, there is no longer any need to modify this page if the database access code changes. Someone who is familiar with the design of the user interface can modify this code without introducing any errors to the database access code.

Model-Controller

The second part of the solution is the following code-behind page:

```csharp
using System;
using System.Data;
using System.Data.SqlClient;

public class Solution : System.Web.UI.Page
{
    protected System.Web.UI.WebControls.Button submit;
    protected System.Web.UI.WebControls.DataGrid MyDataGrid;
    protected System.Web.UI.WebControls.DropDownList recordingSelect;

    private void Page_Load(object sender, System.EventArgs e)
    {
        if(!IsPostBack)
        {
            String selectCmd = "select * from Recording";

            SqlConnection myConnection =
                new SqlConnection(
                    "server=(local);database=recordings;Trusted_Connection=yes");
            SqlDataAdapter myCommand = new SqlDataAdapter(selectCmd, myConnection);

            DataSet ds = new DataSet();
            myCommand.Fill(ds, "Recording");

            recordingSelect.DataSource = ds;
            recordingSelect.DataTextField = "title";
            recordingSelect.DataValueField = "id";
            recordingSelect.DataBind();
        }
    }

    void SubmitBtn_Click(Object sender, EventArgs e)
    {
        String selectCmd =
            String.Format(
            "select * from Track where recordingId = {0} order by id",
            (string)recordingSelect.SelectedItem.Value);

        SqlConnection myConnection =
            new SqlConnection(
                "server=(local);database=recordings;Trusted_Connection=yes");
        SqlDataAdapter myCommand = new SqlDataAdapter(selectCmd, myConnection);

        DataSet ds = new DataSet();
        myCommand.Fill(ds, "Track");

        MyDataGrid.DataSource = ds;
        MyDataGrid.DataBind();
    }
```

```
#region Web Form Designer generated code
override protected void OnInit(EventArgs e)
{
    //
    // CODEGEN: This call is required by the ASP.NET Web Form Designer.
    //
    InitializeComponent();
    base.OnInit(e);
}

/// <summary>
/// Required method for Designer support - do not modify
/// the contents of this method with the code editor.
/// </summary>
private void InitializeComponent()
{
    this.submit.Click += new System.EventHandler(this.SubmitBtn_Click);
    this.Load += new System.EventHandler(this.Page_Load);

}
#endregion
}
```

This code has been moved from the single ASP.NET page into its own file. A few syntactic changes are required to link the two entities together. The member variables defined in the class share the same name as the ones referenced in the Solution.aspx file. The other aspect that must be explicitly defined is how the controller links the events that occur to the actions that must be performed. The **InitializeComponent** method links the two events in this example. The first is the **Load** event, which is linked to the **Page_Load** function. The second is the **Click** event, which triggers the **SubmitBtn_Click** function to run when the Submit button is clicked.

The code-behind feature is an elegant mechanism for separating the view role from the model and controller roles. It may become insufficient when you need to reuse the code that is present in the code-behind class for another page. It is technically possible to reuse the code from the code-behind page, but highly undesirable, due to the increase in coupling of all the pages that share the code-behind class.

Model-View-Controller Refactoring

To resolve the last issue, you need to further separate the model code from the controller. The view code is identical to the code used in the previous implementation.

Model

The following code example describes the model and is dependent on the database only; it does not contain any view-dependent code (code with ASP.NET dependencies):

```
using System;
using System.Collections;
using System.Data;
using System.Data.SqlClient;

public class DatabaseGateway
{
    public static DataSet GetRecordings()
    {
        String selectCmd = "select * from Recording";

        SqlConnection myConnection =
            new SqlConnection(
                "server=(local);database=recordings;Trusted_Connection=yes");
        SqlDataAdapter myCommand = new SqlDataAdapter(selectCmd, myConnection);

        DataSet ds = new DataSet();
        myCommand.Fill(ds, "Recording");
        return ds;
    }

    public static DataSet GetTracks(string recordingId)
    {
        String selectCmd =
            String.Format(
            "select * from Track where recordingId = {0} order by id",
            recordingId);

        SqlConnection myConnection =
            new SqlConnection(
                "server=(local);database=recordings;Trusted_Connection=yes");
        SqlDataAdapter myCommand = new SqlDataAdapter(selectCmd, myConnection);

        DataSet ds = new DataSet();
        myCommand.Fill(ds, "Track");
        return ds;
    }
}
```

This is now the only file that depends on the database. This class is an excellent example of a *Table Data Gateway*. A *Table Data Gateway* holds all the SQL code for accessing a single table or view; selects, inserts, updates, and deletes. Other code calls its methods for all interaction with the database. [Fowler03]

Controller

This refactoring uses the code-behind feature to adapt the model code to the data controls that exist on the page and to map the events that the controller forwards to the specific action methods. Because the model here returns a **DataSet** object, its job is straightforward. This code, like the view code, does not depend on how data is retrieved from the database.

```csharp
using System;
using System.Data;
using System.Collections;
using System.Web.UI.WebControls;

public class Solution : System.Web.UI.Page
{
    protected System.Web.UI.WebControls.Button submit;
    protected System.Web.UI.WebControls.DataGrid MyDataGrid;
    protected System.Web.UI.WebControls.DropDownList recordingSelect;

    private void Page_Load(object sender, System.EventArgs e)
    {
        if(!IsPostBack)
        {
            DataSet ds = DatabaseGateway.GetRecordings();
            recordingSelect.DataSource = ds;
            recordingSelect.DataTextField = "title";
            recordingSelect.DataValueField = "id";
            recordingSelect.DataBind();
        }
    }

    void SubmitBtn_Click(Object sender, EventArgs e)
    {
        DataSet ds =
            DatabaseGateway.GetTracks(
            (string)recordingSelect.SelectedItem.Value);

        MyDataGrid.DataSource = ds;
        MyDataGrid.DataBind();
    }

    #region Web Form Designer generated code
    override protected void OnInit(EventArgs e)
    {
        //
        // CODEGEN: This call is required by the ASP.NET Web Form Designer.
        //
        InitializeComponent();
        base.OnInit(e);
    }

    /// <summary>
    /// Required method for Designer support - do not modify
    /// the contents of this method with the code editor.
    /// </summary>
    private void InitializeComponent()
    {
        this.submit.Click += new System.EventHandler(this.SubmitBtn_Click);
        this.Load += new System.EventHandler(this.Page_Load);

    }
    #endregion
}
```

Tests

Separating the model from the ASP.NET environment makes testing of the model code easier. To test this code inside the ASP.NET environment, you must test the output of the process. This means reading HTML and determining if it is correct, which is tedious and error-prone. The separation of the model so that it can run without ASP.NET allows you to avoid the tedium and test the code in isolation. The following are sample unit tests in NUnit (*http://nunit.org*) for the model code:

```csharp
using System;

using NUnit.Framework;
using System.Collections;
using System.Data;
using System.Data.SqlClient;

[TestFixture]
public class GatewayFixture
{
    [Test]
    public void Tracks1234Query()
    {

        DataSet ds = DatabaseGateway.GetTracks("1234");
        Assertion.AssertEquals(10, ds.Tables["Track"].Rows.Count);
    }

    [Test]
    public void Tracks2345Query()
    {
        DataSet ds = DatabaseGateway.GetTracks("2345");
        Assertion.AssertEquals(3, ds.Tables["Track"].Rows.Count);
    }

    [Test]
    public void Recordings()
    {

        DataSet ds = DatabaseGateway.GetRecordings();
        Assertion.AssertEquals(4, ds.Tables["Recording"].Rows.Count);

        DataTable recording = ds.Tables["Recording"];
        Assertion.AssertEquals(4, recording.Rows.Count);

        DataRow firstRow = recording.Rows[0];
        string title = (string)firstRow["title"];
        Assertion.AssertEquals("Up", title.Trim());
    }
}
```

Resulting Context

Implementing MVC in ASP.NET results in the following benefits and liabilities:

Benefits

- **Reduced dependencies**. An ASP.NET page allows the programmer to implement methods within a page. As the Single ASP.NET Page shows, this can be useful for prototypes and small short-lived Web applications. As the complexity of the page, or the need to share code between pages, increases, it becomes more useful to separate portions of the code.

- **Reduced code duplication**. The **GetRecordings** and **GetTracks** methods in the **DatabaseGateway** class can now be used by other pages. This eliminates the need to copy the methods into multiple views.

- **Separation of duties and concerns**. The skill set for modifying the ASP.NET pages is different from the skill set for writing code that accesses the database. Separating the view and the model, as shown earlier, allows specialists in each area to work in parallel.

- **Optimizing opportunities**. Separating the responsibilities into specific classes, as shown earlier, increases the opportunities for optimization. In the example described previously, the data is loaded from the database every time a request is made. It would be possible to cache the data in certain situations, which could improve the overall performance of the application. This, however, would be difficult or impossible without separating the code.

- **Testability**. Isolating the model from the view makes it possible to test the model outside the ASP.NET environment.

Liabilities

Additional code and complexity. The example shown earlier adds more files and code, which increases the maintenance cost of the code when changes must be made to all three roles. In some cases, making the changes in one file is easier than separating out the changes into multiple files. The extra cost must be weighed against the reasons for separating the code. For small applications, the cost might not be justified.

Related Patterns

- *Table Data Gateway*. This pattern is an object that acts as a gateway to a database table. One instance handles all the roles in a table. [Fowler03]

- *Bound Data Control*. This pattern is a user interface component that is bound to a data source and can render itself on the screen or page.

Acknowledgments

[Fowler03] Fowler, Martin. *Patterns of Enterprise Application Architecture*. Addison-Wesley, 2003.

Page Controller

Context

You decided to use the *Model-View-Controller (MVC)* pattern to separate the user interface components of your dynamic Web application from the business logic. The application you are building constructs the Web pages dynamically, but the navigation between the pages is mostly static.

Problem

How do you best structure the controller for moderately complex Web applications so that you can achieve reuse and flexibility while avoiding code duplication?

Forces

The following forces act on a system within this context and must be reconciled as you consider a solution to the problem:

- The *MVC* pattern often focuses primarily on the separation between the model and the view, while paying less attention to the controller. In many rich-client scenarios, the separation between controller and view is less critical and is often omitted [Fowler03]. In a thin-client application, however, view and controller are inherently separated because the presentation occurs in the client browser, whereas the controller is part of the server-side application. The controller, therefore, warrants a closer examination.

- In dynamic Web applications, multiple user actions can lead to different controller logic, followed by the same page presentation. For example, in a simple Web-based e-mail application, both sending a message and deleting a message from the inbox is likely to return the user to the (refreshed) inbox page. Although the same page is rendered after either activity, the application must perform a different action, based on the previous page and the button the user clicked.

- The code that renders most dynamic Web pages involves very similar steps: verifying user authentication, extracting the page parameters from the query string or the form fields, gathering session information, retrieving data from a data source, rendering the dynamic portion of the page, and adding applicable headers and footers. This can lead to a significant amount of code duplication.

- Scripted server pages (such as ASP.NET) may be easy to create, but can introduce a number of disadvantages as the application grows. Scripted pages provide poor separation between controller and the view, which reduces the opportunities for reuse. For example, if multiple actions lead to the same page, it is difficult to reuse the display code across multiple controllers, because it is intertwined with the controller code. Scripted server pages that intersperse business logic and presentation logic are also more difficult to test and debug. Finally, developing scripted server pages requires expertise both in developing business logic and in rendering visually appealing and efficient HTML pages; these two skill sets are rarely possessed by a single person. Due to these considerations, it makes sense to minimize the scripted server-page code and develop business logic in actual classes.

● As described in the *MVC* pattern, testing user interface code tends to be time-consuming and tedious. If you can separate user-interface-specific code from the actual business logic, testing the business logic becomes simpler and more repeatable. This is true not only for the presentation portion, but also for the controller part of an application.

● Common appearance and navigation tend to improve usability and brand recognition of a Web application. However, common appearance can lead to repetitive presentation code, especially if the code is embedded inside scripted server pages. Therefore, you need a mechanism for improving reuse of presentation logic across pages.

Solution

Use the *Page Controller* pattern to accept input from the page request, invoke the requested actions on the model, and determine the correct view to use for the resulting page. Separate the dispatching logic from any view-related code. Where appropriate, create a common base class for all page controllers to avoid code duplication and increase consistency and testability. Figure 3.7 shows how the page controller relates to the model and view.

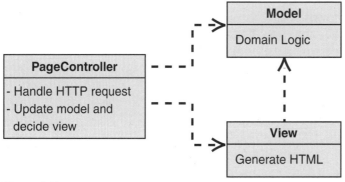

Figure 3.7
Page Controller structure

The page controller receives a page request, extracts any relevant data, invokes any updates to the model, and forwards the request to the view. The view in turn depends on the model for retrieval of data to be displayed. Defining a separate page controller isolates the model from the specifics of the Web request — for example, session management, or the use of query strings or hidden form fields to pass parameters to the page. In this basic form, you create a controller for every link in the Web application. This keeps the controllers simple, because you only have to concern yourself with one action at a time.

Creating a separate controller for each Web page (or action) can lead to significant code duplication. Therefore, you should create a **BaseController** class to incorporate common functions such as validating parameters (see Figure 3.8). Each individual page controller can inherit this common functionality from **BaseController**. In addition to inheriting from a common base class, you can also define a set of helper classes that the controllers can call to perform common functions.

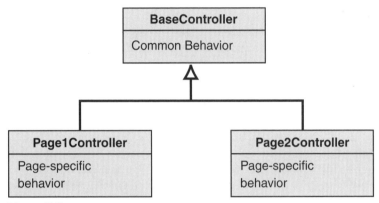

Figure 3.8
Using BaseController to eliminate code duplication

This approach works well if most pages are similar and you can pull the common functions into a single base class. The more page variations you have, the more levels you may have to inject into the inheritance tree. Let's say that all pages parse parameters, but only pages that display lists retrieve data from the database, while pages that require data entry update the model, rather than retrieve data. You could now introduce two new base classes, **ListController** and **DataEntryController**, that both inherit from **BaseController**. The list pages could then inherit from **ListController**, and the data entry pages could inherit from **DataEntryController**. Although this approach may work well in this simple example, the inheritance tree can get rather deep and complicated if you are dealing with a real-life businesses application. You may be tempted to add conditional logic into the base classes to accommodate some of the variants, but doing so violates the principles of encapsulation and makes the base classes a notorious bottleneck for any changes to the system. Therefore, you should consider using helper classes or the *Front Controller* pattern as your application becomes more complex.

Using a page controller for a Web application is such a common need that most Web application frameworks provide a default implementation of the page controller. Most frameworks incorporate the page controller in the form of a server page (for example, ASP, JSP, and PHP). Server pages actually combine the functions of view and controller and do not provide the desired separation between the presentation code and the controller code. Unfortunately, some of the frameworks make it very easy to blend together view-related code with controller-related code and make it difficult to properly separate the controller logic. As a result, the *Page Controller* approach has developed a bad reputation with many developers. Now, many developers associate *Page Controller* with bad design and *Front Controller* with good design. This perception, in fact, resulted from a specific (faulty) implementation choice; both *Page Controller* and the *Front Controller* are perfectly viable architectural choices.

Therefore, it is preferable to separate the controller logic into separate classes that can be called from the server page. The ASP.NET page framework provides an excellent mechanism for achieving this separation, called *code-behind classes*. (See *Implementing Page Controller in ASP.NET*).

Variants

In most cases, the page controller is dependent on the specifics of an HTTP-based Web request. As a result, the page controller code usually contains references to HTTP headers, query strings, form fields, multipart form requests, and so forth. This makes it very hard to test the controller code outside the Web application framework. The only option is to test the controller by simulating HTTP requests and parsing the results. This type of testing is both time-consuming and error prone. Therefore, to improve testability you could separate the Web-dependent and the Web-independent code into two separate classes (see Figure 3.9).

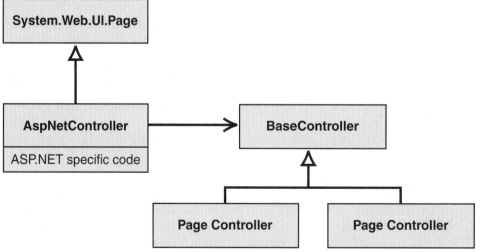

Figure 3.9
Separating the Web-dependent and Web-independent code

In this example, **AspNetController** encapsulates all dependencies on the application framework (ASP.NET). For example, it can extract all incoming parameters from the Web request and pass it to **BaseController** in a way that is independent from the Web interface (for example, in a collection). This approach not only improves testability, but enables you to reuse the controller code with other user interfaces, for example a rich-client interface or a custom scripting language.

The downside of this approach is the additional overhead. You now have an additional class, and each request has to go through a translation before it can be serviced. Therefore, you should keep the environment-specific part of the controller as thin as possible and consider the tradeoffs between reduced dependencies and more efficient development and execution.

Example

See *Implementing Page Controller in ASP.NET*.

Resulting Context

Using the *Page Controller* pattern results in a number of benefits and liabilities.

Benefits

- **Simplicity**. Because each dynamic Web page is handled by a specific controller, the controllers have to deal with only a limited scope and can remain simple. Because each page controller deals with only a single page, *Page Controller* is particularly well-suited for Web applications with simple navigation.
- **Built-in framework features**. In its most basic form, the controller is already built into most Web application platforms. For example, if the user clicks a link in a Web page that leads to a dynamic page generated by an ASP.NET script, the Web server analyzes the URL associated with the link and executes the associated ASP.NET page. In effect, the ASP.NET page is the controller for the action taken by the user. The ASP.NET page framework also provides code-behind classes to execute controller code. Code-behind classes provide better separation between the controller and the view and also allow you to create a controller base class that incorporates common functionality across all controllers. For an example, see *Implementing Page Controller in ASP.NET*.
- **Increased reuse**. Creating a controller base class reduces code duplication and enables you to reuse common code across page controllers. You can reuse code by implementing recurring logic in the base class. This logic is then automatically inherited by all concrete *Page Controller* objects. If the implementation of the logic varies from page to page, you can still use *Template Method* and implement the basic execution structure in the base class; the implementation of specific substeps may vary from page to page.

- **Expandability**. You can expand a page controller quite easily by using helper classes. If the logic inside the controller becomes too complex, you can delegate some of the logic to helper classes. Helper classes also provide another mechanism for reuse, besides inheritance.

- **Separation of developer responsibilities**. Using a *Page Controller* class helps separate responsibilities among members of the development team. The developer of the controller must be familiar with the domain model and the business logic implemented by the application. The designer of the view, on the other hand, can focus on the presentation style of the results.

Liabilities

Due to its simplicity, *Page Controller* is the default implementation for most dynamic Web applications. However, you should be aware of the following limitations:

- **One controller per page**. The key constraint of *Page Controller* is that you create one controller for each Web page. This works well for applications with a static set of pages and a simple navigation path. Some more complex applications require dynamic configuration of pages and navigation maps between them. Spreading this logic across many page controllers would make the application hard to maintain, even if some of the logic could be pulled into the base controller. In addition, the built-in features of the Web framework may reduce the amount of flexibility you have in naming URLs and resource paths (even though you can compensate for some of this with low-level mechanisms like ISAPI filters). In these scenarios, consider using *Front Controller* that intercepts all Web requests and forwards the request to the appropriate handler, based on configurable rules.

- **Deep inheritance trees**. Inheritance seems to be one of the most loved and most hated features of object-oriented programming. Using inheritance alone to reuse common functionality may lead to inflexible inheritance hierarchies. For more detail, see *Implementing Page Controller in ASP.NET*.

- **Dependency on the Web framework**. In the basic form, the page controller still depends on the Web application environment and cannot be tested independently. You can use a wrapper mechanism to decouple the Web-dependent part, but doing so requires an additional level of indirection.

Testing Considerations

Because *Page Controller* is dependent on specifics of the Web application framework (for example, query strings and HTTP headers), you cannot instantiate and test the controller classes outside the Web framework. If you want to run a suite of automated unit tests on the controller class, you would have to start the Web application server for each test case. You would then have to submit HTTP requests in a format that executes the desired function. This configuration introduces many dependencies and side effects into the test. To improve testability, consider separating the business logic (including controller logic as it becomes more complex) from the Web-dependent code.

Related Patterns

For more information, see the following related patterns:

- *Intercepting Filter*. This pattern is another construct to implement recurring functionality inside a Web application. The Web server framework can pass each request through a configurable chain of filters before passing it to the controller. Filters tend to deal with lower-level functions such as decoding, authentication, and session management, whereas *Page Controller* deals with application functionality. Filters also are not usually page-specific.

- *Front Controller*. This pattern is a more complex, but also more powerful alternative to *Page Controller*. *Front Controller* defines a single controller for all page requests, which enables it to make navigational decisions that span multiple pages.

- *Model-View-Controller*. *Page Controller* is an implementation variant of the controller portion of *MVC*.

Acknowledgments

[Fowler03] Fowler, Martin. *Patterns of Enterprise Application Architecture*. Addison-Wesley, 2003.

[Gamma95] Gamma, Helm, Johnson, and Vlissides. *Design Patterns: Element of Reusable Object-Oriented Software*. Addison-Wesley, 1995.

Implementing Page Controller in ASP.NET

Context

You are building a Web application in ASP.NET and you want to take advantage of the event-driven nature of ASP.NET by using the built-in page controller.

Implementation Strategy

The concepts described in the *Page Controller* pattern are implemented in ASP.NET by default. The ASP.NET page framework implements these concepts in such a way that the underlying mechanism of capturing an event on the client, transmitting it to the server, and calling the appropriate method is automatic and invisible to the implementer. The page controller is extensible in that it exposes various events at specific points in the life cycle (see "Page Life Cycle," later in this pattern) so that application-specific actions can be run when they are appropriate.

For example, assume the user is interacting with a Web Forms page that contains one button server control (see "Simple Page Example," later in this pattern). When the user clicks the button control, an event is transmitted as an HTTP post to the server, where the ASP.NET page framework interprets the posted information and associates the raised event with an appropriate event handler. The framework automatically calls the appropriate event handler for the button as part of the framework's normal processing. As a result, you no longer need to implement this functionality. Furthermore, you can use the built-in controller, or you can replace the built-in controller with you own customized controller (see *Front Controller*).

Page Life Cycle

The following list contains the most common stages of the page life cycle in the order in which they occur. It also includes the specific events that are raised and some typical actions that could be performed at the various stages in the processing of the request:

- **ASP.NET page framework initialization (Event: Init)**. This is the first step in the life cycle, which initializes the ASP.NET runtime for the request.

- **User code initialization (Event: Load)**. You should perform common tasks specific to your application, such as opening database connections, when the page controller raises the **Load** event. You can assume that when the **Load** event is raised, server controls are created and initialized, state has been restored, and form controls reflect client-side changes. [Reilly02]

- **Application-specific event handling**. At this stage, you should perform processing specific to your application in response to the events raised by the controller.

- **Cleanup (Event: Unload)**. The page has finished rendering and is ready to be discarded. You should close any database connections that the **Load** event opened and discard any objects that are no longer needed. The Microsoft®.NET Framework closes database connections automatically, after the connection object is garbage collected. However, you do not have any control over when the garbage collection occurs. Therefore, it is good practice to close database connections explicitly to make efficient use of the database connection pool.

Note: There are several more stages of page processing than are listed here. However, they are not used for most page processing scenarios.

Simple Page Example

The first example is a simple page that takes input from the user and then displays the input on the screen. The example illustrates the event-driven model that ASP.NET uses to implement server controls.

Figure 3.10
Simple page

When the user types his or her name and then clicks the Click Here button, the name appears directly below the button, as shown in Figure 3.11.

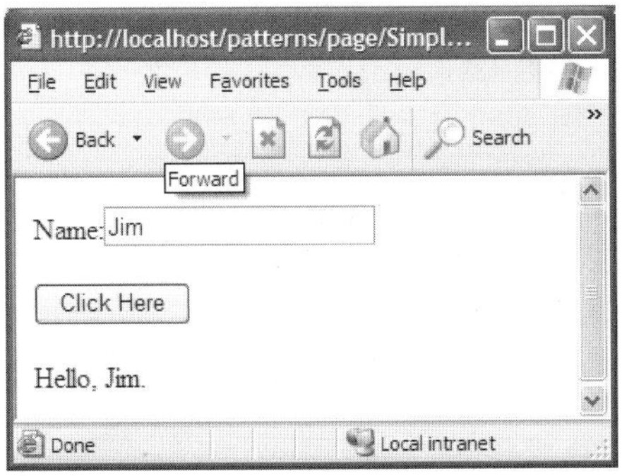

Figure 3.11
Simple page displaying user input

In ASP.NET pages, the user interface programming is divided into two distinct pieces: the visual component, or view, and the logic, which is a combination of the model and the controller. This division separates the visible portion of the page (the view) from the code behind the page with which the page interacts (model and controller).

The visual element is called the Web Forms *page*. The page consists of a file containing static HTML or ASP.NET server controls, or both simultaneously. For this example, the Web Forms page is named SimplePage.aspx and consists of the following code:

```
<%@ Page language="c#" Codebehind="SimplePage.aspx.cs" AutoEventWireup="false"
Inherits="SimplePage" %>
<HTML>
    <body>
        <form id="Form1" runat="server">
            Name:<asp:textbox id="name" runat="server" />
            <p />
            <asp:button id="MyButton" text="Click Here" OnClick="SubmitBtn_Click"
runat="server" />
            <p />
            <span id="mySpan" runat="server"></span>
        </form>
    </body>
</HTML>
```

The logic for the Web Forms page consists of code that you create to interact with the form. The programming logic resides in a file that is separate from the user interface file. This file, referred to as the *code-behind* file, is named SimplePage.aspx.cs:

```
using System;
using System.Web.UI;
using System.Web.UI.WebControls;
using System.Web.UI.HtmlControls;

public class SimplePage : System.Web.UI.Page
{
    protected System.Web.UI.WebControls.TextBox name;
    protected System.Web.UI.WebControls.Button MyButton;
    protected System.Web.UI.HtmlControls.HtmlGenericControl mySpan;

    public void SubmitBtn_Click(Object sender, EventArgs e)
    {
        mySpan.InnerHtml = "Hello, " + name.Text + ".";
    }
}
```

The purpose of this code is to indicate to the page controller that when the user clicks the button, a request will be sent back to the server and the **SubmitBtn_Click** function will be executed.

This implementation shows how simple it is to connect to the events that the controller provides. It also illustrates that code written in this fashion is easier to understand because the application logic is not combined with the low-level code that manages the event dispatching.

Common Look and Feel Example

The following example uses a typical implementation strategy of the page controller to provide a banner that displays dynamic content: the authenticated user's e-mail address (which is retrieved from the database) on every page in the application.

The common implementation is contained in a base class from which all of the page objects in the site inherit. Figure 3.12 shows one of the pages in the site.

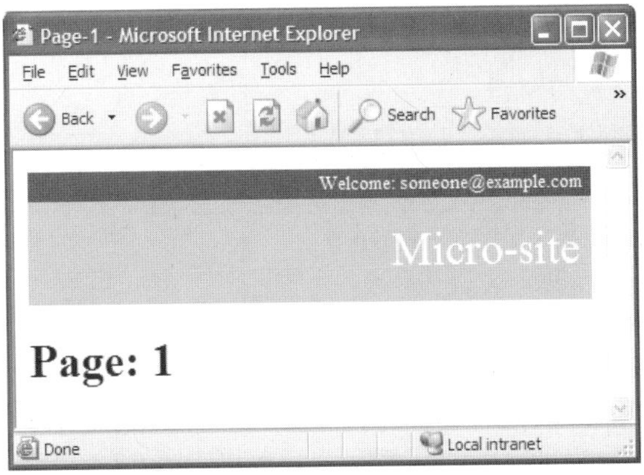

Figure 3.12
Banner displaying dynamic content

The individual pages in the site are responsible for rendering their own content, while the base class is responsible for rendering the header. Because the individual pages inherit from the base class, they all have the same functionality.

This implementation uses a design pattern called *Template Method*. The pattern defines the skeleton of an algorithm in an operation, deferring some steps to subclasses. *Template Method* lets subclasses redefine certain steps of an algorithm without changing the algorithm's structure. [Gamma95]

Applying *Template Method* to this problem involves moving common code from the individual pages into a base class. This ensures that the common code is contained in one place and is easily maintainable. In this example, the base class is named **BasePage** and is responsible for connecting the **Page_Load** method to the **Load** event. After the work associated with the **BasePage**; which is retrieving the user's e-mail address from the database and setting the site name, the **Page_Load** function calls a method named **PageLoadEvent**. Subclasses implement **PageLoadEvent** to perform their own specific Load functionality. Figure 3.13 shows the structure of this solution.

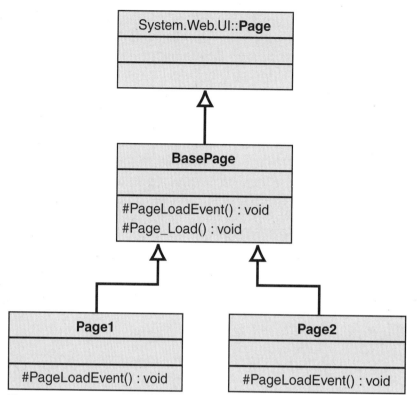

Figure 3.13
Structure of the code-behind pages implementation

When a page is requested, the ASP.NET runtime fires the **Load** event, which in turn calls the **Page_Load** method on **BasePage**. The **BasePage** method retrieves the data it needs and then calls **PageLoadEvent** on the specific page that was requested to perform any page-specific loading that is required. Figure 3.14 shows the page request sequence.

Implementing the common functionality in this manner frees the pages from having to set up the header and also allows for site-wide changes to be made easily. If the header rendering and initialization code is not contained in a single file, the changes must be made to all files that contain code that is related to the header.

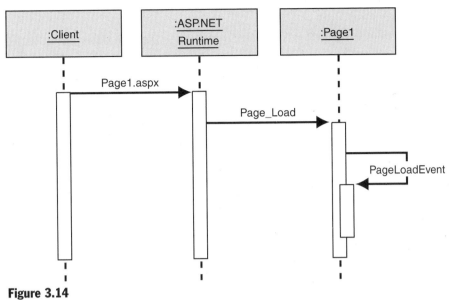

Figure 3.14
Page request sequence

BasePage.cs

The code for the base class implements the following functionality:

- Connects the **Load** event to the **Page_Load** method for request-specific initialization.
- Retrieves the authenticated user's name from the request context and using the **DatabaseGateway** class finds the user's record in the database. The code assigns the **eMail** label to the user's e-mail address.
- Assigns the site name to the **siteName** label.
- Calls the **PageLoadEvent** method, which derived classes can implement for any page-specific loading.

Note: It would be better to define the **BasePage** class as abstract, because doing so would force the implementers to provide an implementation for **PageLoadEvent**. However, in Microsoft Visual Studio® .NET, it is not possible to define this base class as abstract. Instead, the class provides a default implementation that can be overridden by derived classes.

```
using System;
using System.Web.UI;
using System.Web.UI.WebControls;

public class BasePage : Page
{
    protected Label eMail;
    protected Label siteName;
```

```
    virtual protected void PageLoadEvent(object sender, System.EventArgs e)
    {}

    protected void Page_Load(object sender, System.EventArgs e)
    {
        if(!IsPostBack)
        {
            string name = Context.User.Identity.Name;

            eMail.Text = DatabaseGateway.RetrieveAddress(name);
            siteName.Text = "Micro-site";

            PageLoadEvent(sender, e);
        }
    }


    #region Web Form Designer generated code
    override protected void OnInit(EventArgs e)
    {
        //
        //
        // CODEGEN: This call is required by the ASP.NET Web Form Designer.
        //
        InitializeComponent();
        base.OnInit(e);
    }

    /// <summary>
    /// Required method for Designer support - do not modify
    /// the contents of this method with the code editor.
    /// </summary>
    private void InitializeComponent()
    {
        this.Load += new System.EventHandler(this.Page_Load);

    }
    #endregion
}
```

BasePage.inc

Not only do you have to provide a common base class for the logic code behind the page, but you also have to provide a common file that holds the view or UI rendering code. The code is included in each .aspx page. This HTML file is not intended to be displayed on its own. Using a common file enhances your ability to make changes in one place and have them propagate to all the pages that include the file. The following example code shows the common file for this example, named BasePage.inc:

```
<table width="100%" cellspacing="0" cellpadding="0">
    <tr>
        <td align="right" bgcolor="#9c0001" cellspacing="0" cellpadding="0"
width="100%" height="20">
            <font size="2" color="#ffffff">Welcome:
            <asp:Label id="eMail" runat="server">username</asp:Label>  </font>
        </td>
    </tr>
    <tr>
        <td align="right" width="100%" bgcolor="#d3c9c7" height="70">
            <font size="6" color="#ffffff">
            <asp:Label id="siteName" Runat="server">Micro-site Banner</
asp:Label>  </font>
        </td>
    </tr>
</table>
```

DatabaseGateway.cs

This class encapsulates all access to the database for these pages. This is an example of a *Table Data Gateway* [Fowler03] which represents the model code for the pages in this application.

```
using System;
using System.Collections;
using System.Data;
using System.Data.SqlClient;

public class DatabaseGateway
{
    public static string RetrieveAddress(string name)
    {
        String address = null;

        String selectCmd =
            String.Format("select * from webuser where (id = '{0}')",
            name);

        SqlConnection myConnection =
            new
SqlConnection("server=(local);database=webusers;Trusted_Connection=yes");
        SqlDataAdapter myCommand = new SqlDataAdapter(selectCmd, myConnection);

        DataSet ds = new DataSet();
        myCommand.Fill(ds,"webuser");
        if(ds.Tables["webuser"].Rows.Count == 1)
        {
            DataRow row = ds.Tables["webuser"].Rows[0];
```

```
                           address = row["address"].ToString();
                }

                return address;
        }
}
```

Page1.aspx

The following is an example of how to use the common functionality in a page:

```
<%@ Page language="c#" Codebehind="Page1.aspx.cs" AutoEventWireup="false"
Inherits="Page1" %>
<HTML>
    <HEAD>
        <title>Page-1</title>
    </HEAD>
    <body>
        <!-- #include virtual="BasePage.inc" -->
        <form id="Page1" method="post" runat="server">
            <h1>Page:
                <asp:label id="pageNumber" Runat="server">NN</asp:label></h1>
        </form>
    </body>
</HTML>
```

The following directive from the file loads the common HTML for the header:

```
<!-- #include virtual="BasePage.inc" -->
```

Page1.aspx.cs

The code-behind class must inherit from the **BasePage** class and then implement
the **PageLoadEvent** method to do any page-specific loading. In this example, the
page-specific activity is to assign the number 1 to the **pageNumber** label.

```
using System;
using System.Web.UI;
using System.Web.UI.WebControls;

public class Page1 : BasePage
{
    protected System.Web.UI.WebControls.Label pageNumber;

    protected override void PageLoadEvent(object sender, System.EventArgs e)
    {
        pageNumber.Text = "1";
    }
}
```

Testing Considerations

The dependence on the ASP.NET runtime makes testing of the implementation difficult. It is not possible to instantiate classes that inherit from System.Web.UI.Page or the other various classes contained in the environment. This makes it impossible to unit test the individual pieces of the application in isolation. The only remaining way to test this implementation automatically is to generate HTTP requests and then retrieve the HTTP response and determine if the response is correct. This approach is prone to error because you are comparing the text of the response with expected text.

Resulting Context

The built-in ASP.NET page controller functionality results in the following benefits and liabilities:

Benefits

- **Takes advantage of framework features**. The page controller functionality is built into ASP.NET and can be easily extended by connecting application-specific actions to the events exposed by the controller. It is also easy to separate the controller-specific code from the model and view code by using the code-behind feature.

- **Explicit URLs**. The URL that the user enters refers to an actual page in the application. This means that the pages can be bookmarked and entered later. The URLs also tend to have fewer parameters making them easier for users to enter.

- **Increases modularity and reuse**. The Common Look and Feel example demonstrated how you could reuse **BasePage** for many pages without having to modify the **BasePage** class or HTML file.

Liabilities

- **Requires code changes**. To share common functionality, as demonstrated in the Common Look and Feel example, the individual pages have to be modified to inherit from the newly defined base class instead of **System.Web.UI.Page**. The *Intercepting Filter* pattern describes a mechanism for adding common functionality by changing the Web.config file and not the pages themselves.

- **Uses inheritance**. The Common Look and Feel example uses inheritance to share the implementation across multiple pages. Most programmers who learn object-oriented programming initially like inheritance. However, using inheritance to share implementation can often lead to software that is difficult to change. If the base class become complicated with conditional logic, it is better to introduce helper classes or to consider using *Front Controller* instead.

- **Difficult to test**. Because the page controller is implemented in ASP.NET, it is difficult to test in isolation. To improve the testability, you should separate as much functionality out of the ASP.NET – specific code in classes that do not depend on ASP.NET. This enables you to test without having to start the ASP.NET runtime.

Related Patterns

For more information, see the following related patterns:

- *Template Method* [Gamma95]. The BasePage class and the Page_Load method are an example implementation of this pattern.
- *Intercepting Filter*
- *Front Controller*

Acknowledgments

[Gamma95] Gamma, Helm, Johnson, and Vlissides. *Design Patterns: Elements of Reusable Object-Oriented Software*. Addison-Wesley, 1995.

[Reilly02] Reilly, Douglas J. *Designing Microsoft ASP.NET Applications*. Microsoft Press, 2002.

[Fowler03] Fowler, Martin. *Patterns of Enterprise Application Architecture*. Addison-Wesley, 2003.

Front Controller

Context

You have decided to use the *Model-View-Controller (MVC)* pattern to separate the user interface logic from the business logic of your dynamic Web application. You have reviewed the *Page Controller* pattern, but your page controller classes have complicated logic, are part of a deep inheritance hierarchy, or your application determines the navigation between pages dynamically based on configurable rules.

Problem

How do you best structure the controller for very complex Web applications so that you can achieve reuse and flexibility while avoiding code duplication?

Forces

The following are specific aspects of the forces from *Model-View-Controller* that apply to the *Front Controller* pattern.

- If common logic is replicated in different views in the system, you need to centralize this logic to reduce the amount of code duplication. Removing the duplicated code is critical to improving the overall maintainability of the system.

- The retrieval of data is also best handled in one location. A series of views that use the same data from the database is a good example. It is better to implement the retrieval of this data in one place as opposed to having each view retrieve the data and duplicate the database access code.

- As described in *MVC*, testing user interface code tends to be time-consuming and tedious. Separating the individual roles enhances overall testability. This is true not only for the model code, which was described in *MVC*, but also applies to the controller code.

The following forces might persuade you to use *Front Controller* as opposed to *Page Controller*:

- A common implementation of *Page Controller* involves creating a base class for behavior shared among individual pages. However, over time these base classes can grow with code that is not common to all pages. It requires discipline to periodically refactor this base class to ensure that only common behavior is included. For example, you do not want a page to examine a request and decide (based on request parameters) to transfer control to a different page, because this type of decision is more specific to a particular function, rather than common among all the pages.

- To avoid adding excessive conditional logic in the base class, you could create a deeper inheritance hierarchy to remove the conditional logic. For example, in an application that has three functional areas, it might be useful to have a single base class that has common functionality for the application. There might also be another class for each functional area, which inherits from the overall application base class. This type of structure, at first glance, is straightforward, but often leads to a very brittle design and implementation, and to a morass of code.

- The *Page Controller* solution describes a single object per logical page. This solution breaks down when you need to control or coordinate processing across multiple pages. For example, suppose that you have complex configurable navigation, which is stored in XML, in your Web application. When a request comes in, the application must look up where to go next, based on its current state.

- Because *Page Controller* is implemented with a single object per logical page, it is difficult to consistently apply a particular action across all the pages in a Web application. Security, for example, is best implemented in a coordinated fashion. Having security handled by each view or page controller object is problematic because it can be inconsistently applied and can lead to security breaches. An additional solution to this problem is also discussed in *Intercepting Filter.*

- The association of the URL to the particular controller object can be constraining for Web applications. For example, suppose your site has a wizard-like interface for gathering information. This wizard consists of a number of mandatory pages and a number of optional pages based on user input. When implemented with *Page Controller*, the optional pages would have to be implemented with conditional logic in the base class to select the next page.

Solution

Front Controller solves the decentralization problem present in *Page Controller* by channeling all requests through a single controller. The controller itself is usually implemented in two parts: a handler and a hierarchy of commands (see Figure 3.15).

The handler has two responsibilities:

- **Retrieve parameters**. The handler receives the HTTP Post or Get request from the Web server and retrieves relevant parameters from the request.

- **Select commands**. The handler uses the parameters from the request first to choose the correct command and then to transfers control to the command for processing.

Figure 3.16 shows these two responsibilities.

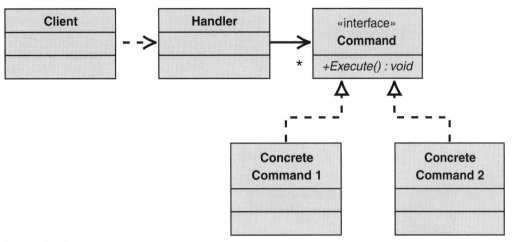

Figure 3.15
Front Controller structure

The commands themselves are also part of the controller. The commands represent the specific actions as described in the *Command* pattern [Gamma95]. Representing commands as individual objects allows the controller to interact with all commands in a generic way, as opposed to invoking specific methods on a common command class. After the command object completes the action, the command chooses which view to use to render the page.

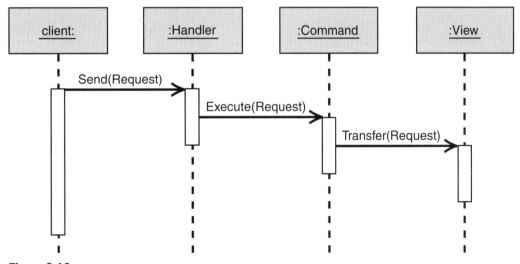

Figure 3.16
Front Controller, typical scenario

Example

See *Implementing Front Controller in ASP.NET Using HTTPHandler.*

Resulting Context

Using the *Front Controller* pattern results in the following benefits and liabilities:

Benefits

- **Centralized control**. *Front Controller* coordinates all of the requests that are made to the Web application. The solution describes using a single controller instead of the distributed model used in *Page Controller*. This single controller is in the perfect location to enforce application-wide policies, such as security and usage tracking.
- **Thread-safety**. Because each request involves creating a new command object, the command objects themselves do not need to be thread safe. This means that you avoid the issues of thread safety in the command classes. This does not mean that you can avoid threading issues altogether, though, because the code that the commands act upon, the model code, still must be thread safe [Fowler03].
- **Configurability**. Only one front controller needs to be configured into the Web server; the handler does the rest of the dispatching. This simplifies the configuration of the Web server. Some Web servers are awkward to configure. Using dynamic commands enables you to add new commands without changing anything [Fowler03].

Liabilities

- **Performance considerations**. *Front Controller* is a single controller that handles all requests for the Web application. Of the two parts, the handler should be examined closely for performance problems, because the handler determines the type of command that performs the request. If the handler must perform a database query or a query of an XML document to make the decision, performance could be very slow as a result.
- **Increased complexity**. *Front Controller* is more complicated than *Page Controller*. It often involves replacing the built-in controller with a custom built *Front Controller*. Implementing this solution increases the maintenance costs and the learning curve for new people.

Testing Considerations

Removing business logic from the views simplifies the testing of the views, because you can then test the views independent from the controller. As described in the *Page Controller* pattern, testing the controller may be hindered by the fact that the controller contains code that makes it dependent on the HTTP run-time environment.

This dependency may be resolved by using a two-stage Web handler as described in Martin Fowler's book, *Patterns for Enterprise Application Architecture* [Fowler03], and in the *Page Controller* pattern. The controller is separated into two parts: a Web handler and a dispatcher. The Web handler retrieves data from the Web request and passes it to the dispatcher in a way that the dispatcher does not depend on the Web server framework (for example, in a generic collection object). This allows for the dispatcher to be tested without the Web server framework being present.

Related Patterns

For more information, see the following related patterns:

- *Intercepting Filter*. This pattern describes another way to implement recurring functionality inside a Web application. *Intercepting Filter* works by passing each request through a configurable chain of filters prior to passing control over to the controller. Filters tend to deal with lower-level functions such as decoding, authorization, authentication, and session management whereas *Front Controller* and *Page Controller* deal with application-level functionality. Another aspect of filter is that they are usually stateless. For example, when a user gets to authorization, the Web server has to authenticate the session. If the user is authenticated the process continues on. If not, the user is redirected elsewhere. One advantage of *Intercepting Filter* is that, in most implementations, the pages themselves do not have to be modified to add additional functionality.

- *Page Controller*. This pattern is a simpler alternative to *Front Controller*. *Page Controller* has a single controller object per page as opposed to the single object for all requests. *Page Controller* is a more appropriate starting point for most applications. Only when the need arises should you turn to *Front Controller*.

Acknowledgments

[Alur01] Alur, Crupi, and Malks. *Core J2EE Patterns: Best Practices and Design Strategies*. Prentice Hall, 2001.

[Fowler03] Fowler, Martin. *Patterns of Enterprise Application Architecture*. Addison-Wesley, 2003.

[Gamma95] Gamma, Helm, Johnson, and Vlissides. *Design Patterns: Elements of Reusable Object-Oriented Software*. Addison-Wesley, 1995.

Implementing Front Controller in ASP.NET Using HTTPHandler

Context

You are building a Web application in ASP.NET. You have evaluated the alternative designs described in *Page Controller* and *Front Controller* and have determined that there is sufficient complexity in your application to warrant implementing *Front Controller*.

Background

An example is helpful to explain how to implement *Front Controller* in ASP.NET and the value provided by centralizing all control through a single controller object, as long as the example is complex enough to demonstrate the issues you will encounter when implementing the pattern.

Note: Because *Page Controller* is built into ASP.NET, the additional effort required to implement *Front Controller* rather than *Page Controller* is very large. In fact, you must build the whole framework for *Front Controller*. You should do so only if your application warrants that amount of complexity. Otherwise, review *Page Controller* to determine whether it is sufficient.

The following example builds on the solution described in *Implementing Page Controller in ASP.NET*. That solution describes two different pages. The pages inherit from a common base class, which is responsible for adding the site header to each page. The implementation is a common choice for *Page Controller* when you want to share behavior between pages. The following is the **BasePage** class from the *Page Controller* example:

```
using System;
using System.Web.UI;
using System.Web.UI.WebControls;

public class BasePage : Page
{
    protected Label eMail;
    protected Label siteName;

    virtual protected void PageLoadEvent(object sender, System.EventArgs e)
    {}

    protected void Page_Load(object sender, System.EventArgs e)
    {
        if(!IsPostBack)
        {
            string name = Context.User.Identity.Name;

            eMail.Text = DatabaseGateway.RetrieveAddress(name);
            siteName.Text = "Micro-site";
```

```
            PageLoadEvent(sender, e);
        }
    }


    #region Web Form Designer generated code
    override protected void OnInit(EventArgs e)
    {
        //
        // CODEGEN: This call is required by the ASP.NET Web Form Designer.
        //
        InitializeComponent();
        base.OnInit(e);
    }

    /// <summary>
    /// Required method for Designer support - do not modify
    /// the contents of this method with the code editor.
    /// </summary>
    private void InitializeComponent()
    {
        this.Load += new System.EventHandler(this.Page_Load);

    }
    #endregion
}
```

The **Page_Load** function is called every time the page is being loaded. It retrieves the e-mail address from the **DatabaseGateway** class (shown in *Implementing Page Controller in ASP.NET*), sets some labels with the data, and then calls **PageLoadEvent** for specialized processing of each page.

One of the criteria for choosing *Front Controller* instead of *Page Controller* is when you have excessive conditional logic in the base class. This example does not use conditional logic in the base class. Therefore, based on this criterion alone, there is no need to implement *Front Controller*.

Changing Requirements

The previous example works very well for its intended purpose. However, it is overly simplistic and not representative of most Web applications. To better approximate the overall complexity of such applications, the requirements for this example call for different headers on the pages, depending on the URL and query parameters.

This example creates two sites: a Micro-site and a Macro-site. Each site consults a different database to retrieve the e-mail address contained in the header. The pages themselves remain unchanged; only the header content is different. In this example, most of the implementation is the same as the previous example. The only class that must be modified is **BasePage**.

```csharp
using System;
using System.Web.UI;
using System.Web.UI.WebControls;

public class BasePage : Page
{
    protected Label eMail;
    protected Label siteName;

    virtual protected void PageLoadEvent(object sender, System.EventArgs e)
    {}

    protected void Page_Load(object sender, System.EventArgs e)
    {
        if(!IsPostBack)
        {
            string site = Request["site"];

            if(site != null && site.Equals("macro"))
                LoadMacroHeader();
            else
                LoadMicroHeader();

            PageLoadEvent(sender, e);
        }
    }

    private void LoadMicroHeader()
    {
        string name = Context.User.Identity.Name;

        eMail.Text = WebUsersDatabase.RetrieveAddress(name);
        siteName.Text = "Micro-site";
    }


    private void LoadMacroHeader()
    {
        string name = Context.User.Identity.Name;

        eMail.Text = MacroUsersDatabase.RetrieveAddress(name);
        siteName.Text = "Macro-site";
    }

    #region Web Form Designer generated code
    override protected void OnInit(EventArgs e)
    {
        //
        // CODEGEN: This call is required by the ASP.NET Web Form Designer.
        //
        InitializeComponent();
        base.OnInit(e);
    }
```

```
/// <summary>
/// Required method for Designer support - do not modify
/// the contents of this method with the code editor.
/// </summary>
private void InitializeComponent()
{
    this.Load += new System.EventHandler(this.Page_Load);

}
#endregion
}
```

As stated previously, the Micro-site and Macro-site each use different databases to retrieve the e-mail address that is contained in the header. The two methods, **LoadMacroHeader** and **LoadMicroHeader**, use different database gateway classes, **WebUsersDatabase** and **MacroUsersDatabase**, to retrieve the address from the database.

The **Page_Load** method's responsibility has changed. In the previous example, it retrieves information from the database. In this implementation, it determines which function, **LoadMicroHeader** or **LoadMacroHeader**, to call and then calls the appropriate method. If you are going to have only two sites, this implementation is sufficient. However, the base class now contains conditional logic. It is up to you how comfortable you feel with that logic contained in this class. Clearly, most developers would flinch if they saw more than a few branches in the code, but two probably would not elicit the same response. The main reason for limiting the conditional logic is that it is more likely to change and cause you to modify the implementation. Because the entire implementation is contained in one file, the changes that you make could affect other sites.

Implementation Strategy

Front Controller is usually implemented in two parts. A **Handler** object receives the individual requests (HTTP Get and Post) from the Web server, retrieves the relevant parameters, and then selects an appropriate command, based on the parameters. The second part of the controller, **Command Processor**, performs the specific actions or commands to satisfy the request. When finished, the commands forward to the view so that the page can be displayed.

Note: This implementation strategy resolves the issues raised in the earlier example. Although this example is probably not sufficient to justify the change to *Front Controller*, it serves to illustrate why you would use *Front Controller*, and the implementation solves problems of this type that are of a far greater complexity. Also, as with most implementations, there is more than one way to implement this pattern; this is just one choice.

Handler

ASP.NET provides a low-level request/response API to service incoming HTTP requests. Each incoming HTTP request that ASP.NET receives is ultimately processed by a specific instance of a class that implements the **IHTTPHandler** interface. This low-level API is ideal for implementing the handler portion of *Front Controller*.

Note: the Microsoft® .NET Framework provides multiple implementation choices for HTTP handlers. For example, in a high-volume environment, you may be able to improve response times with an asynchronous HTTP handler that implements the **IHttpAsyncHandler** interface. This solution uses a synchronous handler for sake of simplicity. For more information about the implementation of asynchronous HTTP handlers, see the Microsoft Developer Network (MSDN®) Web site (*http://msdn.microsoft.com*).

Figure 3.17 shows the structure of the handler portion of the controller.

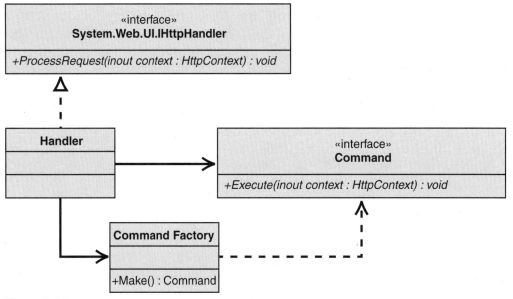

Figure 3.17
Handler portion of the front controller

This solution partitions responsibilities ideally. The **Handler** class handles the individual Web requests and delegates the responsibility of determining the correct **Command** object to the **CommandFactory** class. When the **CommandFactory** returns a **Command** object, the **Handler** calls the **Execute** method on the **Command** to perform the request.

Handler.cs

The following code example shows how the **Handler** class is implemented:

```
using System;
using System.Web;

public class Handler : IHttpHandler
{
    public void ProcessRequest(HttpContext context)
    {
        Command command =
            CommandFactory.Make(context.Request.Params);
        command.Execute(context);
    }

    public bool IsReusable
    {
        get { return true;}
    }
}
```

Command.cs

The **Command** class is an example of the *Command* pattern [Gamma95]. The *Command* pattern is useful in this situation, because you do not want the **Handler** class to depend directly on the commands. They can be returned generically from the **CommandFactory**.

```
using System;
using System.Web;

public interface Command
{
    void Execute(HttpContext context);
}
```

CommandFactory.cs

The **CommandFactory** class is critical to the implementation. It determines, based on parameters from the query string, which command will be created. In this example, if the *site* query parameter is set to *micro* or is not set at all, the factory creates a **MicroSite** command object. If **site** is set to *macro,* the factory creates a **MacroSite** command object. If the value is set to anything else, the factory returns an **UnknownCommand** object for default error handling. This is an example of the *Special Case* pattern [Fowler03].

```
using System;
using System.Collections.Specialized;
```

```
public class CommandFactory
{
    public static Command Make(NameValueCollection parms)
    {
        string siteName = parms["site"];

        Command command = new UnknownCommand();

        if(siteName == null || siteName.Equals("micro"))
            command = new MicroSite();
        else if(siteName.Equals("macro"))
            command = new MacroSite();
        return command;
    }
}
```

Configuring the Handler

HTTP handlers are declared in the ASP.NET configuration as part of a web.config file. ASP.NET defines an **<httphandlers>** configuration section where handlers can be added and removed. For example, ASP.NET maps all requests for Page*.aspx files to the **Handler** class in the application's web.config file:

```
<httpHandlers>
    <add verb="*" path="Page*.aspx" type="Handler,FrontController" />
</httpHandlers>
```

Commands

The commands represent the variability in the Web site. In this example, the functionality to retrieve data from the database for each site is contained in its own class that inherits from a base class named **RedirectingCommand**. The **RedirectingCommand** class implements the **Command** interface. When **Execute** is called on the **RedirectingCommand** class, it first calls an abstract method called **OnExecute** and, on return, transfers to the view. The specific view is retrieved from a class called **UrlMap**. The **UrlMap** class retrieves the map from the application's web.config file. Figure 3.18 shows the structure of the command portion of the solution.

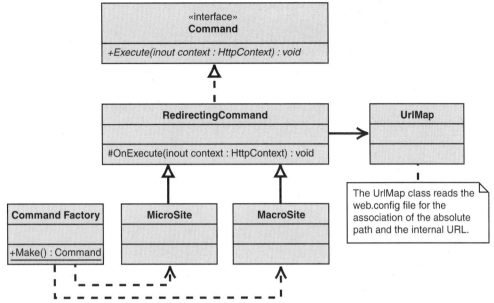

Figure 3.18
Command portion of the front controller

RedirectingCommand.cs

RedirectingCommand is an abstract base class that calls an abstract method named **OnExecute** to perform the specific command and then, on return, transfers to the view that is retrieved from the **UrlMap**.

```
using System;
using System.Web;

public abstract class RedirectingCommand : Command
{
    private UrlMap map = UrlMap.SoleInstance;

    protected abstract void OnExecute(HttpContext context);

    public void Execute(HttpContext context)
    {
        OnExecute(context);

        string url = String.Format("{0}?{1}",
            map.Map[context.Request.Url.AbsolutePath],
            context.Request.Url.Query);

        context.Server.Transfer(url);
    }
}
```

UrlMap.cs

The **UrlMap** class loads configuration information from the application's web.config file. The configuration information associates the absolute path of the requested URL to another URL specified by the file. This allows you to change the actual page to which a user is forwarded when an external page is requested. This provides a great deal of flexibility when changing views, because the actual page is never referenced by the user. The following is the **UrlMap** class:

```
using System;
using System.Web;
using System.Xml;
using System.Configuration;
using System.Collections.Specialized;

public class UrlMap : IConfigurationSectionHandler
{
    private readonly NameValueCollection _commands = new NameValueCollection();

    public const string SECTION_NAME="controller.mapping";

    public static UrlMap SoleInstance
    {
        get {return (UrlMap) ConfigurationSettings.GetConfig(SECTION_NAME);}
    }

    object IConfigurationSectionHandler.Create(object parent,object configContext,
XmlNode section)
    {
        return (object) new UrlMap(parent,configContext, section);
    }

    private UrlMap() {/*no-op*/}

    public UrlMap(object parent,object configContext, XmlNode section)
    {
        try
        {
            XmlElement entriesElement = section["entries"];
            foreach(XmlElement element in entriesElement)
            {
            _commands.Add(element.Attributes["key"].Value,element.Attributes["url"].Value);
            }
        }
        catch (Exception ex)
        {
            throw new ConfigurationException("Error while parsing configuration
section.",ex,section);
        }
    }

    public NameValueCollection Map
```

```
    {
        get { return _commands; }
    }
}
```

The following is an excerpt from the web.config file, which shows the configuration:

```
<controller.mapping>
    <entries>
        <entry key="/patterns/frontc/3/Page1.aspx" url="ActualPage1.aspx" />
        <entry key="/patterns/frontc/3/Page2.aspx" url="ActualPage2.aspx" />
    </entries>
</controller.mapping>
```

MicroSite.cs

The **MicroSite** class is similar to the code in **LoadMicroHeader** earlier in this pattern.
The main difference is that you no longer have any access to the labels that were
contained in the page. Instead, you must add the information to the **HttpContext**
object. The following example shows the **MicroSite** code:

```
using System;
using System.Web;

public class MicroSite : RedirectingCommand
{
    protected override void OnExecute(HttpContext context)
    {
        string name = context.User.Identity.Name;

        context.Items["address"] =
            WebUsersDatabase.RetrieveAddress(name);
        context.Items["site"] = "Micro-Site";
    }
}
```

MacroSite.cs

The **MacroSite** class is similar to **MicroSite** except that it uses a different database
gateway class, **MacroUsersDatabase**. Both classes store information in the passed-in
HttpContext so that the view can retrieve it. The following example shows the
MacroSite code:

```
using System;
using System.Web;


public class MacroSite : RedirectingCommand
{
    protected override void OnExecute(HttpContext context)
    {
```

```
        string name = context.User.Identity.Name;

        context.Items["address"] =
            MacroUsersDatabase.RetrieveAddress(name);
        context.Items["site"] = "Macro-Site";
    }
}
```

WebUsersDatabase.cs

The **WebUsersDatabase** class is responsible for retrieving the e-mail address from the "webusers" database. It is an example of the *Table Data Gateway* [Fowler03] pattern.

```
using System;
using System.Data;
using System.Data.SqlClient;

public class WebUsersDatabase
{
    public static string RetrieveAddress(string name)
    {
        string address = null;

        String selectCmd =
            String.Format("select * from webuser where (id = '{0}')",
            name);

        SqlConnection myConnection =
            new
SqlConnection("server=(local);database=webusers;Trusted_Connection=yes");
        SqlDataAdapter myCommand = new SqlDataAdapter(selectCmd, myConnection);

        DataSet ds = new DataSet();
        myCommand.Fill(ds,"webuser");
        if(ds.Tables["webuser"].Rows.Count == 1)
        {
            DataRow row = ds.Tables["webuser"].Rows[0];
            address = row["address"].ToString();
        }

        return address;
    }

}
```

MacroUsersDatabase.cs

The **MacroUsersDatabase** class is responsible for retrieving the e-mail address from the "macrousers" database. It is an example of the *Table Data Gateway* pattern.

```
using System;
using System.Data;
using System.Data.SqlClient;
```

```
public class MacroUsersDatabase
{
    public static string RetrieveAddress(string name)
    {
        string address = null;

        String selectCmd =
            String.Format("select * from customer where (id = '{0}')",
            name);

        SqlConnection myConnection =
            new
SqlConnection("server=(local);database=macrousers;Trusted_Connection=yes");
        SqlDataAdapter myCommand = new SqlDataAdapter(selectCmd, myConnection);

        DataSet ds = new DataSet();
        myCommand.Fill(ds,"customer");
        if(ds.Tables["customer"].Rows.Count == 1)
        {
            DataRow row = ds.Tables["customer"].Rows[0];
            address = row["email"].ToString();
        }

        return address;
    }

}
```

Views

The last aspect of the implementation is the views. The views from the example in "Changing Requirements" were responsible for retrieving information from the database depending on which site the user is accessing and then displaying the rendered page to the user. Because the database access code has been moved to the command, the views now retrieve the data from the **HttpContext** object. Figure 3.19 on the next page shows the structure of the code-behind classes.

There is still common behavior, so the **BasePage** class is still needed to avoid code duplication.

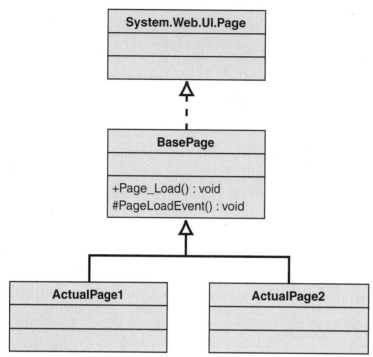

Figure 3.19
Structure of the code-behind classes of the view

BasePage.cs

The **BasePage** class has changed dramatically from the example in "Changing Requirements.". It is no longer responsible for determining which site header to load. It simply retrieves the data that the commands stored in the **HttpContext** object and assigns them to the appropriate label:

```
using System;
using System.Web.UI;
using System.Web.UI.WebControls;

public class BasePage : Page
{
    protected Label eMail;
    protected Label siteName;

    virtual protected void PageLoadEvent(object sender, System.EventArgs e)
    {}

    protected void Page_Load(object sender, System.EventArgs e)
    {
        if(!IsPostBack)
```

```
    {
        eMail.Text = (string)Context.Items["address"];
        siteName.Text = (string)Context.Items["site"];
        PageLoadEvent(sender, e);
    }
}

#region Web Form Designer generated code
#endregion
}
```

ActualPage1.aspx.cs and ActualPage2.aspx

ActualPage1 and **ActualPage2** are the page-specific code-behind classes. They both inherit from **BasePage** to ensure that the header is filled in at the top of the screen:

```csharp
using System;
using System.Web.UI;
using System.Web.UI.WebControls;

public class ActualPage1 : BasePage
{
    protected System.Web.UI.WebControls.Label pageNumber;

    protected override void PageLoadEvent(object sender, System.EventArgs e)
    {
        pageNumber.Text = "1";
    }

    #region Web Form Designer generated code
    #endregion
}

using System;
using System.Web.UI.WebControls;

public class ActualPage2 : BasePage
{
    protected Label pageNumber;

    protected override void PageLoadEvent(object sender, System.EventArgs e)
    {
        pageNumber.Text = "2";
    }

  #region Web Form Designer generated code
    #endregion
}
```

These pages do not have to change when moving from the *Page Controller* implementation to the *Front Controller* implementation.

Testing Considerations

The dependence of the implementation on the ASP.NET runtime makes testing more difficult. It is not possible to instantiate classes that inherit from **System.Web.UI.Page**, **System.Web.UI.IHTTPHandler** or the other various classes contained in the ASP.NET runtime. This makes unit testing of most of the individual pieces of the application impossible. The chosen way to test this implementation automatically is to generate HTTP requests and then retrieve the HTTP response and determine if the response is correct. This approach is error-prone because you are comparing the text of the response with expected text.

CommandFixture.cs

One aspect of the implementation that can be tested is the **CommandFactory**, because it is not dependent on the ASP.NET runtime. Therefore, you can write tests to verify that you get the correct **Command** object in return. The following are NUnit (*http://nunit.org*) tests for the **CommandFactory** class:

```
using System;
using System.Collections.Specialized;
using NUnit.Framework;

[TestFixture]
public class CommandFixture
{
    private static readonly string microKey = "micro";
    private static readonly string macroKey = "macro";

    [SetUp]
    public void BuildCommandFactory()
    {
        NameValueCollection map = new NameValueCollection();
        map.Add(microKey, "MicroSite");
        map.Add(macroKey, "MacroSite");
    }

    [Test]
    public void DefaultToMicro()
    {
        NameValueCollection map = new NameValueCollection();
        Command command = CommandFactory.Make(map);
        Assertion.AssertNotNull(command);
        Assertion.Assert(command is MicroSite);
    }

    [Test]
    public void MicroSiteCommand()
    {
        NameValueCollection map = new NameValueCollection();
        map.Add("site", "micro");
        Command command = CommandFactory.Make(map);
```

```
        Assertion.AssertNotNull(command);
        Assertion.Assert(command is MicroSite);
    }

    [Test]
    public void MacroSiteCommand()
    {
        NameValueCollection map = new NameValueCollection();
        map.Add("site", "macro");
        Command command = CommandFactory.Make(map);
        Assertion.AssertNotNull(command);
        Assertion.Assert(command is MacroSite);
    }


    [Test]
    public void Error()
    {
        NameValueCollection map = new NameValueCollection();
        map.Add("site", "xyzcommand");
        Command command = CommandFactory.Make(map);
        Assertion.AssertNotNull(command);
        Assertion.Assert(command is UnknownCommand);
    }
}
```

Further work could isolate the **Command** class. The **Execute** method has a parameter that is an **HttpContext** object. You could change this parameter to make the object independent of the ASP.NET environment. This would enable you to unit-test the commands outside of the ASP.NET runtime.

Resulting Context

The additional complexity of implementing *Front Controller* results in a number of benefits and liabilities:

Benefits

- **Increased flexibility.** This implementation demonstrates how to centralize and coordinate all requests through the **Handler** class. The **Handler** uses the **CommandFactory** to determine the specific action to perform. This allows the functionality to be modified and extended without changing the **Handler** class. For example, to add another site, a specific command would have to be created and the only class that would have to change is **CommandFactory**.

- **Simplified views.** The views in the *Page Controller* example retrieve data from the database and then render the pages. In *Front Controller*, they no longer depend on the database, because that work is accomplished by the individual commands.

- **Open for extension, but closed to modification**. The implementation provides many opportunities for polymorphic dispatching. For example, the **Handler** simply calls the **Execute** method on the **Command** object, independent of what the method and object are doing. Therefore, you can add additional commands without modifying the **Handler**. The implementation could be extended further by replacing the **CommandFactory** with a different factory for further extension.

- **URL mapping**. The **UrlMap** allows the actual page names to be hidden from the user. The user enters a URL, which is mapped to the specific URL using the web.config file. This increases the flexibility for programmers because there is a level of indirection that is not present in the *Page Controller* implementation.

- **Thread-safety**. The individual command objects, **MicroSite** and **MacroSite**, are created for each request. This means that you do not have to worry about thread safety in these objects.

Liabilities

- **Decreased performance**. This possibility must be examined. All requests are processed through the **Handler** object. It uses the **CommandFactory** to determine which command to create. Although in this case they do not have performance problems, both of these classes should be examined carefully for any potential performance issues.

- **Cruel and unusual punishment**. This implementation is a lot more complicated than *Page Controller*. This implementation does provide more options, but at the cost of complexity and a lot of classes. You must weigh whether or not it is worth it. After you have taken the leap and built the framework, it is easy to add new commands and views. However, due to the implementation of *Page Controller* in ASP.NET, you would not expect to see as many implementations of *Front Controller* as you would in other platforms.

- **Testing considerations**. Because *Front Controller* is implemented in ASP.NET, it is difficult to test in isolation. To improve testability, you should separate functionality out of the ASP.NET–specific code into classes that do not depend on ASP.NET. You can then test these classes without having to start the ASP.NET runtime.

- **Invalid URLs**. Because *Front Controller* determines which view to transfer to, based on input parameters and often the current state of the application, the URLs may not always forward to the same page. This precludes users from saving URLs to access the page at a later time.

Related Patterns

For more information, see the following related patterns:

- *Template Method* [Gamma95]. The **PageLoadEvent** method of the **BasePage** class is an example implementation of *Template Method*.
- *Intercepting Filter*
- *Page Controller*
- *Command* [Gamma95]
- *Factory*. The factories described earlier in this pattern combine elements from both *Factory Method* [Gamma95] and *Abstract Factory* [Gamma95].

Acknowledgments

[Fowler03] Fowler, Martin. *Patterns of Enterprise Application Architecture*. Addison-Wesley, 2003.

[Gamma95] Gamma, Helm, Johnson, and Vlissides. *Design Patterns: Elements of Reusable Object-Oriented Software*. Addison-Wesley, 1995.

Intercepting Filter

Context

Anyone who has built a Web application from scratch realizes that it requires bit more housekeeping work than building an internal client-server application. First, you have to deal with the HTTP and all its quirks such as HTTP headers, multi-part forms, the statelessness of HTTP, character set encoding schemes, Multipurpose Internet Mail Extensions (MIME) types, and URL rewriting. On top of that, you have to deal with security measures such as Secure Sockets Layer (SSL) and user authentication. In many situations, the list continues on to include such items as client browser detection or user activity logging.

Web application server frameworks perform many of these tasks for you, but sometimes you need additional control, or you need to insert your own processing steps before or after the application processes the Web page request.

Problem

How do you implement common pre- and post-processing steps around Web page requests?

Forces

There are many ways to approach this problem, so you will need to consider what forces and tradeoffs are involved:

- It is common practice to separate lower-level functions, such as dealing with HTTP headers, cookies, or character encoding, from the application logic. This enables you to test and reuse the application logic in other environments that may not use a Web client.

- Pre-processing and post-processing features may change at a different pace than application functionality. After you have the character set encoding module working, you are less likely to change it than the code that deals with rendering the HTML page. Therefore, a separation of concerns helps to limit the propagation of changes.

- Many pre-processing and post-processing tasks are common to all Web pages. You should, therefore, try to implement these functions in a central location to avoid code duplication.

- Many of the lower-level functions are not dependent on each other. For example, browser detection and character encoding detection are two independent functions. To maximize reuse, you should encapsulate these functions in a set of composable modules. This enables you to add or remove modules without affecting existing modules.

- In many instances, it is very beneficial to be able to add or remove modules at deployment time rather than at compile-time. For example, you may deploy the character encoding detection module only in the international deployment of the software, but not in the local deployment. Or, you may have a free Web site for anonymous users to which you want to add an authentication module that requires users to sign in. This ability to add or remove modules at deployment time without having to make code changes is often called *deployment-time composability*.

- Because lower-level functions are executed for every single page request, performance is critical. This means two things: do as little as possible and do it efficiently. You do not want to overload these common functions with unnecessary features or decision points, but you do want to minimize access to slower, external resources such as databases. Therefore, you should make each processing step as compact and as efficient as possible.

- You may even consider implementing some of these functions in a different programming language, for example a language that is very efficient at processing character streams (such as C++). On the other hand, using a different language may preclude you from using some of the useful features that the application framework provides (for example, automated memory management and object pooling). Either way, it is a benefit to be able to detach preprocessing from the main application so that you have the choice of using a different programming language if necessary.

- After you create these pre-processing and post-processing functions, you want to be able to reuse them in other Web applications. You want to structure them so that you can reuse one module in another environment without depending on the other modules. You also want to be able to combine existing modules with new modules without having to make any code changes.

Solution

Create a chain of composable filters to implement common pre-processing and post-processing tasks during a Web page request.

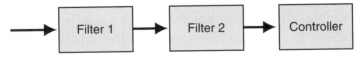

Figure 3.20
Chain of composable filters

The filters form a series of independent modules that can be chained together to execute a set of common processing steps before the page request is passed to the controller object. Because the individual filters implement identical interfaces, they do not have explicit dependencies on each other. Therefore, new filters can be added without affecting existing filters. You can even add filters at deployment time by instantiating them dynamically based on a configuration file.

As much as possible, you should design the individual filters in such as way that they make no assumptions about the presence of other filters. This maintains the composability; that is, the ability to add, remove, or rearrange filters. Also, some frameworks that implement the *Intercepting Filter* pattern do not guarantee the order in which the filters are executed. If you find that you have strong interdependencies between multiple filters, a regular method with calls to helper classes may be the better choice because it guarantees to preserve the constraints in the filters sequence.

In some contexts, the term *Intercepting Filter* is associated with a specific implementation using the *Decorator* pattern [Gamma95]. The solution described here takes a bit more abstract view and considers different implementation options of the *Intercepting Filter* concept.

Filter Chain

A straightforward implementation of *Intercepting Filter* is a filter chain that iterates through a list of all filters. The Web request handler executes the filter chain before passing control to the application logic (see Figure 3.21).

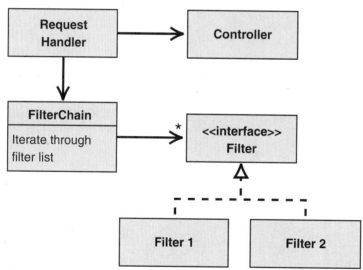

Figure 3.21
Intercepting Filter class diagram

When the Web server receives a page request, **Request Handler** passes control to the **FilterChain** object first. This object maintains a list of all filters and calls each filter in sequence. **FilterChain** can read the sequence of filters from a configuration file to achieve deployment-time composability. Each filter has the chance to modify the incoming request. For example, it can modify the URL or add header fields to be used by the application. After all filters have been executed, **Request Handler** passes control to the controller, which executes the application functionality (see Figure 3.22).

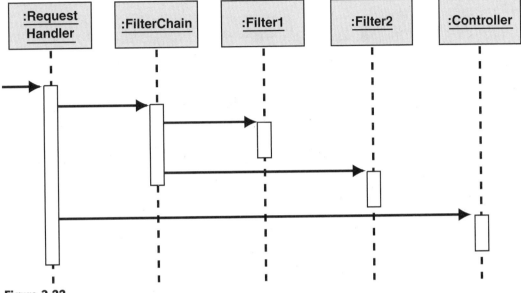

Figure 3.22
Intercepting Filter sequence diagram

One of the key benefits of this design is that filters are self-contained components without any direct dependency on the other filters or the controller, because **FilterChain** invokes each filter. Therefore, a filter does not have to hold a reference to the next filter. The handler passes a context into each filter on which the filter operates. The filter can manipulate the context, for example, by adding information or redirecting the request.

Decorator

An interesting alternative implementation to the *Intercepting Filter* pattern uses the *Decorator* pattern around a *Front Controller*. *Decorator* wraps an object in such a way that it provides the same interface as the original object. As a result, the wrapping is transparent to any other object that references the original object. Because the interface of the original object and wrapper are identical, you can add additional wrappers around the wrapper to create a chain of wrappers that is very similar to a filter chain. Inside each wrapper, you can perform pre-processing and post-processing functions.

Figures 3.23 and 3.24 on the next pages show how this concept can be used to implement *Intercepting Filter*. Each filter implements the **Controller** interface. It also holds a reference to the next object that implements the **Controller** interface, which could be either the actual controller (**concreteController**) or another filter. Even though the filters call each other directly, there is no direct dependency between the filters, because each filter only references the **Controller** interface instead of the next filter class.

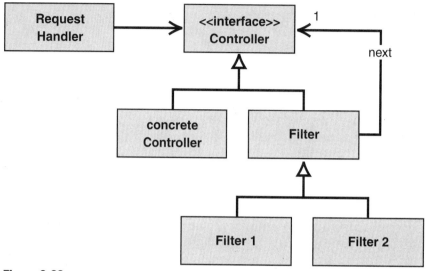

Figure 3.23
Decorator class diagram

Before the filter passes control to the next filter, it has the opportunity to perform pre-processing tasks. Likewise, after the rest of the chain is finished processing the request, the filter has an opportunity to perform post-processing tasks.

The *Decorator* approach avoids the need for a **FilterChain** class that iterates over the filters. Also, the request handler is now completely unaware of the existence of the filters. As far as the request handler is concerned, it simply calls the controller by using the **Controller** interface. This approach usually appears more elegant to hardcore object-oriented developers, but it can be a bit more difficult to figure out what is going on by looking at the code. The *Decorator* approach relates to the Filter Chain approach much as a linked list relates to an array with an iterator.

Even though the object instances have references to each other, you can still compose the chain at runtime. You can instantiate each filter passing along a reference to the **Controller** interface of the next filter object in the chain. That way, you can build the filter chain dynamically from back to front.

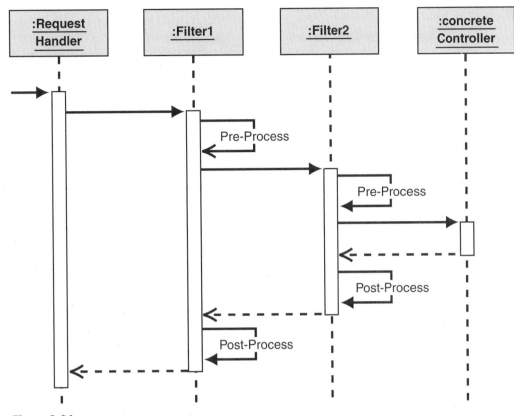

Figure 3.24
Decorator sequence diagram

Event-Driven Filters

In an ideal world, you would design the individual filters in such a way that they were not dependent on the sequence in which they were executed, but the real world rarely works that way. Even if you manage to design the filters independently, they will end up replicating a lot of functionality. For example, each filter that has to analyze the HTTP headers (for example, to do browser detection and extract cookies) will have to parse the headers, extract the header element names, and perform some action on them. It would be much easier if the framework could do some of this work and pass along a collection of all header elements, validated and indexed by element name. This would make the filter development easier and less error-prone, but then all filters would depend on this common header parsing function. This would not be a problem unless a filter had to access the HTTP request stream *before* any header parsing occurred (maybe because you wanted to manipulate or rearrange some header information).

If you want to provide additional base functionality, but still allow filters to be plugged into the request stream, you must define multiple filter chains. Each chain is then executed before or after the framework completes a processing step. For example, you can have a filter chain that is executed before any header parsing occurs and have a second filter chain that is executed *after* the headers are parsed (see Figure 3.25). If you take this concept to its logical conclusion, you can define a whole series of events. You can let the filter decide which event it wants to attach to, based on what function it performs and what services it needs from the framework.

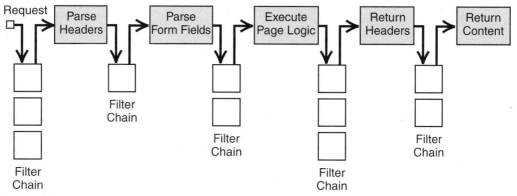

Figure 3.25
Event-driven intercepting filters

This model shares some similarities to the event model described in the *Observer* pattern. In both cases, objects can "subscribe" to events without the original object being dependent on the observers. The object has no dependencies on any specific observers because it calls the observers through an abstract interface. The key difference between *Intercepting Filter* and *Observer* lies in the fact that the observer generally does not modify the source object; it "observes" passively what is going on in the source object. The purpose of *Intercepting Filter*, on the other hand, is to intercept and modify the context in which it is called.

Figure 3.25 also illustrates very well how each filter intercepts the sequence of events inside the Web server framework, hence the name *Intercepting Filter*.

Variations

In most cases, filters are passive in the sense that they manipulate the context, but do not affect flow of execution. In the case of a filter intercepting a Web request, however, you often must design filters so that they redirect the request to a different page. For example, an authentication filter may redirect the request to an error page or to the logon page if the authentication fails.

To illustrate how these filters affect the flow of the Web request, Figure 3.26 shows the sequence of a typical filter scenario, in which the intercepting filter does not intervene in the message flow.

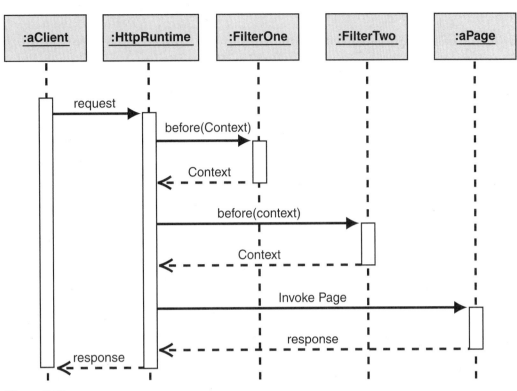

Figure 3.26
Intercepting filter that does not intervene in the message flow

Figure 3.27 shows an alternate sequence in which Filter One redirects the flow to a different page based on the type of request.

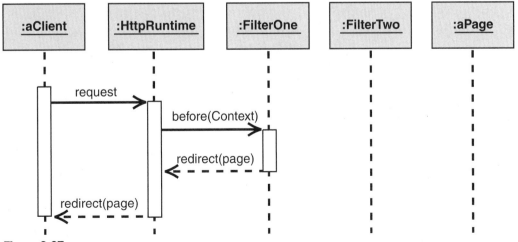

Figure 3.27
Intercepting filter that redirects the message flow

In this scenario, no page is rendered, but a redirect header (HTTP response 302) is produced and is returned to the client. This header causes the client to issue a new request to the URL specified in the redirect header. Because this type of redirection requires a second request from the client browser, it is often referred to as client-side redirect. The main disadvantage is that the client browser has to issue two requests to retrieve the page. This slows down the page display and can also lead to complications with bookmarking, because the client will bookmark the redirected URL, which is generally not good.

Server-side redirects, on the other hand, forward the request to a different page without requiring a roundtrip to the client. They accomplish this by returning control to the **httpRunTime** object, which calls a different *Page Controller* directly, passing along the request context. The transfer happens internally in the server without any involvement of the client. As a result, you do not have to repeat any common preprocessing of the request.

Server-side redirects are used in two common scenarios: URL manipulation can be used in *Intercepting Filter* to allow clients to use virtual URLs to pass parameters to the application. For example, a filter can convert *http://example.com/clientabc* into the URL *http://www.example.com/start.aspx?Client=clientabc*. This manipulation provides a level of indirection that lets the client bookmark a virtual URL that is not affected by internal changes to the application (for example, the migration from .asp to .aspx files). The other common technique that uses server-side redirection is the use of a *Front Controller*. The *Front Controller* processes all page requests in a central component and then passes control to the appropriate command. *Front Controllers* are useful for Web applications with dynamically configurable navigation paths.

Example

Because intercepting filters are such a common need when processing Web requests, most Web frameworks provide mechanisms for the application developer to hook intercepting filters into the request-response process.

The Microsoft® Windows® platform provides two distinct mechanisms:

- The server running Internet Information Services (IIS) provides ISAPI filters. ISAPI filters are low-level constructs that are called before any other processing is performed. As a result, ISAPI filters have a high degree of control over the processing of the request. ISAPI filters are ideal for low-level functions such as URL manipulations. Unfortunately, ISAPI filters should be written in C++ and do not have access to any of the functions incorporated into the Microsoft® .NET Framework.

- The .NET Framework provides the HTTPModule interface. Using a configuration file, filters that implement this interface can be attached to a series of events defined by the framework. For more detail, see *Implementing Intercepting Filter in ASP.NET Using HTTP Module*.

Resulting Context

The *Intercepting Filter* pattern results in the following benefits and liabilities:

Benefits

- **Separation of concerns.** The logic contained in the filters is decoupled from the application logic. Therefore, the application code is not affected when low-level features change (for example, if you move from HTTP to HTTPS or if you migrate session management from URL rewriting to hidden form fields).

- **Flexibility.** The filters are independent of one another. As a result, you can chain together any combination of filters without having to make code changes to any filter.

- **Central configuration.** Due to the composability of filters, you can use a single configuration file to load the filter chain. Rather than working with a lot of source code, you can modify a single configuration file to determine the list of filters to be inserted into the request processing.

- **Deployment-time composability.** *Intercepting Filter* chains can be constructed at runtime based on configuration files. As a result, you can change the sequence of filters during deployment without having to modify code.

- **Reuse.** Because the filters are not dependent on their operating environment, except for the context on which they operate, individual filters can be reused in other Web applications.

Liabilities

- **Order dependency.** Intercepting filters have no explicit dependencies on any other filter. However, filters may make assumptions about the context that is passed to them. For example, some filters may expect certain processing to have occurred before they are invoked. Consider these implicit dependencies when you configure the filter chain. Some frameworks may not guarantee the order of execution across filters. If the program requires a strict sequence, a hard-coded method call may be a better solution than a dynamic filter chain.

- **Shared state.** Filters have no explicit mechanism for sharing state information with one another except to manipulate the context. This is also true for passing information from a filter to the controller. For example, if the filter analyzes the browser type based on header-field values, there is no simple way to pass this information to the application controller. The most common way is to add a fake header field to the request context that contains the filter output. The controller can then extract the fake header field and make a decision based on its value. Unfortunately, you lose any compile-time checking or type safety between the filter and the controller. This is the downside of loose coupling.

Intercepting Filter vs. Controller

Because the intercepting filters are executed right before and after the controller, sometimes it may be difficult to determine whether to implement functionality inside the intercepting filter or inside the controller. The following criteria provide some guidelines when making this decision:

- Filters are better suited to dealing with low-level, transport-related functions such as character-set decoding, decompression, session validation, client-browser type recognition, and traffic logging. These types of operations tend to be well-encapsulated, efficient, and stateless. Therefore, it is easy to chain these operations together without one operation having to pass state information to the other.

- True application functionality that interacts with the model is better taken care of inside the controller or a helper of the controller. These types of functions typically do not possess the kind of composability that filters require.

- In most cases. the processing inside a filter is not dependent on the state of the application; it is executed no matter what. Even though the page controller may contain common functionality, it is best to maintain the opportunity to override the behavior on a case-by-case basis. The controller is better suited to this task than is a chain of filters.

- Many filter implementations (for example, IIS ISAPI filters) execute at a lower layer inside the application server. This gives filters a great deal of control (not much happens before the filter is invoked), but prevents them from accessing many features that the application layer provides, such as session management.

- Because filters are executed for every Web page request, performance is critical. As a result, the framework may limit the choice of implementation language. For example, most ISAPI filters are implemented in a compiled language such as C++. You would not want to have to code complex application logic in C++, if you can have the convenience of coding these pieces in the Microsoft Visual Basic® development system or in the Microsoft Visual C#® development tool with full access to the .NET Framework.

Related Patterns

For more information, refer to the following related patterns:

- *Intercepting Filter* is commonly used in combination with *Front Controller*. [Alur01] and [Fowler03] describe the relationship between the two patterns in detail.

- *Decorator* [Gamma95]. Intercepting filters can be considered decorators around a front controller.

Acknowledgments

[Alur01] Alur, Crupi, and Malks. *Core J2EE Patterns: Best Practices and Design Strategies*. Prentice-Hall, 2001.

[Fowler03] Fowler, Martin. *Patterns of Enterprise Application Architecture*. Addison-Wesley, 2003.

[Gamma95] Gamma, Helm, Johnson, and Vlissides. *Design Patterns: Elements of Reusable Object-Oriented Software*. Addison-Wesley, 1995.

[Buschmann96] Buschmann, Frank, et al. *Pattern-Oriented Software Architecture, Vol 1*. Wiley & Sons, 1996.

[Schmidt00] Schmidt, et al. *Pattern-Oriented Software Architecture, Vol 2*. Wiley & Sons, 2000.

Implementing Intercepting Filter in ASP.NET Using HTTP Module

Context

You are building a Web application in Microsoft® ASP.NET with many different types of requests. Some requests are forwarded to the appropriate page, and others must be logged or modified in some way before being processed.

Implementation Strategy

The ASP.NET implementation of the *Intercepting Filter* pattern is an example of the event-driven filters described in the pattern. ASP.NET provides a series of events during request processing that your application can hook into. These events guarantee the state of the request. Individual filters are implemented with an HTTP module. An HTTP module is a class that implements the **IHttpModule** interface and determines when the filter should be called. ASP.NET includes a set of HTTP modules that can be used by your application. For example, **SessionStateModule** is provided by ASP.NET to supply session state services to an application. You can create your own custom HTTP modules to filter the request or response as needed by your application.

The general process for writing a custom HTTP module is:

- Implement the **IHttpModule** interface.
- Handle the **Init** method and register for the events you need.
- Handle the events.
- Optionally, implement the **Dispose** method if you have to do cleanup.
- Register the module in the web.config file.

Events

The following lists show the events that, when raised during the processing of a request, can be intercepted using ASP.NET. All events are listed in the order in which they occur.

The first list shows the events that are raised before the request is processed:

- **BeginRequest**. This event signals a new request; it is guaranteed to be raised on each request.
- **AuthenticateRequest**. This event signals that the configured authentication mechanism has authenticated the request. Attaching to this event guarantees your filter that the request has been authenticated.
- **AuthorizeRequest**. Like **AuthenticateRequest**, this event signals that the request is now one step further down the chain and has been authorized.

- **ResolveRequestCache**. The output cache module uses this event to short-circuit the processing of requests that have been cached.

- **AcquireRequestState**. This event signals that individual request state should be obtained.

- **PreRequestHandlerExecute**. This event signals that the request handler is about to execute. This is the last event you can participate in before the HTTP handler for this request is called.

The next list shows the events that are raised after the request is processed. The events are listed in the order in which they occur:

- **PostRequestHandlerExecute**. This event signals that the HTTP handler has finished processing the request.

- **ReleaseRequestState**. This event signals that the request state should be stored because the application is finished with the request.

- **UpdateRequestCache**. This event signals that code processing is complete and the file is ready to be added to the ASP.NET cache.

- **EndRequest**. This event signals that all processing has finished for the request. This is the last event called when the application ends.

In addition, the following three per-request events can fire in a nondeterministic order:

- **PreSendRequestHeaders**. This event signals that HTTP headers are about to be sent to the client. This provides an opportunity to add, remove, or modify the headers before they are sent.

- **PreSendRequestContent**. This event signals that content is about to be sent to the client. This provides an opportunity to modify the content before it is sent.

- **Error**. This event signals an unhandled exception.

The following example demonstrates how a request is intercepted after it has been authenticated by the ASP.NET runtime. When the example module, called **UserLogger**, is initialized, it connects a member function, called **OnAuthenticate**, to the **AuthenticateRequest** event. Every time a new request is authenticated, the **OnAuthenticate** function is called. In this example, the **OnAuthenticate** function logs the name of the authenticated user to the Intercepting Filter Pattern application event log.

```
using System;
using System.Web;
using System.Security.Principal;
using System.Diagnostics;

public class UserLogModule : IHttpModule
{
    private HttpApplication httpApp;
```

```
public void Init(HttpApplication httpApp)
{
    this.httpApp = httpApp;
    httpApp.AuthenticateRequest += new EventHandler(OnAuthentication);
}

void OnAuthentication(object sender, EventArgs a)
{
    HttpApplication application = (HttpApplication)sender;
    HttpResponse response = application.Context.Response;

    WindowsIdentity identity =
        (WindowsIdentity)application.Context.User.Identity;

    LogUser(identity.Name);
}

private void LogUser(String name)
{
    EventLog log = new EventLog();
    log.Source = "Intercepting Filter Pattern";
    log.WriteEntry(name,EventLogEntryType.Information);
}

public void Dispose()
{}
}
```

must be added to the web.config file so that the ASP.NET runtime recognizes the module. The following is the configuration file that changes for the **UserLogModule** example module:

```
<httpModules>
    <add name="UserLogModule" type="UserLogModule, ifilter" />
</httpModules>
```

Examples

The following are examples of intercepting filters that are built into Microsoft .NET:

- **DefaultAuthenticationModule**. This filter ensures that an **Authentication** object is present in the **HttpContext** object.

- **FileAuthorizationModule**. This filter verifies that the remote user has Microsoft Windows NT® permissions to access the file requested.

- **FormsAuthenticationModule**. This filter enables ASP.NET applications to use forms authentication.

- **PassportAuthenticationModule**. This filter provides a wrapper around PassportAuthentication services for Passport authentication.

- **SessionStateModule**. This filter provides session-state services for an application.

- **UrlAuthorizationModule**. This filter provides URL-based authorization services for allowing or denying access to specified URLs.
- **WindowsAuthenticationModule**. This filter enables ASP.NET applications to use Microsoft Windows® or Internet Information Services (IIS) authentication.

Testing Considerations

Testing the HTTP modules without the ASP.NET runtime is not possible. Therefore, a slightly different implementation strategy must be employed to separate as much of the functionality as possible from the class that implements the **IHttpModule** interface. In the previous example, the code that logs the user name does not require the ASP.NET runtime. This functionality can be placed in its own class, called **UserLog**, which is independent of ASP.NET. The **UserLogAdapter** class, which implements the **IHttpModule** interface, can use the **UserLog** class. This enables other classes to use the **UserLog** class and also enables you to test it without the ASP.NET environment. The following is the same functionality as described previously, but implemented in a way that allows the logging functionality to be tested without the ASP.NET runtime:

```
using System;
using System.Diagnostics;

public class UserLog
{
    public static void Write(String name)
    {
        EventLog log = new EventLog();
        log.Source = "Intercepting Filter Pattern";
        log.WriteEntry(name,EventLogEntryType.Information);
    }
}

using System;
using System.Web;
using System.Security.Principal;

public class UserLogAdapter
{
    private HttpApplication httpApp;

    public void Init(HttpApplication httpApp)
    {
        this.httpApp = httpApp;
        httpApp.AuthenticateRequest += new EventHandler(OnAuthentication);
    }

    void OnAuthentication(object sender, EventArgs a)
    {
        HttpApplication application = (HttpApplication)sender;
        HttpResponse response = application.Context.Response;
```

```
            WindowsIdentity identity =
                (WindowsIdentity)application.Context.User.Identity;

            UserLog.Write(identity.Name);
    }

    public void Dispose()
    {}
}
```

Resulting Context

The implementation of the *Intercepting Filter* pattern results in the following benefits and liabilities:

Benefits

- **Uses event-driven filters**. The ASP.NET runtime provides numerous events, which enable the programmer to hook into the right place to add their functionality. This is beneficial, because they can assume the current state of the request based on the event. For example, if the event is **AuthenticateRequest**, you can assume that the request is authenticated prior to your filter being called.
- **Enables flexible configuration**. The modules are added or removed by editing the web.config file. The source code does not have to be changed, and the ASP.NET runtime does not have to be restarted.
- **Alleviates order dependency**. One of the liabilities of *Intercepting Filter* is that filters should not be order-dependent. Because the ASP.NET implementation uses events, it alleviates the problem by using events to indicate that certain processing has occurred.

Liabilities

Testing of classes that implement the **IHttpModule** interface is difficult or impossible without testing the full ASP.NET runtime.

Related Patterns

For more information, see *Adapter* [Gamma95]. The *Adapter* pattern was used in "Testing Considerations" to help isolate the core functionality and to enhance testability.

Acknowledgments

[Gamma95] Gamma, Helm, Johnson, and Vlissides. *Design Patterns: Elements of Reusable Object-Oriented Software*. Addison-Wesley, 1995.

Page Cache

Context

You are working with a Web-based application that presents dynamic information to users. You have observed that many users access a specific page without the dynamic information changing.

Problem

How can you improve the response time of dynamically generated Web pages that are requested frequently but consume a large amount of system resources to construct?

Forces

The following forces act on a system within this context and must be reconciled as you consider a solution to the problem:

- Generating a dynamic Web page consumes a variety of system resources. When the Web server receives a page request, the server usually has to retrieve the requested information from an external data source, such as a database or a Web service. Access to these resources often occurs over a limited pool of resources, such as database connections, sockets, or file descriptors. Because a Web server typically handles many concurrent requests, contention for these pooled resources may delay the page request until a resource becomes available. After the request has been sent to the external data source, the results still have to be transformed into HTML code for display.

- One obvious approach to making systems faster is to buy more hardware. This option may be appealing because hardware is cheap (or so the vendors say) and the program does not have to change. On the other hand, more hardware only helps until you reach its physical limitations. Network limitations, such as data transfer rates, or latency make these physical limitations more apparent.

- A second approach to making systems faster is to do less (processing) work. This approach requires more effort from developers, but can provide enormous increases in performance. The following paragraphs explore the challenges that this approach poses.

The following paragraphs use a weather example to show how extra development effort can relieve the processing load. If 10,000 users view the weather forecast for London within one hour, a default Web server implementation may connect to the weather service 10,000 times, and render 10,000 HTML pages with images of clouds and rain, even though it rains all day. To reduce processing, you could just get the actual weather forecast during the first request, render the HTML page, and then save that pre-rendered page for later use. When the next request for London weather arrives, the system could return the saved page to the client browser; there would be no need to connect to the weather service or render another page.

This would save CPU cycles to render redundant HTML pages and improve response times. The cost, however, would be the memory allocated to store the pre-rendered pages. Providing the weather forecast for each postal code may require that you store thousands of weather forecast pages. (There are thousands of postal codes in the United States alone.) To figure out which page the user is requesting, you would also need to index the pre-rendered pages by postal code, or possibly additional parameters such as which Web browser the user is running (the HTML may differ slightly by browser). Also, you may receive a lot more requests for the weather in a large city than for a small town. Likewise, the forecast may change more often in some regions than in others. Therefore, you need to be smart about which pages you are pre-rendering and how long you keep them around before you re-render them.

Another item to consider is the composition of the page. Maybe you want to display a combination page with the weather and the current stock prices. Because stock prices change more often than the weather, you can no longer store the complete page. You can store pieces of the page, but then you must manage each page component separately and reassemble it from pre-rendered components as requests arrive.

Yet another consideration is the variability of the pages. For example, the weather data may not change, but the page may still look different for different users based on user preferences such as language, color, browser, and device (computer, Personal Digital Assistant (PDA), or phone). If you store the rendered page, you have to store each version separately. If you store the weather data, however, you save a trip to the weather service, but you still have to render the page. So you use a few more CPU cycles, but need to cache much less information. For a more detailed description of this approach, see *Page Data Caching*.

Solution

Use a page cache for dynamic Web pages that are accessed frequently, but change less often.

Structure

The basic structure of a page cache is relatively simple. The Web server maintains a local data store with pre-rendered pages (see Figure 3.28).

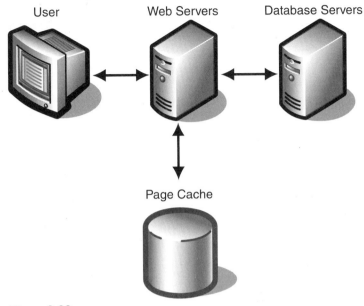

Figure 3.28
Basic page cache configuration

Dynamics

The following sequence diagrams make it clear why a page cache can improve performance. The first sequence diagram (Figure 3.29, on the next page) depicts the initial state where the desired page is not yet cached (a so-called cache miss). In this scenario, the Web server must access the database, render the HTML page, store it in the cache, and then return the page to the client browser. Note that this process is slightly slower than the scenario without caching because it performs the following extra steps:

- Determines whether the page is cached
- Stores the page in the cache after it is rendered into HTML

Neither step should take very long in comparison to the database access and the HTML generation. Because this scenario requires extra processing, however, you must ensure a good series of cache hits after the system goes through the steps associated with a cache miss, which are shown in Figure 3.29 on the next page.

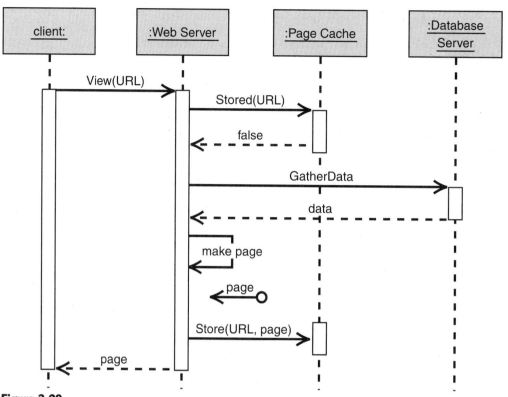

Figure 3.29
Sequence for a cache miss (when the page is not in the cache)

In the cache hit scenario shown in Figure 3.30, the page is already in the cache. A cache hit saves cycles by skipping the database access, the page rendering, and the storing of the page.

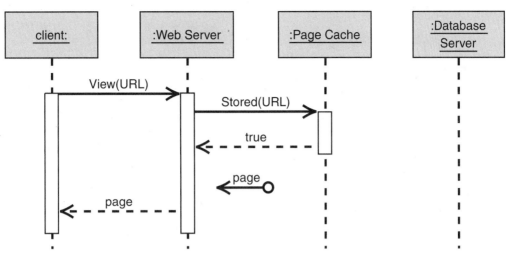

Figure 3.30
Sequence for a cache hit (when the page is in the cache)

Implementation

Caching strategies are an extensive topic that cannot be covered exhaustively in a single pattern. Nevertheless, it is important to discuss the considerations that are most relevant when implementing a solution that includes *Page Cache*.

A *Page Cache* solution consists of the following key mechanisms:

- Page (or page fragments) storage
- Page indexing
- Cache refresh

The following paragraphs discuss each of these mechanisms.

Page Storage

A page cache must store pre-rendered pages so that the system can retrieve them quickly. You also want to be able to store as many pages as possible to increase the chances of a cache hit. When it comes to storage, you usually face a tradeoff between speed, size, and cost. Assuming that you do not have unlimited funds at hand, the choice is usually between small or fast. Smaller caches can live in memory and can be very fast. Larger disk storage caches offer more storage, but are significantly slower.

To reach the best compromise between speed and size, you must be careful about which pages you cache. Some pages will be accessed much more frequently than others, so, ideally, you should cache only the popular pages and forget about the rarely used ones. This decision is not always easy to make, because usage patterns tend to vary. Many caches implement strategies such as Least Frequently Used (LFU) to remove pages that have been used infrequently since being stored. Other caching schemes let the user specify the caching strategy for each individual page.

The next most important decision is how big the pieces in the cache should be. Storing complete pages enables quick page display after a page hit, because the system retrieves the page from the cache and immediately sends it to the client without any other action. However, if some portions of the page change frequently and others do not (for example, a page with weather and stock prices), storing complete pages could lead to a lot of extra storage. Storing smaller pieces improves the chances of a page hit, but also requires more storage overhead (there are more pieces to index) and more CPU consumption (testing the cache for multiple segments and assembling the final page). For a description on how to assemble pages from cached segments, see *Page Fragment Caching.*

Page Indexing

It is also important to consider how the system locates pages in the cache. The simplest method for a system to locate pages is by URL. If a page does not depend on any other factors, you can retrieve it from the cache simply by comparing the requested URL to the URLs of the pages stored in the cache. However, this scenario rarely occurs. Almost all dynamic pages are built based on parameters such as user preferences, query strings, form fields, and internal application state. For example, the weather page in the earlier example depends on the postal code that users enter. So the system may have to store multiple instances of one page, based on the parameter. In the postal code example, this could translate to thousands of pages. This is inefficient because weather services do not actually maintain the forecast for every postal code, but rather by city or region. If you know how the weather service translates postal codes into weather regions, you can reduce the number of cached pages by an order of magnitude and increase the average hit rate. As always, the more information you have, the more efficient you can be. You can use *Vary-By-Parameter Caching* to implement this type of caching, where the page content depends on parameters.

Cache Refresh

How long the system keeps items in the cache is also important. Storing pages for a fixed amount of time is the simplest method (see *Implementing Page Cache in ASP.NET Using Absolute Expiration*). This method may not always be sufficient, however. In the weather example, if an unusual weather pattern such as a cold front or a hurricane is approaching a major city, you may want to update every 15 minutes. You can resolve these issues by tying the caching duration to external events. For example, you may choose to flush the cache when an external event arrives (for example, late-breaking news), forcing the page to be re-rendered when the next request arrives.

Some caching strategies try to pre-render pages during low-traffic periods. This approach can be very effective if you have predictable traffic patterns and you can hold pages long enough to avoid refreshing during peak traffic times.

Resulting Context

Page Cache results in the following benefits and liabilities:

Benefits

- **Conserves CPU cycles required to render pages**. This results in faster response times and increases the scalability of the Web server to a larger number of concurrent users.

- **Eliminates unnecessary round-trips to the database or other external data sources**. This benefit is particularly important, because these external sources usually provide only a limited number of concurrent connections that must be shared by all concurrent page requests in a resource pool. Frequent access to external data sources can quickly bring a Web server to an abrupt halt due to resource contention.

- **Conserves client connections**. Each concurrent connection from a client browser to the Web server consumes limited resources. The longer it takes to process a page request, the longer the connection resource is tied up.

- **Enables concurrent access by many page requests**. Because a page cache is primarily a read-only resource, it can be multithreaded rather easily. Therefore, it prevents resource contention that can occur when the system accesses external data sources. The only portion that must be synchronized is the cache update, so the considerations around frequency of update are most critical to good performance.

- **Increases the availability of the application**. If the system accesses an external data source to render pages, it depends on the data source being available. Page caching enables the system to deliver cached pages to the clients even when the external source becomes unavailable; the data may not be current, but it is likely better than no data at all.

Note: If this function is critical to your caching strategy, consider using *Page Data Cache*, which can provide more flexibility for external data sources.

Liabilities

- **Displays information that is not current**. If the cache refresh mechanism is configured incorrectly, the Web site could display invalid data, which could be confusing or even harmful. For example, an overly extended caching interval in a live stock feed could become very costly for the user who makes purchasing decisions based on the data.

- **Requires CPU and memory (RAM or disk) resources**. Caching pages' that are not frequently viewed or setting refresh intervals that are too short can incur additional overhead and actually decrease server performance. As with all performance measures, perform a thorough analysis using actual measurements and performance indicators to determine the correct settings. Hasty decisions, such as caching every page, can do more harm than good.

- **Adds complexity to the system and can make it more difficult to test and debug**. In most cases, you should develop and test the application without caching and then enable caching options during the performance-tuning phase.

- **Requires additional security considerations**. This implication of caching is often overlooked. When a Web server is processing concurrent requests for confidential information from multiple users, it is important to avoid crossover between these requests. Because the page cache is a global entity, an improperly configured page cache may deliver a page to the browser that was originally rendered for another user. This may not be an issue with weather forecasts, but would pose a serious problem if, for example, the system displayed a user's bank statement to another user.

- **Can produce dramatically inconsistent response times**. Although delivering pages quickly in 99 percent of the cases is surely better than delivering slow pages every time, a caching strategy that is over-optimized for cache hits and under-optimized for cache misses can cause sporadic timeouts. This concern is particularly relevant for Web services as opposed to simple HTML pages.

Related Patterns

The following patterns describe various strategies for implementing *Page Cache*:

- *Implementing Page Cache in ASP.NET Using Absolute Expiration*. This pattern inserts a directive into each page that is to be cached. The directive specifies the refresh interval in seconds. The refresh interval does not depend on external events, and the cache cannot be flushed.

- *Vary-By-Parameter Caching*. This pattern uses a variation of *Absolute Expiration* that enables the developer to specify parameters that affect the contents of the page. As a result, the cache stores multiple versions of the page, which are indexed by the parameter values.

- *Sliding Expiration Caching*. This pattern is similar to *Absolute Expiration* in that the page is valid for a specified time. However, the refresh interval is reset on each request. For example, you could use sliding expiration caching to cache a page for a maximum of 10 minutes. As long as requests for the page are made within 10 minutes, the expiration is postponed for another 10 minutes.

Implementing Page Cache in ASP.NET Using Absolute Expiration

Context

You are building a Web application in ASP.NET and you want to cache pages to improve performance. You have evaluated the alternatives presented in *Page Cache* and have determined that absolute expiration is an adequate strategy.

Implementation Strategy

Page caching increases request response throughput by caching the content generated from dynamic pages. Page caching is enabled by default in ASP.NET, but output from any given response is not cached unless a valid expiration policy is defined. To define the expiration policy, you can use either the low-level **OutputCache** API or the high-level @ **OutputCache** directive.

When page caching is enabled, the first **GET** request to the page creates a page cache entry. The page cache entry serves subsequent **GET** or **HEAD** requests until the cached response expires.

The page cache respects the expiration policy for pages. If a page is cached with an expiration policy of 60 seconds, the page is removed from the output cache when 60 seconds have elapsed. If the cache receives another request after that time, it executes the page code and refreshes the cache. This type of expiration policy is called *absolute expiration*, which means that a page is valid until a certain time.

The following example demonstrates a way to use the **@OutputCache** directive to cache responses:

```
<%@ OutputCache Duration="60" VaryByParam="none" %>

<html>
  <script language="C#" runat="server">
    void Page_Load(Object sender, EventArgs e)
    {
        TimeMsg.Text = DateTime.Now.ToString("G");
    }
  </script>

  <body>
    <h3>Using the Output Cache</h3>

    <p>Last generated on: <asp:label id="TimeMsg" runat="server"/>
  </body>
</html>
```

The example displays the time when the response was generated. To see output caching in action, invoke the page and note the time at which the response was generated. Then refresh the page and note that the time has not changed, indicating that the second response is being served from the cache.

The following line activates page caching on the response:

```
<%@ OutputCache Duration="60" VaryByParam="none" %>
```

This directive simply indicates that the page should be cached for 60 seconds and that the page does not vary according to any **GET** or **POST** parameters. Requests received in the first 60 seconds are satisfied from the cache. After 60 seconds, the page is removed from the cache; the next request caches the page again.

Testing Considerations

The caching of pages makes testing more difficult. For example, if you change a page and then view it in the browser, you may not see the updated page because the browser displays the page from the cache, rather than a newly generated page. Ideally, you can turn off the caching of pages and run tests that do not require caching. After these tests run successfully, you can enable caching and then run the tests that require caching.

Resulting Context

Using absolute expiration to implement *Page Cache* in ASP.NET results in the following benefits and liabilities:

Benefits

- **This is by far the simplest method of caching pages in ASP.NET**. Absolute expiration may be sufficient in many cases and is clearly an excellent place to begin, provided that you analyze the usage patterns of the Web application to determine which pages you cache. Also consider the volatility of the dynamic content on the page. For example, a weather page may have an expiration policy of 60 minutes, because the weather does not change very quickly. However, a Web page that displays a stock quote may not be cacheable at all. To determine the correct expiration time, you must know the most frequently viewed pages and understand the volatility of the data the pages contain.

- **You can set different expiration policies for different pages**. Doing so enables you to cache only frequently accessed pages and not waste cache space on pages that are accessed infrequently. It also allows you to refresh pages containing volatile data more often than others.

Liabilities

- **Dynamic content on cached pages may become invalid**. This is because the page expiration is based on time rather than content. In the example described previously, the time is displayed on the page in seconds. Because the page is built every 60 seconds, the seconds field is invalid immediately after the page is built. The ramifications of the invalid data in this example are small. If you are displaying a time-sensitive financial quote, for example, and extreme accuracy is required, consider a caching strategy that ensures that you never display invalid data. (See *Page Data Caching*.)

  This strategy does not accommodate passing parameters to the page. Dynamic pages are often parameterized. For example, a weather page may be parameterized by postal code. Unless you want to create separate pages and URLs for thousands of postal codes (42,000 in the United States, for example), you cannot use absolute expiration to cache this page. Vary-By-Parameter Caching resolves this issue.

- **Absolute expiration works well only if the whole page stays the same**. In many applications, large portions of a page change rarely (great candidates for caching), but are coupled with other sections that change frequently (cannot be cached). Because absolute expiration caches only whole pages, it cannot take advantage of localized changes such as this. *Page Fragment Caching* may be a better choice in these circumstances, because it can cache portions of a page. HTML frames provide another option to simulate fragments of pages. However, frames have known issues in Web browsers, such as navigation and printing problems.

- **There is no way to flush the cached pages**. The pages remain in the cache until they expire or the server is restarted. This makes testing problematic. It can also be difficult in situations where data changes rarely, but if a change occurs you cannot afford a delay. For example, updating the weather forecast every two hours is probably sufficient in most cases. However, if a hurricane is approaching, you may not want to wait two hours before updating the weather forecast.

- **You must alter the code in each page to change the expiration policy**. Because the expiration policy can only be changed in the code, there is no mechanism to turn off caching for the entire application.

- **Storing pages in a cache requires disk space on the server**. In the example described earlier, the small page would not require much disk space. As the content on each page and the number of pages in the cache increase, however, the demands for disk space on the Web server will also increase.

Variants

The following patterns explain alternate implementations of *Page Cache:*

- *Vary-By-Parameter Caching*
- *Sliding Expiration Caching*

Related Patterns

For related page cache designs and implementation strategies, see the following patterns:

- *Page Data Caching*
- *Page Fragment Caching*

Observer

Context

In object-oriented programming, objects contain both data and behavior that, together, represent a specific aspect of the business domain. One advantage of using objects to build applications is that all manipulation of the data can be encapsulated inside the object. This makes the object self-contained and increases the potential for reuse of the object in other applications. However, objects cannot simply work in isolation. In all but the most trivial applications, objects must collaborate to accomplish more complex tasks. When objects collaborate, the objects may have to notify each other when an object changes state. For example, the *Model-View-Controller* pattern prescribes the separation of business data (the model) and the presentation logic (the view). When the model changes, the system must notify the view so that it can refresh the visual presentation and accurately reflect the model's state. In other words, the view is dependent on the model to inform it of changes to the model's internal state.

Problem

How can an object notify other objects of state changes without being dependent on their classes?

Forces

A solution to this problem has to reconcile the following forces and considerations:

- The easiest way to inform dependent objects of a state change is to call them directly. However, direct collaboration between objects creates dependency between their classes. For example, if the model object calls the view object to inform it of changes, the model class is now also dependent on the view class. This kind of direct coupling between two objects (also called tight coupling) decreases the reusability of classes. For example, whenever you want to reuse the model class, you have to also reuse the view class because the model makes calls to it. If you have more than one view, the problem is compounded.

- The need to decouple classes occurs frequently in event-driven frameworks. The framework must be able to notify the application of events, but the framework cannot be dependent on specific application classes.

- Likewise, if you make a change to the view class, the model is likely to be affected. Applications that contain many tightly coupled classes tend to be brittle and difficult to maintain, because changes in one class could affect all the tightly coupled classes.

- If you call the dependent objects directly, every time a new dependent is added, the code inside the source object has to be modified.

- In some cases, the number of dependent objects may be unknown at design time. For example, if you allow the user to open multiple windows (views) for a specific model, you will have to update multiple views when the model state changes.

- A direct function call is still the most efficient way to pass information between two objects (second only to having the functionality of both objects inside a single object). As a result, decoupling objects with other mechanisms is likely to adversely affect performance. Depending on the performance requirements of the application, you may have to consider this tradeoff.

Solution

Use the *Observer* pattern to maintain a list of interested dependents (observers) in a separate object (the subject). Have all individual observers implement a common *Observer* interface to eliminate direct dependencies between the subject and the dependent objects (see Figure 3.31).

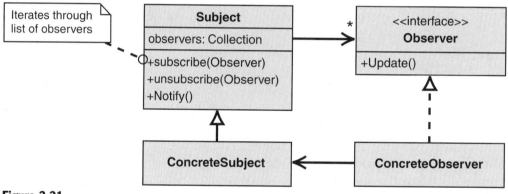

Figure 3.31
Basic Observer structure

When a state change occurs in the client that is relevant to the dependent objects, **ConcreteSubject** invokes the **Notify()** method. The **Subject** superclass maintains a list of all interested observers so that the **Notify()** method can loop through the list of all observers and invoke the **Update()** method on each registered observer. The observers register and unregister for updates by calling the **subscribe()** and **unsubscribe()** methods on **Subject** (see Figure 3.32). One or more instances of **ConcreteObserver** may also access **ConcreteSubject** for more information and therefore usually depend on the **ConcreteSubject** class. However, as Figure 3.31 illustrates, there is no direct or indirect dependency from the **ConcreteSubject** class on the **ConcreteObserver** class.

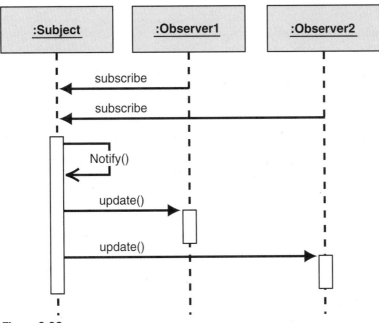

Figure 3.32
Basic Observer interaction

With this generic way of communicating between the subject and observers, collaborations can be built dynamically instead of statically. Due to the separation of notification logic and synchronization logic, new observers can be added without modifying the notification logic, and notification logic can also be changed without affecting the synchronization logic in observers. The code is now much more separate, and thus easier to maintain and reuse.

Notifying objects of changes without incurring a dependency on their classes is such a common requirement that some platforms provide language features to perform this function. For example, the Microsoft® .NET Framework defines the notion of delegates and events to accomplish the *Observer* role. Therefore, you would rarely implement the *Observer* pattern explicitly in .NET, but should use delegates and events instead. Most .NET developers will think of the *Observer* pattern as a complicated way to implement events.

The solution presented in Figure 3.31 shows the **ConcreteSubject** class inheriting from the **Subject** class. The **Subject** class contains the implementations of the methods to add or remove observers and to iterate through the list of observers. All **ConcreteSubject** has to do is to inherit from **Subject** and call **Notify()** when a state change occurs. In languages that only support single inheritance (such as Java or C#), inheriting from **Subject** precludes the class from inheriting from any other class. This can be a problem because in many cases **ConcreteSubject** is a domain object that may inherit from a domain object base class. Therefore, it is a better idea to replace the **Subject** class with a **Subject** interface and to provide a helper class for the implementation (see Figure 3.33). This way, you do not exhaust your single superclass relationship with the **Subject** class but can use the **ConcreteSubject** in another inheritance hierarchy. Some languages (for example, Smalltalk) even implement the **Subject** interface as part of the **Object** class, from which every class inherits implicitly.

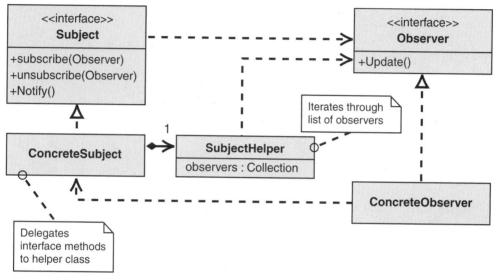

Figure 3.33
Using a helper class to avoid inheriting from the Subject class

Unfortunately, you now have to add code to each class that inherits from the **Subject** interface to implement the methods defined in the interface. This task can become very repetitious. Also, because the domain object coincides with **ConcreteSubject**, it cannot differentiate between different types of state changes that would be associated with different subjects. This only allows observers to subscribe to all state changes of **ConcreteSubject**, even though you may want to be more selective (for example, if the source object contains a list, you may want to be notified of updates, but not of insertions). You could have the observers filter out notifications that are not relevant, but that makes the solution less efficient, because **ConcreteSubject** calls all the observers just to find out that they are really not interested.

You can resolve these issues by separating the subject completely from the source class (see Figure 3.34). Doing so reduces **ConcreteSubject** to the implementation of the **Subject** interface; it has no other responsibilities. This allows **DomainObject** to be associated with more than one ConcreteSubject so that you can differentiate between different types of events for a single domain class.

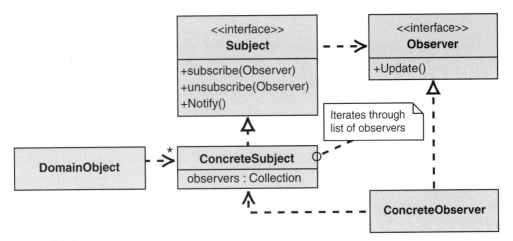

Figure 3.34
Separating DomainObject and Subject

The event and delegate features in the .NET Framework implement this approach as a language construct so that you do not even have to implement your own **ConcreteSubject** classes anymore. Basically, events replace the **ConcreteSubject** classes, and delegates implement the role of the **Observer** interface.

Propagating State Information

So far, this solution has described how a client object can notify the observers when a state change occurs, but has not yet discussed how the observers find out which state the client object is in. There are two mechanisms for passing this information to the observers:

- **Push model**. In the push model, the client sends all relevant information regarding the state change to the subject, which passes the information on to each observer. If the information is passed in a neutral format (for example, XML), this model keeps the dependent observers from having to access the client directly for more information. On the other hand, the subject has to make some assumptions about which information is relevant to the observers. If a new observer is added, the subject may have to publish additional information required by that observer. This would make the subject and the client once again dependent on the observers — the problem you were trying to solve in the first place. So when using the push model, you should err on the side of inclusion when determining the amount of information to pass to the observers. In many cases, you would include a reference to the subject in the call to the observer. The observers can use that reference to obtain state information.

- **Pull model**. In the pull model, the client notifies the subject of a state change. After the observers receive notification, they access the subject or the client for additional data (see Figure 3.35) by using a **getState()** method. This model does not require the subject to pass any information along with the **update()** method, but it may require that the observer call **getState()** just to figure out that the state change was not relevant. As a result, this model can be a little more inefficient. Another possible complication occurs when the observer and the subject run in different threads (for example, if you use RMI to notify the observers). In this scenario, the internal state of the subject may have changed again by the time the observer obtains the state information through the callback. This may cause the observer to skip an operation.

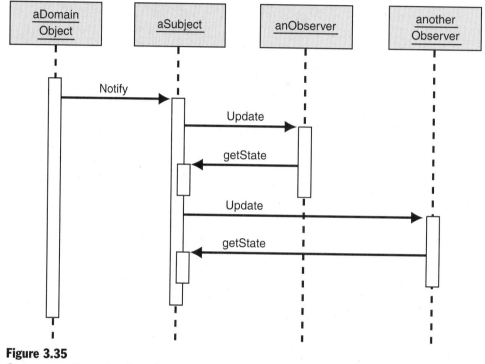

Figure 3.35
State propagation using the pull model

When to Trigger an Update

When implementing the *Observer* pattern, you have two options for managing the triggering of the update. The first option is to insert the call to **Notify()** in the client right after each call to **Subject** that affects an internal state change. This gives the client full control over the frequency of the notification, but also adds extra responsibility to the client, which can lead to errors if the developer forgets to call **Notify()**. The other choice is to encapsulate the call to **Notify()** inside each state-changing operation of **Subject**. This way, a state change always causes **Notify()** to be called without additional action from the client. The downside is that several nested operations might cause multiple notifications. Figure 3.36 shows an example of this in which Operation A calls Sub-Operation B and an observer might receive two calls to its **Update** method.

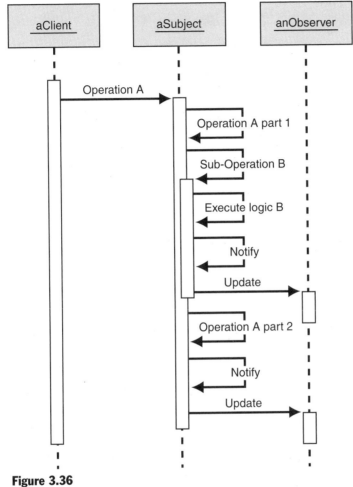

Figure 3.36
Extraneous notifications

Calling multiple updates for a single, but nested operation can cause some ineffi-ciency, but also leads to more serious side effects: The subject could be in an invalid state when the nested **Notify** method is invoked at the end of Operation B (see Figure 3.36) because Operation A has only been processed part of the way. In this case, the nested notify should be avoided. For example, Operation B can be extracted out into a method without notification logic and can rely on the call to **Notify()** inside Operation A. *Template Method* [Gamma95] is a useful construct for making sure the observers are notified only once.

Observers Affecting State Change

In some cases, an observer may change the state of the subject while it is processing the **update()** call. This could lead to problems if the subject automatically calls **Notify()** after each state change. Figure 3.37 shows why.

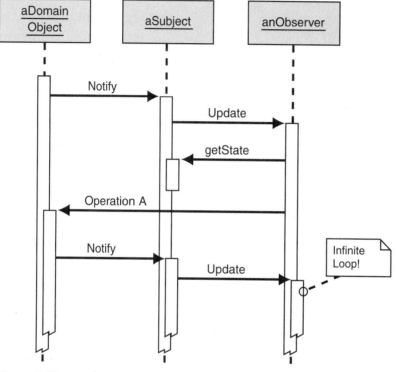

Figure 3.37

Modifying object state from within Update causes an infinite loop

In this example, the observer performs Operation A in response to the state change notification. If Operation A changes the state of **DomainObject**, it then triggers another call to **Notify()**, which in turn calls the **Update** method of the observer again. This results in an infinite loop. The infinite loop is easy to spot in this simple example, but if relationships are more complicated, it may be difficult to determine the dependency chain. One way to reduce the likelihood of infinite loops is to make the notification interest-specific. For example, in C#, use the following interface for subject, where Interest could be an enumeration of all types of interest:

```
interface Subject
{
public void addObserver(Observer o, Interest a);
public void notify(Interest a);
...
```

```
}

interface Observer
{
    public void update(Subject s, Interest a);
}
```

Allowing observers to be notified only when an event related to their specific interest occurs reduces the dependency chain and helps to avoid infinite loops. This is equivalent to defining multiple, more narrowly defined, event types in .NET. The other option for avoiding the loop is to introduce a locking mechanism to keep the subject from publishing new notifications while it is still inside the original **Notify()** loop.

Example

See *Implementing Observer in .NET*.

Resulting Context

Because *Observer* supports loose coupling and reduces dependencies, should you loosely couple every pair of objects that depend on each other? Certainly not. As is the case with most patterns, one solution rarely solves all problems. You need to consider the following tradeoffs when employing the *Observer* pattern.

Benefits

- **Loose coupling and reduced dependencies**. The client is no longer dependent on the observers because it is isolated through the use of a subject and the **Observer** interface. This advantage is used in many frameworks where application components can register to be notified when (lower-level) framework events occur. As a result, the framework calls the application component, but is not dependent on it.

- **Variable number of observers**. Observers can attach and detach during runtime because the subject makes no assumptions about the number of observers. This feature is useful in scenarios where the number of observers is not known at design time (for example, if you need an observer for each window that the user opens in the application).

Liabilities

- **Decreased performance**. In many implementations, the update() methods of the observers may execute in the same thread as the subject. If the list of observers is long, the **Notify()** method may take a long time. Abstracting object dependencies does not mean that adding observers has no impact on the application.

- **Memory leaks**. The callback mechanism (when an object registers to be called later) used in *Observer* can lead to a common mistake that results in memory leaks, even in managed C# code. Assuming that an observer goes out of scope but forgets to unsubscribe from the subject, the subject still maintains a reference to the observer. This reference prevents garbage collection from reallocating the memory associated with the observer until the subject object is destroyed as well. This can lead to serious memory leaks if the lifetime of the observers is much shorter than the lifetime of the subject (which is often the case).

- **Hidden dependencies**. The use of observers turns explicit dependencies (through method invocations) into implicit dependencies (via observers). If observers are used extensively throughout an application, it becomes nearly impossible for a developer to understand what is happening by looking at the source code. This makes it very difficult to understand the implications of code changes. The problem grows exponentially with the levels of propagation (for example, an observer acting as **Subject**). Therefore, you should limit the use of observers to few well-defined interactions, such as the interaction between model and view in the *Model-View-Controller* pattern. The use of observers between domain objects should generally be cause for suspicion.

- **Testing/Debugging difficulties**. As much as loose coupling is a great architectural feature, it can make development more difficult. The more you decouple two objects, the more difficult it becomes to understand the dependencies between them when looking at the source code or a class diagram. Therefore, you should only loosely couple objects if you can safely ignore the association between them (for example, if the observer is free of side effects).

Related Patterns

For more information, see *Implementing Observer in .NET*.

Acknowledgments

[Gamma95] Gamma, Helm, Johnson, and Vlissides. *Design Patterns: Elements of Reusable Object-Oriented Software*. Addison-Wesley, 1995.

Implementing Observer in .NET

Context

You are building an application in Microsoft® .NET and you have to notify dependent objects of state changes without making the source object depend on the dependent objects.

Background

To explain how to implement *Observer* in .NET and the value provided by limiting the dependencies between objects, the following example refactors a solution, which has a bidirectional dependency, first into an implementation based on the *Observer* pattern defined in *Design Patterns* [Gamma95], then into a modified form of the *Observer* pattern for languages that have single inheritance of implementation, and finally into a solution that uses the .NET Framework language constructs delegates and events.

The example problem has two classes, **Album** and **BillingService** (See Figure 3.38).

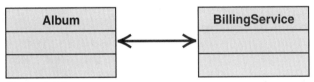

Figure 3.38
Example UML static diagram

These two objects interact to play albums and to charge end-users each time an album is played.

Album.cs

The following example shows the implementation of the **Album** class:

```
using System;

public class Album
{
    private BillingService billing;
    private String name;

    public Album(BillingService billing,
            string name)
    {
        this.billing = billing;
        this.name = name;
    }
}
```

```
    public void Play()
    {
        billing.GenerateCharge(this);

        // code to play the album
    }

    public String Name
    {
        get { return name; }
    }
}
```

BillingService.cs

The following example shows the implementation of the **BillingService** class:

```
using System;

public class BillingService
{
    public void GenerateCharge(Album album)
    {
        string name = album.Name;
        // code to generate charge for correct album
    }
}
```

These classes have to be created in a specific order. Because the **Album** class needs the **BillingService** object for construction, it must be constructed last. After the objects are instantiated, the user is charged every time the **Play** method is called.

Client.cs

The following class, **Client**, demonstrates the construction process:

```
using System;

class Client
{
    [STAThread]
    static void Main(string[] args)
    {
        BillingService service = new BillingService();
        Album album = new Album(service, "Up");

        album.Play();
    }
}
```

This code works, but there are at least two issues with it. The first is a bidirectional dependency between the **Album** class and the **BillingService** class. **Album** makes method calls on **BillingService**, and **BillingService** makes method calls on **Album**. This means that if you need to reuse the **Album** class somewhere else, you have to include **BillingService** with it. Also, you cannot use the **BillingService** class without the **Album** class. This is not desirable because it limits flexibility.

The second issue is that you have to modify the **Album** class every time you add or remove a new service. For example, if you want to add a counter service that keeps track of the number of times albums are played, you must modify the **Album** class's constructor and the **Play** method in the following manner:

```csharp
using System;

public class Album
{
    private BillingService billing;
    private CounterService counter;
    private String name;

    public Album(BillingService billing,
            CounterService counter,
                string name)
    {
        this.billing = billing;
        this.counter = counter;
        this.name = name;
    }

    public void Play()
    {
        billing.GenerateCharge(this);
        counter.Increment(this);

        // code to play the album
    }

    public String Name
    {
        get { return name; }
    }
}
```

This gets ugly. These types of changes clearly should not involve the **Album** class at all. This design makes the code difficult to maintain. You can, however, use the *Observer* pattern to fix these problems.

Implementation Strategy

This strategy discusses and implements a number of approaches to the problems described in the previous section. Each solution attempts to correct issues with the previous example by removing portions of the bidirectional dependency between **Album** and **BillingService**. The first solution describes how to implement the *Observer* pattern by using the solution described in *Design Patterns* [Gamma95].

Observer

The *Design Patterns* approach uses an abstract **Subject** class and an **Observer** interface to break the dependency between the **Subject** object and the **Observer** objects. It also allows for multiple **Observers** for a single **Subject**. In the example, the **Album** class inherits from the **Subject** class, assuming the role of the concrete subject described in the *Observer* pattern. The **BillingService** class takes the place of the concrete observer by implementing the **Observer** interface, because the **BillingService** is waiting to be told when the **Play** method is called. (See Figure 3.39.)

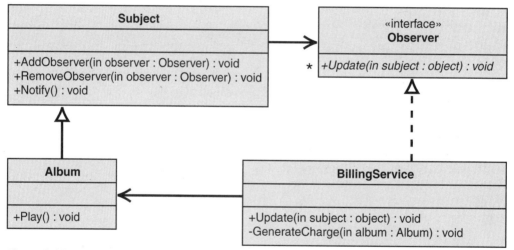

Figure 3.39
Observer class diagram

By extending the **Subject** class, you eliminate the direct dependence of the **Album** class on the **BillingService**. However, you now have a dependency on the **Observer** interface. Because **Observer** is an interface, the system is not dependent on the actual instances that implement the interface. This allows for easy extensions without modifying the **Album** class. You still have not removed the dependency between **BillingService** and **Album**. This one is less problematic, because you can easily add new services without having to change **Album**. The following examples show the implementation code for this solution.

Observer.cs

The following example shows the **Observer** class:

```
using System;

public interface Observer
{
    void Update(object subject);
}
```

Subject.cs

The following example shows the **Subject** class:

```
using System;
using System.Collections;

public abstract class Subject
{
    private ArrayList observers = new ArrayList();

    public void AddObserver(Observer observer)
    {
        observers.Add(observer);
    }

    public void RemoveObserver(Observer observer)
    {
        observers.Remove(observer);
    }

    public void Notify()
    {
        foreach(Observer observer in observers)
        {
            observer.Update(this);
        }
    }
}
```

Album.cs

The following example shows the **Album** class:

```
using System;

public class Album : Subject
{
    private String name;

    public Album(String name)
    { this.name = name; }
```

```
public void Play()
{
   Notify();

   // code to play the album
}

public String Name
{
   get { return name; }
}
}
```

BillingService.cs

The following example shows the **BillingService** class:

```
using System;

public class BillingService : Observer
{
   public void Update(object subject)
   {
      if(subject is Album)
         GenerateCharge((Album)subject);
   }

   private void GenerateCharge(Album album)
   {
      string name = album.Name;

      //code to generate charge for correct album
   }
}
```

You can verify in the example that the **Album** class no longer depends on the **BillingService** class. This is very desirable if you need to use the **Album** class in a different context. In the "Background" example, you would need to bring along the **BillingService** class if you wanted to use **Album**.

Client.cs

The following code describes how to create the various objects and the order in which to do it. The biggest difference between this construction code and the "Background" example is how the **Album** class finds out about **BillingService**. In the "Background" example, **BillingService** was passed explicitly as a construction parameter to **Album**. In this example, you call a function named **AddObserver** to add the **BillingService**, which implements the **Observer** interface.

```
using System;

class Client
{
    [STAThread]
    static void Main(string[] args)
    {
        BillingService billing = new BillingService();
        Album album = new Album("Up");

        album.AddObserver(billing);

        album.Play();
    }
}
```

As you can see, the **Album** class has no references to the billing service. All it has to do is to inherit from the **Subject** class. The **Client** class passes a reference to an instance of the **BillingService** to the album, but the language runtime automatically casts the **BillingService** reference into a reference to the **Observer** interface. The **AddObserver** method (implemented in the **Subject** base class) deals only with references to the **Observer** interface; it does not mention the billing service either. This, therefore, eliminates the dependency of the **Album** class to anything related to billing services. However, there still are a number of issues:

- **Use of inheritance to share the Subject implementation**. The Microsoft Visual Basic® .NET development system and the C# language allow for single inheritance of implementation and multiple inheritance of interfaces. In this example, you need to use single inheritance to share the **Subject** implementation. This precludes using it to categorize **Albums** in an inheritance hierarchy.

- **Single observable activity**. The **Album** class notifies the observers whenever the **Play** method is called. If you had another function, such as **Cancel**, you would have to send the event along with the **Album** object to the services so they would know if this were a **Play** or **Cancel** event. This complicates the services, because they are notified of events that they may not be interested in.

- **Less explicit, more complicated**. The direct dependency is gone, but the code is less explicit. The initial implementation had a direct dependency between **Album** and **BillingService**, so it was easy to see how and when the **GenerateCharge** method was called. In this example, **Album** calls the **Notify** method in **Subject**, which iterates through a list of previously registered **Observer** objects and calls the **Update** method. This method in the **BillingService** class calls **GenerateCharge**. If you are interested in a great description of the virtues of being explicit, see "To Be Explicit," Martin Fowler's article in *IEEE Software* [Fowler01].

Modified Observer

The primary liability of *Observer* [Gamma95] is the use of inheritance as a means for sharing the **Subject** implementation. This also limits the ability to be explicit about which activities **Observer** is interested in being notified about. To solve these problems, the next part of the example introduces the modified *Observer*. In this solution, you change the **Subject** class into an interface. You also introduce another class named **SubjectHelper**, which implements the **Subject** interface (See Figure 3.40).

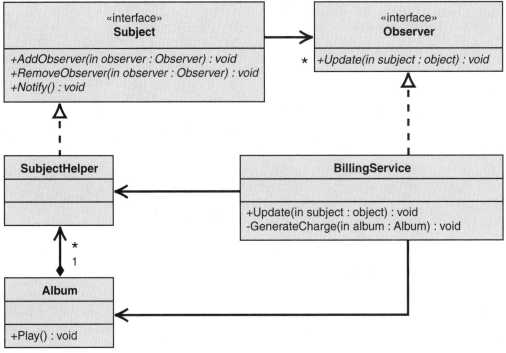

Figure 3.40
Modified Observer class diagram

The **Album** class contains **SubjectHelper** and exposes it as a public property. This allows classes like **BillingService** to access the specific **SubjectHelper** and indicate that it is interested in being notified if **Album** changes. This implementation also allows the **Album** class to have more than one **SubjectHelper**; perhaps, one per exposed activity. The following code implements this solution (the **Observer** interface and **BillingService** class are omitted here because they have not changed).

Subject.cs

In the following example, **Notify** has changed because you now have to pass the **Subject** into the **SubjectHelper** class. This was unnecessary in the *Observer* [Gamma95] example because the **Subject** class was the base class.

```
using System;
using System.Collections;

public interface Subject
{
    void AddObserver(Observer observer);
    void RemoveObserver(Observer observer);
    void Notify(object realSubject);
}
```

SubjectHelper.cs

The following example shows the newly created **SubjectHelper** class:

```
using System;
using System.Collections;

public class SubjectHelper : Subject
{
    private ArrayList observers = new ArrayList();

    public void AddObserver(Observer observer)
    {
        observers.Add(observer);
    }

    public void RemoveObserver(Observer observer)
    {
        observers.Remove(observer);
    }

    public void Notify(object realSubject)
    {
        foreach(Observer observer in observers)
        {
            observer.Update(realSubject);
        }
    }
}
```

Album.cs

The following example shows how the **Album** class changes when using **SubjectHelper** instead of inheriting from the **Subject** class:

```
using System;

public class Album
{
    private String name;
    private Subject playSubject = new SubjectHelper();
```

```
    public Album(String name)
    { this.name = name; }

    public void Play()
    {
        playSubject.Notify(this);

        // code to play the album
    }

    public String Name
    {
        get { return name; }
    }

    public Subject PlaySubject
    {
        get { return playSubject; }
    }
}
```

Client.cs

The following example shows how the **Client** class changes:

```
using System;

class Client
{
    [STAThread]
    static void Main(string[] args)
    {
        BillingService billing = new BillingService();
        CounterService counter = new CounterService();
        Album album = new Album("Up");

        album.PlaySubject.AddObserver(billing);
        album.PlaySubject.AddObserver(counter);

        album.Play();
    }
}
```

You can probably already see some of the benefits of reducing coupling between the classes. For example, the **BillingService** class did not have to change at all, even though this refactoring rearranged the implementation of **Subject** and **Album** quite a bit. Also, the **Client** class is easier to read now, because you can specify to which particular event you attach the services.

The modified *Observer* solution clearly solves the problems from the previous solution. In fact, it is the preferred implementation for languages that only have single inheritance of implementation. However, this solution still shows the following liabilities:

- **More complicated**. The original solution consisted of two classes that talked directly to each other in an explicit fashion; now you have two interfaces and three classes that talk indirectly, and a lot of code that was not there in the first example. No doubt, you are starting to wonder if that dependency was not so bad in the first place. Keep in mind, though, that the two interfaces and the **SubjectHelper** class can be reused by as many observers as you want. So it is likely that you will have to write them only once for the whole application.

- **Less explicit**. This solution, like *Observer* [Gamma95], makes it difficult to determine which observer is observing the changes to **Subject**.

So this solution makes good object-oriented design, but requires you to create a lot of classes, interfaces, associations, and so on. Is all of that really necessary in .NET? The answer is, "no," as the following example shows.

Observer in .NET

The built-in features of .NET help you to implement the *Observer* pattern with much less code. There is no need for the **Subject**, **SubjectHelper**, and **Observer** types because the common language runtime makes them obsolete. The introduction of delegates and events in .NET provides a means of implementing *Observer* without developing specific types.

In the .NET-based implementation, an event represents an abstraction (supported by the common language runtime and various compilers) of the **SubjectHelper** class described earlier in "Modified Observer." The **Album** class exposes an event type instead of **SubjectHelper**. The observer role is slightly more complicated. Rather than implementing the **Observer** interface and registering itself with the subject, an observer must create a specific delegate instance and register this delegate with the subject's event. The observer must use a delegate instance of the type specified by the event declaration; otherwise, registration will fail. During the creation of this delegate instance, the observer provides the name of the method (instance or static) that will be notified by the subject. After the delegate is bound to the method, it may be registered with the subject's event. Likewise, this delegate may be unregistered from the event. Subjects provide notification to observers by invocation of the event. [Purdy02]

The following code examples highlight the changes you must make to the example in "Modified Observer" to use delegates and events.

Album.cs

The following example shows how the **Album** class exposes the event type:

```
using System;

public class Album
{
    private String name;

    public delegate void PlayHandler(object sender);
    public event PlayHandler PlayEvent;

    public Album(String name)
    { this.name = name; }

    public void Play()
    {
        Notify();

        // code to play the album
    }

    private void Notify()
    {
        if(PlayEvent != null)
            PlayEvent(this);
    }

    public String Name
    {
        get { return name; }
    }

}
```

BillingService.cs

As the following example shows, the changes to the **BillingService** class from the example in "Modified Observer" only involve removing the implementation of the **Observer** interface:

```
using System;

public class BillingService
{
    public void Update(object subject)
    {
        if(subject is Album)
            GenerateCharge((Album)subject);
    }

    private void GenerateCharge(Album theAlbum)
    {
```

```
        //code to generate charge for correct album
    }
}
```

Client.cs

The following example shows how the **Client** class has been modified to use the new event that is exposed by the **Album** class:

```
using System;

class Client
{
    [STAThread]
    static void Main(string[] args)
    {
        BillingService billing = new BillingService();
        Album album = new Album("Up");

        album.PlayEvent += new Album.PlayHandler(billing.Update);
        album.Play();
    }
}
```

As you can see, the structure of the program is nearly identical to the previous example. The built-in features of .NET replace the explicit *Observer* mechanism. After you get used to the syntax of delegates and events, their use becomes more intuitive. You do not have to implement the **SubjectHelper** class and the **Subject** and **Observer** interfaces described in "Modified Observer." These concepts are implemented directly in the common language runtime.

The greatest benefit of delegates is their ability to refer to any method whatsoever (provided that it conforms to the same signature). This permits any class to act as an observer, independent of what interfaces it implements or classes it inherits from. While the use of the **Observer** and **Subject** interfaces reduced the coupling between the observer and subject classes, use of delegates completely eliminates it. For more information on this topic, see "Exploring the Observer Design Pattern," in the MSDN® developer program library [Purdy02].

Testing Considerations

Because delegates and events completely eliminate the bidirectional assembly between **Album** and **BillingService**, you can now write tests for each class in isolation.

AlbumFixture.cs

The **AlbumFixture** class describes example unit tests in NUnit (*http://www.nunit.org*) that verify that the **PlayEvent** is fired when the **Play** method is called:

```
using System;
using NUnit.Framework;

[TestFixture]
public class AlbumFixture
{
    private bool eventFired;
    private Album album;

    [SetUp]
    public void Init()
    {
        album = new Album("Up");
        eventFired = false;
    }

    [Test]
    public void Attach()
    {
        album.PlayEvent += new Album.PlayHandler(OnPlay);
        album.Play();

        Assertion.AssertEquals(true, eventFired);
    }

    [Test]
    public void DoNotAttach()
    {
        album.Play();
        Assertion.AssertEquals(false, eventFired);
    }

    private void OnPlay(object subject)
    {
        eventFired = true;
    }
}
```

Resulting Context

The benefits of implementing *Observer* in .NET with the delegates and events model clearly outweigh the potential liabilities.

Benefits

Implementing *Observer* in .NET provides the following benefits:

- **Eliminates dependencies**. The examples clearly showed that the dependency was eliminated from the **Album** and **BillingService** classes.

- **Increases extensibility**. The "Observer in .NET" example demonstrated how easy it was to add new types of observers. The **Album** class is an example of the Open/Closed Principle, first written by Bertrand Meyer in *Object-Oriented Software Construction, 2nd Edition* [Bertrand00], which describes a class that is open to extension but closed to modification. The **Album** class embodies this principle because you can add observers of the **PlayEvent** without modifying the **Album** class.

- **Improves testability**. "Testing Considerations" demonstrated how you could test the **Album** class without having to instantiate **BillingService**. The tests verified that the **Album** class worked correctly. The tests also provide an excellent example of how to write **BillingService**.

Liabilities

As shown in the example, the implementation of *Observer* is simple and straightforward. However, as the number of delegates and events increases, it becomes difficult to follow what happens when an event is fired. As a result, the code can become very difficult to debug because you must search through the code for the observers.

Related Patterns

For more background on the concepts discussed here, see the following related patterns:

- *Observer*
- *Model-View-Controller*

Acknowledgments

[Fowler03] Fowler, Martin. *Patterns of Enterprise Application Architecture*. Addison-Wesley, 2003.

[Fowler01] Fowler, Martin. "To Be Explicit." *IEEE Software*, November/December 2001.

[Purdy02] Purdy, Doug; Richter, Jeffrey. "Exploring the Observer Design Pattern." *MSDN Library*, January 2002. Available at: *http://msdn.microsoft.com/library /default.asp?url=/library/en-us/dnbda/html/observerpattern.asp*.

[Gamma95] Gamma, Helm, Johnson, and Vlissides. *Design Patterns: Elements of Reusable Object-Oriented Software*. Addison-Wesley, 1995.

[Bertrand00] Meyer, Bertrand. *Object-Oriented Software Construction, 2nd Edition*. Prentice-Hall, 2000.

4

Deployment Patterns

"What do you mean it doesn't run in production? It ran fine in the development environment." — Anonymous developer

Building enterprise class solutions involves not only developing custom software, but also deploying this software into a production server environment. This is where software development efforts intersect with systems infrastructure efforts. Bringing these two disciplines together effectively requires a common understanding of the issues involved and a strong set of application and system infrastructure skills. The required skills are rarely found in a single team; therefore, deployment activities often involve the collaboration of several teams, with each team contributing specialized skills. To simplify discussion, this chapter assumes that there are two teams: the application development team and the system infrastructure team.

Bringing Teams Together

The application development team is responsible for developing and maintaining a set of software components that fulfill the application's requirements. This team is primarily concerned with meeting functional requirements quickly and flexibly. Its members seek to manage complexity by creating software abstractions that make the system easy to extend and maintain.

The system infrastructure team is responsible for building and maintaining the servers and network infrastructure. Its members are primarily concerned with such operational requirements as security, availability, reliability, and performance. Stability and predictability are critical success factors, which are primarily addressed by controlling change and by managing known good configurations.

The forces acting on the application development team are quite different from the forces acting on the system infrastructure team. The result is an inherent tension between the two teams. If this tension is not addressed, the resulting solution may be optimized for one team or the other, but it will not be an optimal business solution. Resolving the tension is a critical element for delivering a holistic, software-intensive enterprise solution that is optimized for the overall needs of the business.

The patterns in this chapter help reduce the tension between the teams by offering guidance on how to optimally structure your applications and technical infrastructure to efficiently fulfill the solution's requirements. The patterns then discuss how to map the software structure to the hardware infrastructure. Specifically, this chapter presents a set of patterns that enable you to:

- Organize your software application into logical layers.
- Refine your logical layering approach to provide and consume services.
- Organize your hardware into physical tiers, so you can scale out.
- Refine your physical tier strategy in a three-tiered configuration.
- Allocate processes to processors with a deployment plan.

Patterns Overview

Although the concepts of layer and tier are often used interchangeably, the patterns in this chapter make a strong distinction between the two terms. A *layer* is a logical structuring mechanism for the elements that make up your software solution; a *tier* is a physical structuring mechanism for the system infrastructure. The first set of patterns in this cluster deals with the logical structuring of the software application into layers. The second set of patterns explores the physical structuring of the system infrastructure into tiers. Figure 4.1 shows both sets of patterns and their interrelationships.

Application   **Deployment**   **Infrastructure**

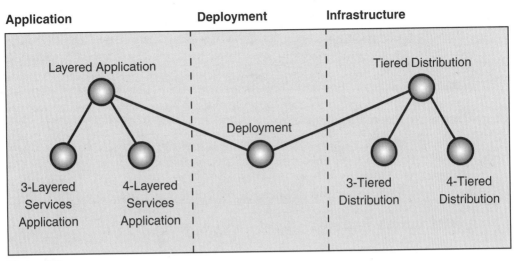

Figure 4.1
Deployment cluster

Application Patterns

The first pattern in this cluster, *Layered Application,* organizes a software application into a set of logical layers for the purpose of managing dependencies and creating pluggable components. The pattern defines exactly what a layer is and then describes how to define your own layers. It also describes some additional techniques that build on and amplify the benefits of using a layered application. One of the key benefits of *Layered Application* is that the well-defined interfaces and strong dependency management gives you a great deal of flexibility in deploy an application. Although it is very hard to distribute a single-layered application across multiple servers, it is much easier to divide the application at layer boundaries and distribute the different parts to multiple servers. Not every layer boundary makes a good distribution boundary, however, because the forces that mold your layering decisions are different from the forces that shape your distribution decisions. For more information, see *Deployment Plan.*

Layered Application is applied extensively throughout the software development world. A common implementation of the pattern for enterprise applications is three-layered application. This implementation defines three layers: presentation, business, and data. Although you can add more layers, these three layers are almost always needed for enterprise business applications.

Most enterprise applications are now developed using a component-based approach. Although many definitions of a component exist, the simplest definition is that a *component* is a unit of self-contained software functionality that can be independently deployed. Components can be plugged into and out of an execution environment that exposes an agreed-on set of interfaces at runtime. This pluggability offers a great deal of flexibility when it comes to deployment. The self-contained aspect of components makes them the smallest units at which deployment decisions can be made.

Three-Layered Services Application refines *Layered Application* to provide specific structuring guidance for enterprise applications that collaborate with other enterprise applications in a larger service-oriented architecture. It expands on the typical three layers described earlier and defines a set of component types for each layer.

Infrastructure Patterns

The next set of patterns in this cluster focuses on the physical infrastructure. The context for these patterns is an infrastructure that supports an application distributed over more than one server. Specifically, these patterns do not address mainframe or other large multiprocessor infrastructure configurations.

Tiered Distribution organizes the system infrastructure into a set of physical tiers to provide specific server environments optimized for specific operational requirements and system resource usage. A single-tiered infrastructure is not very flexible; the servers must be generically configured and designed around the strictest of operational requirements and must support the peak usage of the largest consumers of system resources. Multiple tiers, on the other hand, enable multiple environments. You can optimize each environment for a specific set of operational requirements and system resource usage. You can then deploy components onto the tier that most closely matches their resource needs and enables them to best meet their operational requirements. The more tiers you use, the more deployment options you will have for each component.

Three-Tiered Distribution refines *Tiered Distribution* to provide specific guidance on structuring the infrastructure for Web applications with basic security and other operational requirements. The pattern suggests that the solution's servers be organized into three tiers: client, Web application, and data. The client and data tiers are self-explanatory, and the Web application tier hosts application business components as well as the Web presentation components. For solutions with more stringent security and operational requirements, you may want to consider moving the Web functionality into its own tier.

Bringing Applications and Infrastructure Together

The final pattern in the cluster is *Deployment Plan*, which describes a process for allocating components to tiers. During this process, it is critical to ensure proper communication between the application development and system infrastructure teams. All the previous patterns increase the deployment flexibility of the software application and the systems infrastructure. *Deployment Plan* builds on this deployment flexibility, which provides more options for the teams to resolve conflicts of interest. Resolving these conflicts increases the chance of delivering a solution that provides optimum business value. The pattern concludes by describing four common models that typically result when this process is applied to enterprise applications: simple Web application, complex Web application, extended enterprise, and rich client.

Deployment Patterns

Table 4.1 lists the patterns included in the deployment cluster, along with the problem statements for each, which should serve as a roadmap to the patterns.

Table 4.1: Deployment Patterns

Pattern	Problem
Layered Application	How do you structure an application to support such operational requirements as maintainability, reusability, scalability, robustness, and security?
Three-Layered Services Application	How do you layer a service-oriented application and then determine the components in each layer?
Tiered Distribution	How should you structure your servers and distribute functionality across them to efficiently meet the operational requirements of the solution?
Three-Tiered Distribution	How many tiers should you have, and what should be in each tier?
Deployment Plan	How do you determine which tier you should deploy each of your components to?

Layered Application

Context

You are designing a complex enterprise application that is composed of a large number of components across multiple levels of abstraction.

Problem

How do you structure an application to support such operational requirements as maintainability, reusability, scalability, robustness, and security?

Forces

When structuring your application, you must reconcile the following forces within the context of your environment:

- Localizing changes to one part of the solution minimizes the impact on other parts, reduces the work involved in debugging and fixing bugs, eases application maintenance, and enhances overall application flexibility.

- Separation of concerns among components (for example, separating the user interface from the business logic, and separating the business logic from the database) increases flexibility, maintainability, and scalability.

- Components should be reusable by multiple applications.

- Independent teams should be able to work on parts of the solution with minimal dependencies on other teams and should be able to develop against well-defined interfaces.

- Individual components should be cohesive.

- Unrelated components should be loosely coupled.

- Various components of the solution are independently deployed, maintained, and updated, on different time schedules.

- Crossing too many component boundaries has an adverse effect on performance.

- To make a Web application both secure and accessible, you need to distribute the application over multiple physical tiers. This enables you to secure portions of the application behind the firewall and make other components accessible from the Internet.

- To ensure high performance and reliability, the solution must be testable.

Solution

Separate the components of your solution into layers. The components in each layer should be cohesive and at roughly the same level of abstraction. Each layer should be loosely coupled to the layers underneath. *Pattern-Oriented Software Architecture, Vol 1* [Buschmann96] describes the layering process as follows:

> Start at the lowest level of abstraction — call it Layer 1. This is the base of your system. Work your way up the abstraction ladder by putting Layer J on top of Layer J-1 until you reach the top level of functionality — call it Layer N.

Figure 4.2 shows how this layering scheme would look.

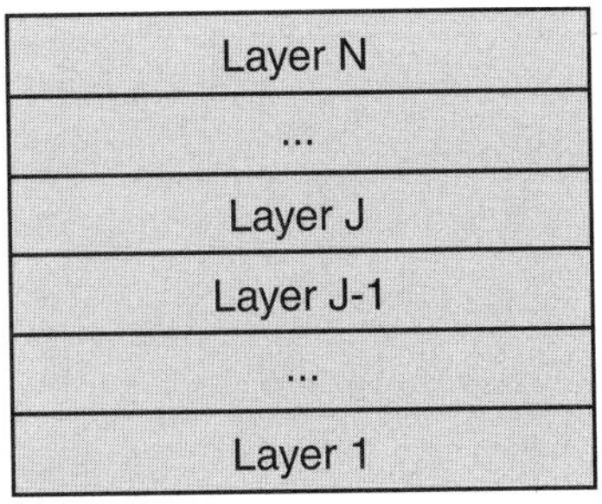

Layer N
...
Layer J
Layer J-1
...
Layer 1

Figure 4.2
Layers

Structure

The key to *Layered Application* is dependency management. Components in one layer can interact only with peers in the same level or components from lower levels. This helps reduce the dependencies between components on different levels. There are two general approaches to layering: strictly layered and relaxed layered.

A strictly layered approach constrains components in one layer to interacting only with peers and with the layer directly below. If the application is layered as shown in Figure 2, for example, Layer J can only interact with components from Layer J-1, Layer J-1 can only interact with Layer J-2, and so on.

A relaxed layered application loosens the constraints such that a component can interact with components from any lower layer. Therefore, in Figure 2, not only can Layer J interact with Layer J-1, but with layers J-2 and J-3.

The relaxed approach can improve efficiency because the system does not have to forward simple calls from one layer to the next. On the other hand, the relaxed approach does not provide the same level of isolation between the layers and makes it more difficult to swap out a lower layer without affecting higher layers.

For large solutions involving many software components, it is common to have a large number of components at the same level of abstraction that are not cohesive. In this case, each layer may be further decomposed into one or more cohesive subsystems. Figure 4.3 on the next page demonstrates a possible UML notation for representing layers that are composed of multiple subsystems.

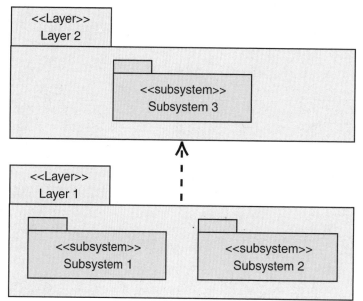

Figure 4.3
UML representation of layers composed of subsystems

The basic *Layered Application* pattern is often augmented with the following techniques:

- **Layer Supertype** [Fowler03]. If the components in the layer share a set of common behaviors, you extract those behaviors into a common class or component from which all the components in the layer inherit. Not only does this ease maintenance and promote reuse, it also reduces the dependencies between layers by allowing the common behaviors to be invoked through a runtime reference to the supertype instead of a specific component.

- **Abstract interface**. An abstract interface is defined for each component in a layer that is called by components in a higher level. The higher layers access the lower-level components through the abstract interfaces instead of calling the components directly. This allows the implementation of the lower-level components to change without affecting the higher-level components.

- **Layer Facade**. For larger systems, it is common to use the *Facade* pattern to provide a single unified interface to a layer or subsystem instead of developing an abstract interface for each exposed component [Gamma95]. This gives you the lowest coupling between layers, because higher-level components only reference the facade directly. Be sure to design your facade carefully. It will be difficult to change in the future, because so many components will depend on it.

Dynamics

There are basically two modes of interaction within the layered application:

- Top-down
- Bottom-up

In the *top-down* mode, an external entity interacts with the topmost layer of the stack. The topmost layer uses one or more services of the lower-level layers. In turn, each lower level uses the layers below it until the lowest layer is reached.

For the sake of discussion, this pattern assumes that the external entity is a client application and the layered application is for a server-based application that exposes its functionality as a set of services. Figure 4.4 is a UML sequence diagram that depicts a common top-down scenario.

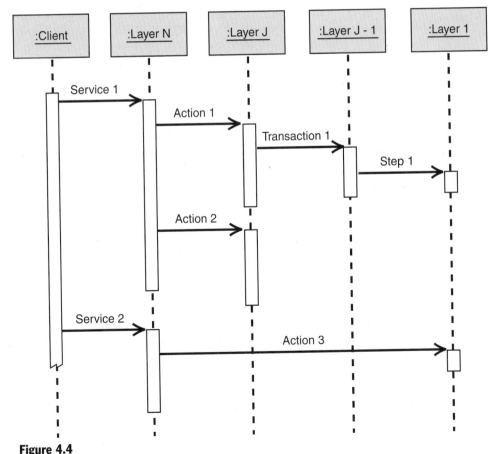

Figure 4.4
Sequence diagram of a top-down scenario

In this scenario, the client application consumes a set of services offered by a server-based application. These services are exposed by the topmost layer of the server application. Therefore, the client only must interact with the topmost layer and has no direct knowledge of any lower layers. A couple of factors are worth noting.

First, a single incoming invocation can result in multiple outgoing invocations. The invocation of Service 1 on Layer N illustrates this case. This quite often occurs when a higher-level service aggregates the results of several lower-level services or coordinates the execution of multiple lower services that must be executed in a particular order. For example, an ASP.NET page might feed the output of a customer domain component to an order component whose output is in turn fed to an invoice component.

Second, this scenario illustrates the relaxed layered approach. The implementation of Service 2 bypasses all the intermediate layers and calls Layer 1 directly. A common example of this is a presentation layer accessing a data access layer directly, bypassing any intermediate business logic layers. Data maintenance applications often use this approach.

Third, an invocation of the service at the top layer does not necessarily invoke all of the layers. This concept is illustrated by the Service 1 to Action 2 sequence, which occurs when a higher level can process an invocation on its own or has cached the results of an earlier request. For example, domain components quite often cache results of database queries, which remove the need to invoke the data access layer for future invocations.

In the *bottom-up* mode, Layer 1 detects a situation that affects higher levels. The following scenario assumes that Layer 1 is monitoring the state of some external entity such as the file system of the server on which the server application is running. Figure 4.5 depicts a typical bottom-up scenario as a UML sequence diagram.

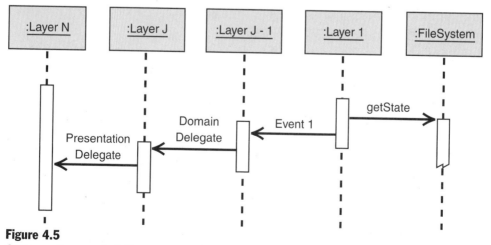

Figure 4.5
Sequence diagram of a bottom-up scenario

In this scenario, Layer 1 is monitoring the state of the local file system. When it detects a change, it fires an event exposed by a component from the J-1 layer. This component then invokes a callback delegate of Layer J, where the state of the domain layer is updated. The domain component then notifies Layer N that it has been updated by a delegate provided by Layer N for that purpose.

As in the first scenario, an input at one level can result in multiple outputs. A lower layer can notify any layer higher than it, not just the next higher layer. And finally, a notification does not necessarily have to percolate up the entire chain.

Take careful notice of how differently the layers interact in the bottom-up scenario as opposed to the top-down scenario. In the top-down scenario, higher layers call lower layers directly and thus are dependent on them. In the bottom-up scenario, however, lower layers communicate with higher layers through events, callbacks, and delegates. This level of indirection is required to keep lower layers from being dependent on higher layers. Making lower layers dependent on higher layers reduces quite a few of the benefits that the layered architecture provides.

Implementation

There are basically two approaches to implementing the *Layered Application* pattern:

- Create your own layering scheme
- Reuse an existing layering scheme

Creating Your Own Layering Scheme

Buschmann provides a great discussion about implementing your own layered application. A brief overview is provided here, but it is highly recommended that you study the *Layers* pattern in Buschmann if you need to define your own layered application. The outline of the process is as follows:

- Use a well-defined set of criteria to group the functionality of the solution into a set of layers and define the services that each layer provides. This is an iterative process in which you will likely try multiple combinations of criteria, numbers of levels, functionality decomposition, and service assignments. UML sequence diagrams describing the interactions of layers and solution components are an ideal tool for understanding the tradeoffs involved with each candidate layering scheme.

- Define the interfaces between each level and the protocols they require to communicate with each other. To avoid making lower levels dependent on higher levels, use techniques such as asynchronous messaging, callbacks, and events for communications that need to travel up the stack. Again, UML sequence diagrams are a great tool for ensuring that you have a complete and consistent set of interfaces. The diagrams give you a visual clue of the granularity or chattiness of your interface and protocols. Be particularly aware of the number of times you cross a layer boundary for a given scenario and look for opportunities to refactor your design to reduce the number of boundary crossings. A key design decision is to determine how much coupling should exist between levels. Do components in Layer J directly access components in Layer J-1? This makes higher levels dependent on lower-level implementation details. Patterns such as *Facade* and other decoupling techniques should be explored to minimize this type of coupling.

- Design the implementation of the layers. Traditional object-oriented design techniques work quite well for this task. Be sure to consider patterns such as *Adapter, Bridge,* and *Strategy* [Gamma95] to enable the switching out of multiple implementations of a given layer's interface. This capability is especially valuable when it comes to testing the interfaces and level implementations. Another critical design decision is how to handle errors. A consistent error-handling strategy must be defined across all the levels. Consider the following when designing your error-handling strategy:

  - Try to deal with the error at the lowest level possible.

  - Avoid exposing lower-level abstractions to higher levels through the exception handling mechanism.

  - If you must escalate an exception up the stack, convert lower-level exceptions to exceptions that have some meaning to the handling layer.

Reusing an Existing Layering Scheme

The other approach is to reuse an existing reference layered application to provide structure for your applications. The canonical three-layered application consists of the following three layers: presentation, domain, and data source. Even something as simple as this goes a long way towards achieving the benefits of the *Layered Application* pattern. An enhanced version of the canonical model is discussed in *Layered Services Application*.

Martin Fowler has found the use of mediating layers between the presentation and domain layers as well as between the domain and data source layers useful at times. For more information, see Fowler's book, *Patterns of Enterprise Application Architecture* [Fowler03].

Testing Considerations

Layered Application enhances testability in several ways:

- Because each layer interacts with the other layers only through well-defined interfaces, it is easy to plug in alternative implementations of a layer. This allows some testing on a layer before the layers it depends on are complete. In addition, an alternative implementation that immediately returns a set of known good data can be substituted for a layer that takes a long time to compute a correct answer, thus speeding up test execution. This ability is greatly enhanced if the layered supertype, abstract interface, and layer facade techniques are used, because they further decrease the dependencies between layers.

- It is easier to test individual components, because the dependencies between components are constrained such that components in higher levels can only call components in lower levels. This helps to isolate individual components for testing and facilitates swapping out lower-level components with special-purpose testing components.

Example

It is quite common for enterprise application architects to compose their solutions into the following three layers:

- **Presentation**. This layer is responsible for interacting with the user.
- **Business**. This layer implements the business logic of the solution.
- **Data**. This layer encapsulates the code that accesses the persistent data stores such as a relational database.

For more information, see the *Three-Layered Services Application* pattern.

Resulting Context

Layered Application generally results in the following benefits and liabilities:

Benefits

- Maintenance of and enhancements to the solution are easier due to the low coupling between layers, high cohesion between the layers, and the ability to switch out varying implementations of the layer interfaces.
- Other solutions should be able to reuse functionality exposed by the various layers, especially if the layer interfaces are designed with reuse in mind.
- Distributed development is easier if the work can be distributed at layer boundaries.
- Distributing the layers over multiple physical tiers can improve scalability, fault-tolerance, and performance. For more information, see the *Tiered Distribution* pattern.
- Testability benefits from having well-defined layer interfaces as well as the ability to switch out various implementations of the layer interfaces.

Liabilities

- The extra overhead of passing through layers instead of calling a component directly can negatively affect performance. To help offset the performance hit, you can use the relaxed layers approach, in which higher layers can directly call lower layers.
- Development of user-intensive applications can sometime take longer if the layering prevents the use of user interface components that directly interact with the database.

- The use of layers helps to control and encapsulate the complexity of large applications, but adds complexity to simple applications.
- Changes to lower-level interfaces tend to percolate to higher levels, especially if the relaxed layered approach is used.

Acknowledgments

[Buschmann96] Buschmann, Frank, et al. *Pattern-Oriented Software Architecture, Vol 1*. Wiley & Sons, 1996.

[Fowler03] Fowler, Martin. *Patterns of Enterprise Application Architecture*. Addison-Wesley, 2003.

[Gamma95] Gamma, Helm, Johnson, and Vlissides. *Design Patterns: Elements of Reusable Object-Oriented Software*. Addison-Wesley, 1995.

Three-Layered Services Application

Context

You are designing a *Layered Application*. You want to expose some of the core functionality of your application as services that other applications can consume, and you want your application to consume services exposed by other applications.

Problem

How do you layer a service-oriented application and then determine the components in each layer?

Forces

In addition to the forces discussed in *Layered Application*, the following forces apply:

- You always want to minimize the impact of adding services to an existing application.
- Services are often exposed to clients outside the corporate firewall, and therefore have different security and operational requirements than do business components.
- Communicating with other services involves significant knowledge of protocols and data formats.
- You want to separate the concerns of your components so that you are only changing them for one reason, such as to isolate your business logic from the technology required to access an external service.

Solution

Base your layered architecture on three layers: presentation, business, and data. This pattern presents an overview of the responsibilities of each layer and the components that compose each layer. For more information, see the article, "Application Architecture for .NET: Designing Applications and Services." [PnP02].

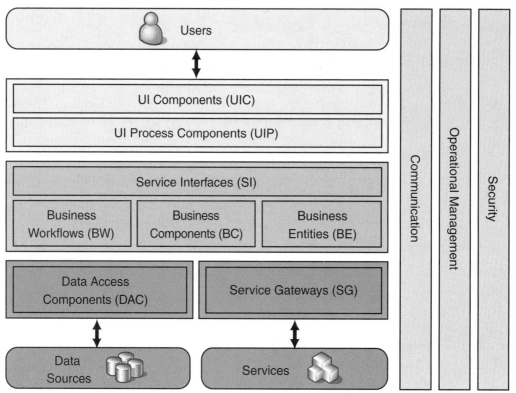

Figure 4.6
Three-Layered Services Application

Three-Layered Services Application, as presented here, is basically a relaxed three-layered architecture. The three layers are:

- **Presentation**. The presentation layer provides the application's user interface (UI). Typically, this involves the use of Windows Forms for smart client interaction, and ASP.NET technologies for browser-based interaction.

- **Business**. The business layer implements the business functionality of the application. The domain layer is typically composed of a number of components implemented using one or more .NET–enabled programming languages. These components may be augmented with Microsoft® .NET Enterprise Services for scalable distributed component solutions and Microsoft BizTalk® Server for workflow orchestration.

- **Data** The data layer provides access to external systems such as databases. The primary .NET technology involved at this layer is ADO.NET. However, it is not uncommon to use some .NET XML capabilities here as well.

Each layer should be structured as described in the following paragraphs.

Presentation Layer

For most business applications, a form metaphor is used to structure the presentation layer. The application consists of a series of forms (pages) with which the user interacts. Each form contains a number of fields that display output from lower layers and collect user input.

Two types of components that implement forms-based user interfaces are:

- User interface components
- User interface process components

User Interface Components

For rich-client applications, this pattern uses UI components from the System.Windows.Forms namespace of the .NET Framework. For Web applications, this pattern uses ASP.NET components. If the standard .NET components do not meet your needs, .NET supports subclassing of the standard UI components, as well as plugging your own custom components into the framework.

User Interface Process Components

Complex user interfaces often require many highly complex forms. To increase reusability, maintainability, and extensibility, you can create a separate user interface process (UIP) component to encapsulate dependencies between forms and the logic associated with navigating between them. You can apply the same concept to the dependencies, validation, and navigation between components of a single form. These UIP components are typically custom components that are based on design patterns such as *Front Controller*, *Application Controller* [Fowler03], and *Mediator* [Gamma95].

The interaction between UI and UIP components often follows the *Model-View-Controller* or *Presentation-Abstraction-Controller* [Buschmann96] pattern.

Business Layer

Large enterprise applications are often structured around the concepts of business processes and business components. These concepts are addressed through a number of components, entities, agents, and interfaces in the business layer.

Business Components

In *Business Component Factory*, Peter Herzum and Oliver Sims define a business component as follows:

> The software implementation of an autonomous business concept or business process. It consists of all the software artifacts necessary to represent, implement, and deploy a given business concept as an autonomous, reusable element of a larger distributed information system. [Herzum00]

Business components are the software realization of business concepts. They are the primary units of design, implementation, deployment, maintenance, and management for the life cycle of the business application. Business components encapsulate the business logic, also called business rules. These rules constrain the behavior of a business concept to match the needs of a particular company. For example, the business rule that determines whether a given customer is approved for a line of credit may be encapsulated in the customer business component for small solutions. For larger solutions, it is likely that all credit-related business logic is encapsulated in a separate credit component.

Note: *Three-Layered Services Application* diverges from the Herzum and Oliver definition in that business processes components are separated into their own class: Business Workflow Components.

Business Workflows

Business processes reflect the macro-level activities that the business performs. Examples include order processing, customer support, and procurement of materials. These business processes are encapsulated by business workflow components that orchestrate one or more business components to implement a business process. For example, a ProcessOrder business workflow component may interact with Customer, Order, and Fulfillment business components to carry out the Process Order business process. You can use any .NET language to develop custom business workflow components. Alternatively, you can use BizTalk Server to define the business process and automatically orchestrate the business components.

Business Entities

Business entities are data containers. They encapsulate and hide the details of specific data representation formats. For instance, a business entity may initially encapsulate a recordset obtained from a relational database. Later, that same business entity may be modified to wrap an XML document with minimal impact to the rest of the application.

Business and business workflow components can interact with independent business entity components, or they can use a business entity to set their own state and then discard the business entity. Business entities are often used as *Data Transfer Objects* [Fowler03]. The data access components will often return business entities instead of database-specific structures. This helps significantly in isolating database-specific details to the data layer.

Service Interfaces

An application may expose some of its functionality as a service that other applications can use. A service interface presents this service to the outside world. Ideally, it hides the implementation details and exposes only a course-grained business interface. Service interfaces are often implemented using XML Web services.

If you are using a domain model, classes in your domain model are often realized by one or more domain layer components.

Data Layer

Most business applications must access data that is stored in corporate databases, which are most often relational databases. Data access components in this data layer are responsible for exposing the data stored in these databases to the business layer.

Data Access Components

Data access components isolate the business layer from the details of the specific data storage solution. This isolation provides the following benefits:

- Minimizes the impact of a change in database provider.
- Minimizes the impact of a change in data representation (for example, a change in database schema).
- Encapsulates all code that manipulates a particular data item in one place. This greatly simplifies testing and maintenance.

ADO.NET can be used directly as the data access components for simple applications. More complex applications may benefit from developing a set of classes over ADO.NET that help you to manage the complexities of object-relational mapping.

Service Gateways

Business components often must access internal and external services or applications. A service gateway is a component that encapsulates the interface, protocol, and code required to use such services. For example, a business solution often requires information from the accounting system to complete a business process. The solution would delegate all interaction with the accounting system to a service gateway. The service gateway makes it much easier to change the external service provider. The service gateway can even simulate the external service to facilitate testing of the domain layer.

Foundation Services

In addition to the three standard layers, *Three-Layered Services Application* defines a set of foundation services that all layers can use. These services fall into three basic categories:

- **Security**. These services maintain application security.
- **Operational management**. These services manage components and associated resources, and also meet operational requirements such as scalability and fault tolerance.
- **Communication**. These are services, such as .NET remoting, SOAP, and asynchronous messaging, which provide communication between components.

Resulting Context

Using *Three-Layered Services Application* results in the following benefits and liabilities:

Benefits

The three layers prescribed by this pattern are a great starting point for designing your own solutions. You accrue most of the benefits of the *Layered Architecture* pattern while minimizing the negative effects of having to cross too many layers.

Liabilities

For complex solutions, it may be necessary to further divide the domain layer, especially if reuse is a high priority or if you are designing a family of solutions based on a common set of components. In such cases, it is common to replace the one business layer described in this pattern with the following three layers (For details, see Larman02):

- **Application**. The application layer contains business components that are unique to the application.
- **Domain**. The domain layer contains business components that are common within the business domain. Examples include components related to the insurance, energy, or banking industry.
- **Business services**. The business services layer contains business components that provide common business functionality such as financial, product, and order functionality.

One user interface layer may be insufficient for solutions that provide complex user interfaces. Data validation, command processing, printing, and undo/redo are a few examples of functionality that may require additional layering.

Acknowledgments

[Buschmann96] Buschmann, Frank, et al. *Pattern-Oriented Software Architecture.* John Wiley & Sons Ltd, 1996.

[Fowler03] Fowler, Martin. *Patterns of Enterprise Application Architecture.* Addison-Wesley, 2003.

[Gamma95] Gamma, Helm, Johnson, and Vlissides. *Design Patterns: Elements of Reusable Object-Oriented Software.* Addison-Wesley, 1995.

[Herzum00] Herzum, Peter and Sims, Oliver. *Business Component Factory.* John Wiley and Sons, Inc., 2000.

[Larman02] Larman, Craig. *Applying UML and Patterns.* Prentice-Hall PTR, 2002.

[PnP02] *patterns & practices*, Microsoft Corporation. "Application Architecture for .NET: Designing Applications and Services." *MSDN Library.* Available at: *http://msdn.microsoft.com/library/default.asp?url=/library/en-us/dnbda/html/distapp.asp.*

Tiered Distribution

Context

You are designing the physical infrastructure on which your complex distributed enterprise application will be hosted. You have decided to distribute your application over multiple servers rather than over multiple processors on a multiprocessor computer.

After you have made the decision to distribute your application over multiple computers, you need to consider the consequences from the following three perspectives:

- **System architecture**. This perspective is fundamentally about servers. Key aspects of this perspective include the number of servers, the role each server plays in the solution, the relationship between servers, and how the multiple servers collaborate together to meet system-level operational requirements.

- **Application architecture**. This perspective is fundamentally concerned with components. Key aspects of this perspective include packaging components into deployment units, mapping deployment units to operating system processes, and mapping these processes to servers.

- **Application administration**. This perspective is fundamentally concerned with executable modules, such as DLLs and executable files. Key aspects of this perspective include packaging components into executable modules, delivering and installing the executable modules onto the correct servers, and then configuring them.

This pattern addresses the system architecture perspective. Specifically, it addresses the role each server plays in a solution.

Problem

How should you structure your servers and distribute functionality across them to efficiently meet the operational requirements of the solution?

Forces

The following forces act on a system within this context and must be reconciled as you consider a solution to the problem:

- Components of your application each consume different amounts of resources, such as memory, processor capacity, file handles, IO sockets, disk space, and so on.

- Servers must be configured to provide an efficient environment for solution components.

- A single-server configuration is not likely to meet the requirements of all the components deployed within a complex enterprise application.

- Different servers have different scalability profiles that are determined by the type of components they host. For example, the size of a database may increase at a different rate than the number of users of the solution.

- Different servers have different security requirements that are determined by the type of components they host. For example, components that present information to the user often have different security requirements than components that implement business logic.

- The techniques for meeting availability, reliability and fault-tolerance requirements vary by type of component. For example, the solution's database may be hosted on a single server that is configured for maximum fault-tolerance and high availability, while the Web components may achieve high availability and fault-tolerance through arranging a group of Web servers into a server farm.

- Performance, political, or legal considerations may dictate the geographic locations of specific servers and the components they host. For example, databases containing sensitive corporate information may be hosted at secure corporate data centers, but the application servers that contain the business logic may reside at a third-party hosting facility.

- Every computer boundary that a component invocation crosses adversely affects performance. Component invocations that cross the network are much slower than component invocations in the same application domain or process.

- Licensing considerations may constrain the deployment of software components to specific servers.

Solution

Structure your servers and client computers into a set of physical tiers. A tier is composed of one or more computers that share one or more of the following characteristics:

- **System resource consumption profile**. The components hosted on the tier's servers may use a set of system resources, such as memory, sockets, and I/O channels, in a similar way. For instance, a solution may have a tier dedicated to Web servers and another to database servers. The Web servers consume a lot of network sockets and file descriptors, while the database servers consume a lot of file I/O bandwidth and disk space. Using multiple tiers enables you to optimize both the server configuration in the Web tier for Web access and the server configuration in the data tier for data access.

- **Operational requirements**. The servers in a tier often share common operational requirements, such as security, scalability, availability, reliability, and performance. For example, servers in a Web tier are often configured in a server farm for scalability and reliability, but the servers in a data tier are often configured as highly available clusters.

Although tiered distribution affects all operational requirements, it has the most impact on the system-level operational requirements, such as system security, scalability, and availability.

- **Design constraints**. A tier may be dedicated to servers that share a common design constraint. For instance, an organization's security policy may dictate that only Web servers are allowed on the public side of the perimeter network (also known as DMZ, demilitarized zone, and screened subnet), and that conversely, all application logic and corporate databases must reside on the corporate side of the perimeter network.

The word "layer" is often used interchangeably with tier. However, this set of patterns makes a distinction between the two. Conceptually, a tier is the hardware equivalent of a software architecture layer (See *Layered Application*). Whereas layers logically structure your application's components, tiers physically structure your solution's servers. A useful heuristic for determining the number of tiers in a solution is to count the number of computers involved in realizing a use case. Do not count computers that are only loosely associated with a use case, such as display terminals, Web proxies, caches, and file servers. The rest of this pattern refers to this heuristic as the *tiering heuristic*.

Example

To provide a better understanding of just what a tier is, and the value provided by distributing your solution over multiple tiers, the following discussion works through an example of refactoring a monolithic single-tiered solution into a multi-tiered solution. The example is an order-processing application, and only considers one use case: Process Order. This use case is responsible for allowing a customer service representative to enter an order into the system.

Single-Tiered Solution

Initially, the solution was designed for use by customer service agents and was deployed on a mainframe with the rest of the company's mission-critical applications. Figure 4.7 shows this distribution.

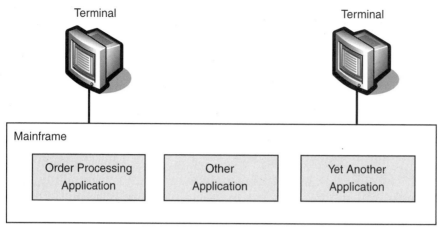

Figure 4.7
Single-tiered distribution

According to the tiering heuristic, Figure 4.7 is a single-tiered application. One computer does all the processing. The terminal does not perform any processing in support of the use case other than to accept input and provide output to the application's users.

Deployment and administration are very easy, because only one computer is involved.

As the number of users and the load each user puts on the system increase, more resources such as memory, processors, and disk space will be added to the system. Eventually, the expansion capabilities of the single computer will be exhausted and a second computer will be required. For mainframe-class computers, the cost associated with adding a new computer can be very high. This factor severely limits the options for scalability. At some point, adding a new user will cost you an additional mainframe and the associated infrastructure.

The terminal has no processing power of its own. All work is done on the mainframe, and the quality of the user experience is limited due to the limited user-interface functionality.

As long as all the users of the system are within the company's intranet, the security of the solution is quite high. Most companies add additional security precautions if the mainframe is exposed to the Internet.

Two-Tiered Solution

Several factors caused the company to switch to a two-tiered solution. First, the customer service representatives required more robust user interfaces. Second, the desire to take orders 24 hours per day affected the mainframe's batch-processing windows. Third, performance of the order-processing system was sometimes unacceptable when the mainframe was under a high load.

As a result of these factors, the order-processing system was removed from the mainframe and was rearchitected as a two-tiered fat-client solution. The fat-client architecture puts most of the business logic on the client tier, leaving the other tier to host the solution's database. Figure 4.8 shows this distribution.

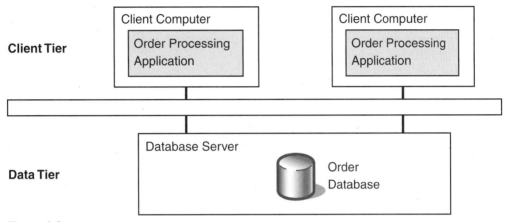

Figure 4.8
Two-tiered distribution

The Process Order use case now involves two computers and thus is a two-tiered solution according to the tiering heuristic. The user interacts with the order application on the client computer, and the order application then obtains the data required for the use case from the data tier.

Deployment and administration are now more complicated. The application must be distributed, installed, and configured on each client computer, and a separate installation for the server components (in this case, just the database) must be maintained.

Scalability significantly improves over the single-tiered solution. Each user has his or her own dedicated computer, so the only limit to scalability is how many concurrent users the database servers can handle. Compared to a mainframe, the database server is relatively low cost and can be dedicated to the order-processing application. This allows the database server to be optimized for the usage patterns of the order-processing application. If a single database server is ever unable to handle the load, an additional database server can be added.

Each user computer has it own processor and a robust graphical user interface. The order processing takes advantage of this by offering a much more interactive user interface that ultimately results in increased productivity from the customer service agents and lower error rates for the data entered.

Security is more complex in the two-tiered solution. Users typically log on to the client application. Additionally, the data tier often requires a separate authentication process. This requires the administration of two separate security systems and increases the number of potential security vulnerabilities.

Three-Tiered Solution

To better serve key customers, the company decided to expose its order processing application to some of its key customers through an extranet. To minimize deployment issues, the company decided to rearchitect the solution to allow access through a Web browser and rich-client interfaces. Figure 4.9 shows this distribution.

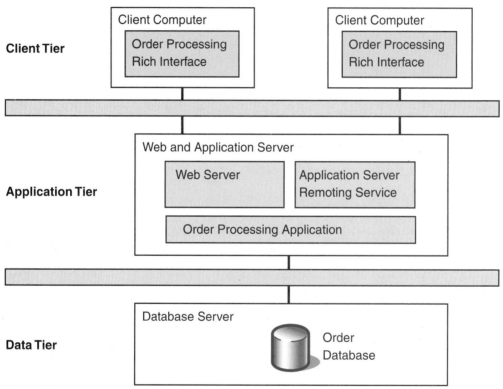

Figure 4.9
Three-tiered distribution

For more details about this distribution, see *Three-Tiered Distribution*. The following section discusses the effects of moving the example to a three-tiered distribution.

The Process Order use case now involves three computers and therefore is a three-tiered solution. The Web interface provides a basic interface to the order-processing system that allows customers to perform common operations fairly efficiently. For more complex tasks, customers must contact their customer support representative, who uses the rich interface to carry out the task. The business logic has been extracted out of the client tier and placed in its own application tier where many users can share it. This application tier invokes the services of the data tier for its data needs.

According to the tiering heuristic, it is the number of computers involved in processing a use case that determines the number of tiers, and not the number of computers per tier. For example, it is common for Web-based solutions to have multiple servers in the application tier arranged in a load balanced configuration. Because only one computer in the tier is involved with a given use-case instance, the tier adds only one computer to the tier count. Similarly, because the load balancer does not fundamentally advance the use-case processing, it does not count toward the tier count either.

Deployment and administration tasks are simpler than with two-tiered distribution, because most of the application logic is deployed on a centralized server. Therefore, clients usually do not have to be updated for application changes that do not require user interfaces changes. This is especially true for the browser-based user interfaces, which involve virtually no deployment effort. The rich interface that the customer support agents use involves somewhat more distribution effort, but the effort required is still significantly less than that involved in a fat-client installation.

The application tier is often the scalability bottleneck in Web applications. Not only does the application tier handle the Web server responsibilities, it also performs all of the business logic processing for the solution. The application tier is most often deployed in a server farm to achieve scalability and fault tolerance. A server farm is a set of identical servers with a load balancer that distributes work evenly across the server set. For more information, see *Server Farm*.

Configuring and tuning the application tier is more difficult due to the need to balance the differing server resource requirements of the Web server components and business processing components.

The database tier is virtually the same as described in a two-tiered distribution.

Computers on the client tier typically follow one of two strategies. For Web applications, the client tier uses the Web browser environment for interacting with the user. Minimal configuration and tuning of the client computers is required, other than adjusting network connectivity parameters and browser settings. As noted earlier, this significantly reduces the client's deployment and administrative costs. For rich applications, the client application uses the computer resources on the client computers to significantly enhance the user experience. Additionally, some tasks can be offloaded from the application tier at the expense of increasing the client computer's deployment and administration burden.

The security concerns of three-tiered distribution are similar to those of two-tiered distribution. However, the main security issue for this example is the fact that the solution is now exposed to users who are external to the company. As a result, a firewall configuration known as a perimeter network is usually placed between the application and data tiers. The application tier is on the public side of the perimeter network, because it also hosts the Web server, and most security professionals do not grant external users access to servers on the corporate side of the perimeter network.

Four-Tiered Solution

The company has decided to expose its order-processing application to all its customers over the Internet. Therefore, to increase security and scalability, the company has once again rearchitected its solution by separating the Web servers and applications servers into their own tiers. Figure 4.10 shows this distribution.

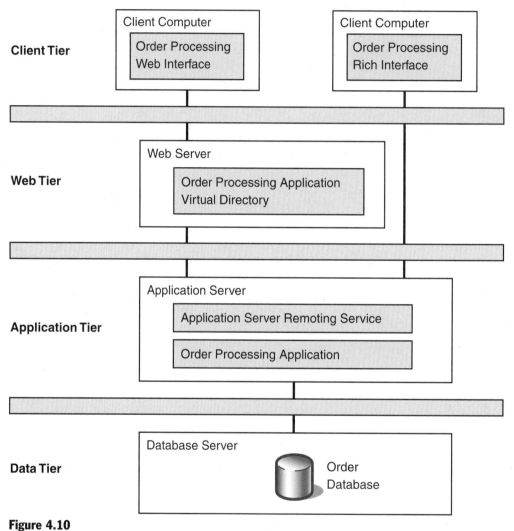

Figure 4.10
Four-tiered distribution

The Process Order use case now involves four computers and therefore is a four-tiered solution. The flow is the same as for three tiers, except that the Web servers have been separated into an additional tier, which adds one computer to the tier count.

Because four-tiered distribution is very similar to three-tiered distribution, much of the earlier discussion applies here. The primary areas where the two distributions differ are configuration, scalability, and security.

The servers in the Web tier consume a different set of resources than servers in the application tier. Therefore, separating them into separate tiers allows the two different server types to optimize their resource usage. The servers on the Web tier can now be optimized for Web server use, which typically involves lots of network sockets and I/O throughput; the application tier servers can be optimized for processing business transactions, which typically involves maximizing processor utilization, threading, and database connections.

The Web tier typically addresses scalability and fault-tolerance through a *Server Farm* as described earlier. The application tier addresses the same concerns through the use of *Server Cluster*. A server cluster is a set of servers configured for high-availability that appear to clients as one super server. For more information, see *Server Cluster*.

Separating the Web servers into a new tier enables the Web tier to be placed within the perimeter network and the application tier servers to be placed on the corporate side of the perimeter network. Now, if a fault allows unauthorized access to the Web server, sensitive information hosted on the application servers is not exposed.

Summary

The refactoring exercise in this pattern demonstrated several criteria for structuring your solution's tiers:

- Tiers were used to allow servers and client computers to be optimized for specific tasks, such as interacting with users, serving Web pages, and hosting databases.
- Tiers were used to separate servers that had different security profiles.
- Tiers were used to separate servers that had different scalability and fault-tolerance requirements.
- Tiers were used to reduce the administration and deployment overhead required of distributed applications.

You can address the vast majority of distribution scenarios by following one of the *Tiered Distribution* implementation patterns, such as *Three-Tiered Distribution*. If none of the implementation patterns address your requirements, see *Application Deployment* for guidance on how to design your own deployment solution.

Resulting Context

This pattern results in a number of benefits and liabilities.

Benefits

The resulting context of the solution described in this pattern has the following benefits:

- Each tier can be optimized for specific resource usage profiles. For instance, servers in tiers that interact with a large number of client computers can be optimized for socket and file handle usage.
- Each tier can have a different security profile.
- Each tier can be designed for different operational characteristics. For instance, Web tiers usually achieve scalability and fault-tolerance through server farms, whereas database tiers usually achieve the same through server clusters.
- Each tier can be separately modified to respond to changes in load, requirements, hosting strategy, and so on. For example, you can scale out a Web tier to accept an increase in the number of users, independent of scaling up the database servers to accept an increase in the transactional throughput. This flexibility tends to reduce overall total cost of ownership, because servers can be added and removed as the business requirements and technical environment change.
- Tiers can be deployed to meet geographical, political, and legal requirements.
- Tiers ease some of the administrative and deployment burden associated with distributed solutions.

Liabilities

The benefits of the solution described in this pattern are offset by the following liabilities:

- Each tier involved in processing a client request degrades performance and adds application and system management overhead.
- Server clusters and server farms add cost and complexity to your infrastructure.

Related Patterns

For more information, see the following related patterns:

- *Server Farm*
- *Server Cluster*
- *Application Server*
- *Three-Tiered Distribution*
- *Deployment Plan*

Acknowledgments

[PnP02] *patterns & practices*, Microsoft Corporation. "Application Architecture for .NET: Designing Applications and Services." *MSDN Library*. Available at: *http://msdn.microsoft.com/library/default.asp?url=/library/en-us/dnbda/html/distapp.asp*.

Three-Tiered Distribution

Context

Your are implementing a distributed solution using the *Tiered Distribution* pattern.

Problem

How many tiers should you have, and what should be in each tier?

Forces

The forces discussed in *Tiered Distribution*, apply to this pattern as well. For a discussion of those general forces, see *Tiered Distribution*. The following forces apply specifically to the *Three-Tiered Distribution* pattern:

- The load on your database is significant enough that you want to dedicate a server (or entire cluster) to the database.
- Your security policy mandates that corporate databases must not be hosted on servers that are directly connected to the Internet.
- You have a large number of users who have their own computer or device for accessing the solution. For example, you have a Web application with a large number of users accessing a common application.
- You must be able to scale the client tier to handle a significant increase in the number of users.
- Your clients need to execute transactions against a shared database, and you want to share business logic across solutions.
- The scalability requirements of the clients, application logic, and databases are significantly different.

Solution

Structure your application around three physical tiers: client, application, and database. Figure 4.11 shows this three-tiered distribution.

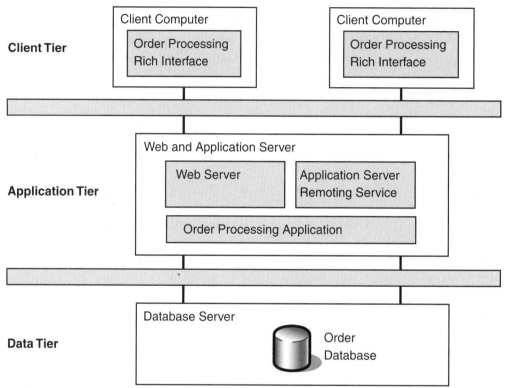

Figure 4.11
Three-tiered distribution

Client Tier

The client tier interacts with the users of the solution. If your application conforms to *Three-Layered Services Application*, this tier hosts the presentation layer components.

Hardware

For Web applications, the client tier consists of the user workstations, PDAs, and other devices that host a Web browser. For service-oriented solutions, this tier consists of the computers and devices that consume the service.

Computers in the client tier are independent of each other and should not have hard-coded references to application tier resources; instead, they should use naming services such as Domain Name System (DNS), Lightweight Directory Access

Protocol (LDAP), or Universal Description, Discovery, and Integration (UDDI) to find servers and services.

The number of computers in this tier can be quite large. Web applications essentially have an infinite number of computers in this tier. Solutions often need to scale up to handle a large increase in the number of users and their associated computers. The client tier does not impose any limit on the number of computers it contains, or how fast you can add computers. However, all the computers in the client tier must eventually interact with the application tier. The scalability of the application tier ultimately constrains the ability of the client tier to handle new users or increased workload per user.

Software

The operating system and solution software on the client tier is configured and optimized for responsive user interaction and must provide the following two services at a minimum:

- A mechanism for presenting the solution's user interface. For Web applications, this mechanism is a Web browser. For rich clients, it may be a custom UI framework, or may even be provided by the operating system.
- The software infrastructure required to communicate with other tiers. An example for rich clients would be TCP/IP sockets. HTTP would provide this service for Web applications.

Security

The client tier quite often exists in a separate security context from that of the other tiers, and individual computers within the tier are often in their own context. Many solutions must be able to adapt the security context of the client tier to the application tier.

The network infrastructure for Web-based enterprise applications is often based on a perimeter network (also known as DMZ, demilitarized zone, and screened subnet). The client tier is, by definition, on the public side of the perimeter network.

Application Tier

The servers in the application tier are responsible for hosting the application's business components and, in the case of Web applications, the Web servers as well. If your application conforms to *Three-Layered Services Application*, this tier hosts the business layer.

Hardware

The computers in the application tier are servers, the configuration of which must balance between the conflicting resource requirements of an application server and a Web server.

Because application tier servers are Web servers, this tier often must contain multiple servers configured as a *Server Farm* to meet scalability and fault-tolerance operational requirements. As you add users to the client tier and the performance of the solution diminishes beyond acceptable parameters, you must add servers to the farm. For details concerning scalability and fault-tolerance characteristics of server farms, see *Server Farm*.

Software

The servers in the application tier have both Web server and application server software installed. The application server software provides the execution context for the application logic. For an overview of the application server concept, see *Application Server*. For an example of the software infrastructure that this tier requires, see *Implementing Application Server Using Windows Server 2003*.

If your solution is a Web application, the server must be optimized for security and network connectivity. Otherwise, the server configuration should reflect the resource requirements of your business components and application server. Avoid hard-coding references to specific databases in the application. Use a configuration file, registry, or naming service to option references to the proper databases.

Security

The servers in this tier usually reside within the same security context. Therefore they can interact with each other using a common security infrastructure.

If a perimeter network is used, the combined application and Web server is usually deployed in there. This has the adverse affect of increasing the exposure of sensitive business logic to the public Internet. Consider the *Four-Tiered Distribution* pattern if your security requirements dictate that sensitive business logic must be kept on the corporate side of the perimeter network.

Data Tier

The servers in the data tier host the databases that the solution requires. If your application conforms to the *Three-Layered Services Application* pattern, this tier hosts the data layer.

Hardware

The computers in the data tier are sized and configured as enterprise servers. The servers are optimized for I/O throughput and hard-disk utilization. If the scalability and fault-tolerance operational requirements dictate that you have multiple servers in this tier, they are almost always configured as a server cluster. A server cluster is typically used in this case, because all the servers must manipulate a shared state (for example, the database), and because server-class computers have a very high limit on disk space and disk I/O capacity. For details concerning scalability and fault-tolerance characteristics of server clusters, see *Server Cluster*.

Software

Data tier servers host database management systems such as Microsoft® SQL Server™ 2000. Usually, reporting and data analysis software is also deployed on this tier. Database software that is specifically tuned for use in a clustered environment is required to maximize the benefit from a clustered server environment.

Security

Because of the need to protect corporate data assets, the data tier often has the most stringent security requirements of all the tiers. Typically, access to these servers is limited to the application servers and database administrator workstations. For solutions with stringent security requirements, the data tier may be deployed on its own subnet on the network.

If a perimeter network is used, the data tier is almost always on the corporate side of the perimeter network. Some very security-conscious solutions even have a second perimeter network between the application and data tiers.

Resulting Context

The *Three-Tiered Distribution* pattern results in a number of benefits and liabilities.

Benefits

Using this pattern results in the following benefits:

- Scalability and fault tolerance are strongly supported by configuring the application tier as a server farm and the database tier as a server cluster.
- Separating the client computer from the application logic supports the development and distribution of thin-client applications.
- Each tier can operate within its own security context.
- Having the Web server and business components on the same computer, and quite often in the same process, increases performance.

Liabilities

The following liabilities offset the benefits of using *Three-Tiered Distribution*:

- Business logic is directly exposed to the client tier, which can be a significant security risk for Web applications.
- Hardware for supporting a Web server is significantly cheaper than hardware for supporting both a Web server and an application server. Therefore, the incremental cost of adding a new user is usually higher for this solution than for a solution where the Web servers are separated from the application servers.

Related Patterns

For more information, see the following related patterns:

- *Tiered Distribution*
- *Application Server*
- *Server Farm*
- *Server Cluster*

Acknowledgments

[PnP02] *patterns & practices*, Microsoft Corporation. "Application Architecture for .NET: Designing Applications and Services." *MSDN Library*. Available at: *http://msdn.microsoft.com/library/default.asp?url=/library/en-us/dnbda/html/distapp.asp*.

Deployment Plan

Context

You have developed a component-based application that is logically structured into layers, as described in *Three-Layered Services Application.* You want to distribute it onto a set of servers that are physically structured into tiers, as described in *Tiered Distribution.*

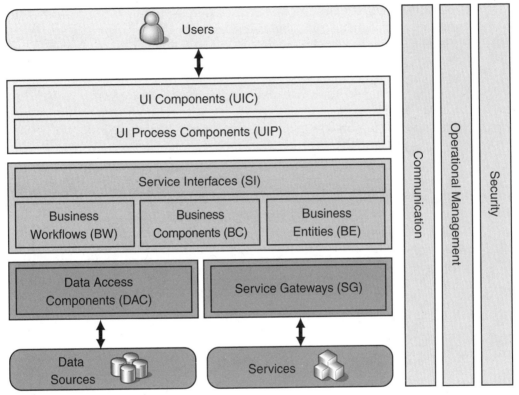

Figure 4.12
Three-Layered Services Application

Problem

How do you determine which tier you should deploy each of your components to?

Forces

When determining which tier to deploy your components onto, you must consider the following forces within the context of your environment:

- *Layered Application* mostly concerns managing design dependencies between components, while *Tiered Distribution* concerns optimizing the runtime server configuration to meet system-level operational requirements. Therefore, the criteria for structuring your application into layers are fundamentally different from the criteria used for optimizing physical component deployment. For example, one of the driving forces for assigning components to layers is to minimize the dependencies between components in different layers. Conversely, a primary driver for optimizing component deployment is to match a component's resource consumption profile to an appropriate server. This implies that a direct mapping of layers to tiers is often not the best distribution strategy. For instance, the Open Systems Interconnection (OSI) network protocol stack reference model is structured into seven layers. Seven different servers, each hosting a separate layer, are not required or even recommended.

- The people who structure the application into layers are often not the same people who structure the hardware infrastructure. People in these two groups often have different skill sets with few skills in common. For example, application architects focus on application components and the relationships between components, while system architects focus on the servers and the networks that connect them.

- Each additional tier to which components must be deployed adds complexity, deployment effort, and cost. Deploying all components to one tier is relatively simple. As you add more tiers, it becomes harder to determine which component goes where. Similarly, it takes relatively little effort to deploy all of your components to one location; after you add additional tiers, though, you have to put extra effort into your build and deployment process to decide which component goes where. Finally, each additional tier adds fixed and recurring costs for the additional hardware composing the tier.

- The components that compose your application each consume a different amount of resources such as memory, processor utilization, file handles, IO sockets, and disk space. There are two approaches for assigning components to tiers based on this force: *specialized tiers* and *general purpose tiers*. Specialized tiers are optimized for hosting components with specific resource utilization profiles. Because the servers in the specialized tier are optimized for a specific profile, each server can host many more components that meet that profile than can a generically configured server. Therefore, using specialized tiers usually results in more tiers with fewer servers per tier. On the other hand, servers in a general purpose tier are generically configured, and so the deployment decision basically becomes: how many components each server can hold before a given system resource is completely consumed. Using general purpose tiers usually results in fewer tiers with more servers per tier.

- Different components have different operational requirements such as security, availability, and fault-tolerance. For example, components that are accessed from the Web have different security requirements than do components that are on the corporate side of the perimeter network (also known as DMZ, demilitarized zone, and screened subnet). The same two approaches described for the previous force work here as well. Specialized tiers can be added to host components with specific operational requirements, or a general purpose tier can be configured to meet all operational requirements.

- Security requirements often drive you to add tiers, with each tier hosting components that have common security requirements. Beside the added complexity, deployment effort, and cost noted earlier, each additional tier adds to the overall security risk. Each additional tier also adds new servers and other infrastructure that must be secured.

- Business, political, or legal considerations may require specific components of a solution to be hosted at specific geographic locations. For example, databases containing sensitive corporate information may need to be hosted at secure corporate data centers, while the application servers that contain the business logic may reside at a third-party hosting facility.

- Every process and server boundary that a component invocation crosses adversely affects response time. Component invocations that cross process boundaries are several times slower than in-process invocations, while component invocations that cross the network are an order of magnitude slower than component invocations in the same process.

Solution

The application architects must meet with the system architects to create a deployment plan that describes which tier each of the application's components will be deployed to. Key to the success of this meeting is that both parties are starting from a set of high-quality requirements that are precisely specified down to a testable level. For example, a requirement stated as "The application must be scalable" is not specific enough to be testable. A more testable requirement would be: "The application must support 50 concurrent users with two second response time at launch and must scale up to 500 concurrent users with three second response time." This requirement is also phrased in a way that both system and application architects can understand. In addition starting from specific requirements, both parties must be intimately aware of the technical, legal, and business constraints that will be imposed on the solution.

Based on these requirements and constraints, the application architects define a set of components as specified in *Three-Layered Services Application*, and the system architects define a set of tiers as specified in *Tiered Distribution*. The discussion between the two parties while performing this mapping often causes significant changes to the components and tiers as each party becomes aware of the other's perspective.

You start the meeting by mapping the component roles defined in *Three-Layered Services Application* to tiers, using the forces described earlier as a guide. For example, user interface components may be mapped to the Web tier, whereas business components are almost always mapped to the application tier.

The next step is to go through each component in the application and assign it to a tier. In most cases, you can assign a component to a tier by determining what role it plays in the application and then assigning it to the corresponding tier identified for that role in the previous step. However, some components inevitably have unique operational or resource requirements that will cause them to be mapped to alternative tiers. Although these special cases are expected, too many of them indicate that you may need to modify the initial mapping of roles to tiers.

While assigning components to tiers, you may be unable to find a tier that is a good match for a component. When this happens, the two teams must work together and determine the cost and benefits of modifying the component to better work with the infrastructure, or modifying the infrastructure to better suit the component.

Several common deployment plan models for enterprise applications have been identified, based on *Three-Layered Services Application*: simple Web application, complex Web application, extended enterprise application, and smart client application.

Simple Web Application

The simple Web application configuration deploys all components into a single general-purpose tier. This configuration, which is shown in Figure 4.13, is the least complex and simplest configuration to understand.

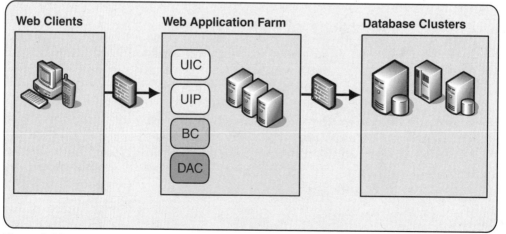

Figure 4.13
Simple Web application deployment

Complex Web Application

The complex Web application configuration, shown in Figure 4.14, separates the presentation and domain components and deploys them to different tiers that have been specialized to address their unique requirements.

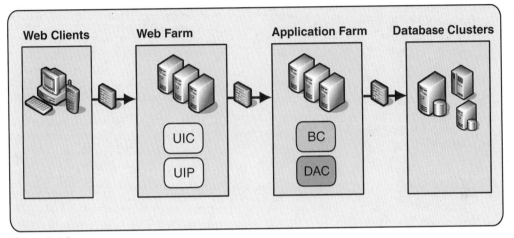

Figure 4.14
Complex Web application deployment

The user interface components (UIC) and user interface process components (UIP) are exposed to the Internet and can potentially interact with numerous clients. Because these presentation layer components are often exposed outside a company's firewall, they typically have much more restrictive security requirements than do components that are not exposed. Also, many organizations mandate that servers exposed to the Internet cannot contain any sensitive data. Therefore, putting the presentation layer components into a separate tier and configuring that tier for maximum security greatly increases the overall security of the solution with minimal impact on the components that have less severe security requirements.

Because presentation layer components are exposed to the Internet, their performance and scalability requirements typically differ from those of domain and data access layer components. Presentation layer components are often optimized to handle many concurrent users who interact with the components in bursts. Domain and data access layer components are often optimized to handle a steady stream of requests from a relatively few number of sources. It can be difficult to configure a single tier to adequately support both sets of optimizations. Therefore, the solution is to use two tiers, each optimized for the type of components they host.

Extended Enterprise Application

Extended enterprise applications consume services provided by other applications and may also expose functionality as services to be consumed by other applications. Figure 4.15 on the next page shows this deployment configuration.

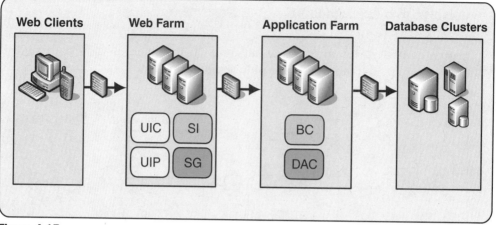

Figure 4.15
Extended enterprise application deployment

The reasons for placing the service gateways (SG) and service interfaces (SI) in the Web tier are the same as for placing the presentation components in the Web tier, as discussed earlier in this pattern.

Smart Client Application

The smart client configuration deploys the user interface components onto the client tier instead of the Web tier. The primary motivation for moving the presentation components to the client tier is that rich user interfaces demand a high degree of interactivity with the user. Mainstream Web technology does not support these rich user interface requirements. Figure 4.16 shows the smart client configuration with the additional tier.

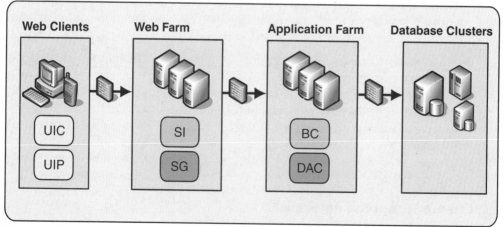

Figure 4.16
Smart client application deployment

Note: Large enterprise applications tend to look like a composite of one or more of the models discussed in this pattern. For instance, while most business components of an extended enterprise application run in the application server, a few might run in the Web farm and one or two might run in the browser for performance reasons.

Resulting Context

The meeting between the application development and system infrastructure teams is critical for successful application deployment. The resulting deployment plan provides the following benefits:

- Assigns components to tiers to meet the requirements of both teams.
- Facilitates communication between the two teams and defines the contract that both teams agree to abide by. If one of the teams cannot fulfill its commitments, then the two teams must get together and redefine a new contract.

Note: The meeting between the application development and system infrastructure teams will not produce an optimum deployment plan unless the corporate culture recognizes the equal importance of both the application and system architecture views. Both teams must be flexible and willing to seek compromises that enable both teams to fulfill their requirements.

5

Distributed Systems Patterns

In today's connected world, enterprise applications increasingly run distributed across multiple servers, connect to remote data sources and Web services, and are accessible over the Internet. Distributed computing is powerful, but it is not without challenges. Networks are inherently unreliable, and communicating with remote servers is slow when compared to local interprocess communication. In addition, running a program simultaneously across multiple computers can introduce a host of concurrency and synchronization issues.

Instance-Based vs. Service-Based Collaboration

Distributed computing can be based on two distinct architectural styles, according to Business Component Factory [Herzum00]:

- Instance-based collaboration
- Service-based collaboration

Instance-based collaboration extends the model of object-oriented computing across network boundaries. A component can instantiate remote object instances, pass references to these remote objects around, invoke methods on the remote objects, and de-allocate them. The advantage of this approach is that the same object-oriented programming model used inside the application applies to the distributed components. Most runtime platforms incorporate support for instance-based collaboration so that a developer has to make no (or few) special provisions to access a remote object versus a local object. This simplifies developing a distributed solution tremendously, often to the point where previously co-located objects can be distributed during deployment time without requiring any code changes to the application. Instance-based collaboration also gives the consumer of a remote object fine-grained control over the lifetime of the remote object, allowing more efficient usage of remote resources.

The ease-of-use of instance-based collaboration, however, comes at the expense of a complex interaction model and tight coupling between consumer and provider. Instance-based interaction requires a specific instance of a remote object to be addressable over the network, introducing the complexities of lifetime and instance management into the communications protocol. For this reason, most platforms that support instance-based collaboration do not provide interoperability with other platforms.

Service-based collaboration addresses some of these challenges by exposing only a "manager-like" or "coordinator-like" interface to potential consumers. Consumers can invoke a method on this interface but they do not have lifetime control over any remote objects This simplifies the interaction tremendously and enables the use of standard protocols that support interoperability across platforms.

However, service-based collaborations do not provide the continuity of using an object-oriented programming model for both local and remote objects. This means that you have to track the state of a conversation between objects explicitly, something you did not have to worry about when using instance-based collaboration. Also, while standards-based protocols improve interoperability, they require the application to convert application-internal data types into a common format that is understood by each communicating endpoint, which may involve additional transformation logic.

Near Links vs. Far Links

Another way to think about distributed systems is to consider each system as a collection of processing nodes connected by links. The nodes represent actual server machines while the links represent the network that connects these machines together. The links within the system fall within two classifications: near links or far links.

Near links are those that reside in the same enterprise, are connected reliably and do not require interoperability. Far links include all other links and include any link that spans the Internet.

If your distributed system spans near links only, then instance-based collaboration may be optimal. Using instance-based collaboration, you can expand the power of object-oriented development across machine boundaries while taking advantage of your platform infrastructure to optimize speed, navigate type systems, and handle marshalling details for you. Technology choices here would include .NET remoting and Enterprise Services within the Microsoft® .NET Framework.

On the other hand, if your distributed system spans far links, then service-based collaboration is usually a better choice. Interacting with a service that offers up a "coordinator-like" interface allows the service to be responsible for implementation and shields the user of the service from implementation details. Service interfaces often return messages, which offer less coupling than remote procedure calls. The best messages are those that contain both a header and a body, which allow the receiver to act upon the message autonomously. Technology choices here would include capabilities such as Web services.

The balance of this chapter will describe patterns usually associated with instance-based collaboration and near links. Patterns usually associated with service-based collaborations and far links are further described in Chapter 6, "Services Patterns."

Distributed Computing Challenges

The core of a distributed architecture is the ability to invoke a method on an object or communicate with services that reside in a different process and possibly on a different computer. Although this does not sound difficult, you must address a surprisingly long list of issues:

- How do you instantiate a remote object?

- If you want to invoke a method on an existing object, how do you obtain a reference to this object?

- Network protocols transport only byte streams, not objects. How can you invoke a method over a byte stream?

- What about security? Can anyone invoke a method on the remote object?

- Most networks are inherently unreliable. What happens if the remote object is unreachable? What if the remote object receives the method invocation but cannot send the response because of network problems?

- Calling a remote object can be much slower than invoking a local method. Do you want to invoke the remote method asynchronously so that you can continue processing locally while the remote object processes the request?

The list of questions continues. Fortunately, the features in the .NET Framework take care of most of these issues, allowing developers to create distributed applications without having to deal with many of the nasty details. These features make remote invocation almost transparent to the programmer, at least at the syntactic level. This simplicity can be deceiving, however, because developers still must understand some of the underlying principles of remote communication to write robust and efficient distributed applications. The Distributed Systems patterns cluster helps developers make informed design decisions when implementing distributed applications.

Using Layered Application

The secret to creating an easy-to-use infrastructure for distributed systems is *Layered Application*. A distributed services layer relies on lower layers, such as the TCP/IP stacks and socket communication layers, but hides the details of these layers from upper layers that contain the application and business logic layers. This arrangement allows the application developer to work at a higher level of abstraction without having to worry about such details as TCP/IP packets and network byte ordering. It also allows lower layers to be replaced without any impact on the upper layers. For example, you can switch to a different transport protocol (for example HTTP instead of straight TCP/IP) without changing code at the application layer.

One way to make remote invocation easy for developers is to use a *Proxy* [Gamma95]. A proxy is a local stand-in object with which the client object communicates. When the client creates an instance of the remote object, the infrastructure creates a proxy object that looks to the client exactly like the remote type. When the client invokes a method on that proxy object, the proxy invokes the remoting infrastructure. The remoting infrastructure routes the request to the server process, invokes the server object, and returns the result to the client proxy, which passes the result to the client object. Because all of this happens behind the scenes, the client object may be completely unaware that the other object resides on a different computer. This not only makes developing distributed applications easier, it also allows you to distribute objects after the program has been developed while only minimally changing the application code.

Patterns Overview

The Distributed Systems patterns cluster focuses on two primary concepts: remote invocation and coarse-grained interfaces.

Remote Invocation

The *Broker* pattern describes how to locate a remote object and invoke one of its methods without introducing the complexities of communicating over a network into the application. This pattern establishes the basis for most distributed architectures, including .NET remoting.

Design

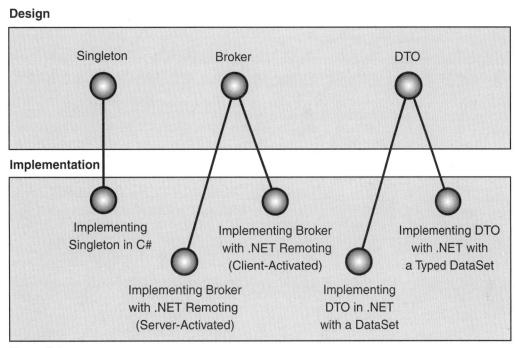

Figure 5.1
Patterns in the Distributed Systems cluster

One of the guiding principles of the .NET Framework is to simplify complex program-ming tasks without taking control away from the programmer. In accordance with this principle, .NET remoting allows the developer to choose from a number of remoting models, as described in the following paragraphs.

Local Copy

The simplest remoting model creates a local copy of the remote object in the client process. Any subsequent method invocations on this object are truly local calls. This model avoids many of the complications inherent in distributed computing but has a number of shortcomings. First, computing is not really distributed because you are running a local copy of an object in your own process space. Second, any updates you make to the object's state are lost because they occur only locally. Finally, an object is usually remote because it requires a remote resource or because the pro-vider of the remote object wants to protect access to its internals. Copying the object instance to the local process not only defeats both of these goals but also adds the overhead of shipping a complete object over a remote channel. Because of these limitations, the only application of object copying that this chapter discusses is the *Data Transfer Object* pattern.

Server-Activated Objects

Invoking the methods directly on the remote object is a better model than working on a local copy. However, you can invoke a method on a remote object only if you have a reference to it. Obtaining a reference to the remote object requires the object to be instantiated first. The client asks the server for an instance of the object, and the server returns a reference to a remote instance. This works well if the remote object can be viewed as a service. For example, consider a service that verifies credit card numbers. The client object submits a credit card number and receives a positive or negative response, depending on the customer's spending (and payment) habits. In this case, you are not really concerned with the instance of the remote object. You submit some data, receive a result, and move on. This is a good example of a *stateless* service, a service in which each request leaves the object in the same state that it was in before.

Not all remote object collaborations follow this model, though. Sometimes you want to call the remote object to retrieve some data that you can then access in subsequent remote calls. You must be sure that you call the same object instance during subsequent calls. Furthermore, when you are finished examining the data, you would like the object to be deallocated to save memory on the server. With *server-activated objects*, you do not have this level of control over object instances. Server-activated objects offer a choice of only two alternatives for lifetime instance management:

- Create a new instance of the object for each call.
- Use only a single instance of the remote object for all clients (effectively making the object a *Singleton*).

Neither of these options fits the example where you want to access the same remote instance for a few function calls and then let the garbage collector have it.

Client-Activated Objects

Client-activated objects give the client control over the lifetime of the remote objects. The client can instantiate a remote object almost as it would instantiate a local object, and the garbage collector removes the remote objects after the client removes all references to the object instance. This level of control comes at a price, though. To use client activation, you must copy the assembly available to the client process. This contradicts the idea that a variety of clients should be able to access the remote objects without further setup requirements.

You can have the best of both worlds, though, by creating a server-activated object that is a factory object for server objects. This factory object creates instances of other objects. The factory itself is stateless; therefore, you can easily implement it as a server-activated singleton. All client requests then share the same instance of the factory. Because the factory object runs remotely, all objects it instantiates are remote objects, but the client can determine when and where to instantiate them.

Coarse-Grained Interfaces

Invoking a method across process and network boundaries is significantly slower than invoking a method on an object in the same operating system process.

Many object oriented design practices typically lead to designing objects with fine-grained interfaces. These objects may have many fields with associated getters and setters and many methods, each of which encapsulates a small and cohesive piece of functionality. Because of this fine-grained nature, many methods must be called to achieve a desired result. This fine-grained interface approach is ideal for stand-alone applications because it supports many desirable application characteristics such as maintainability, reusability, and testability.

Working with an object that exposes a fine-grained interface can greatly impede application performance, because a fine-grained interface requires many method calls across process and network boundaries. To improve performance, remote objects must expose a more coarse-grained interface. A coarse-grained interface is one that exposes a relatively small set of self-contained methods. Each method typically represents a high-level piece of functionality such as Place Order or Update Customer. These methods are considered self-contained because all the data that a method needs is passed in as a parameter to the method.

Data Transfer Object

The *Data Transfer Object* pattern applies the coarse-grained interface concept to the problem of passing data between components that are separated by process and network boundaries. It suggests replacing many parameters with one object that holds all the data that a remote method requires. The same technique also works quite well for data that the remote method returns.

There are several options for implementing a data transfer object (DTO). One technique is to define a separate class for each different type of DTO that the solution needs. These classes usually have a strongly typed public field (or property) for each data element they contain. To transfer these objects across networks or process boundaries, these classes are serialized. The serialized object is marshaled across the boundary and then reconstituted on the receiving side. Performance and type safety are the key benefits to this approach. This approach has the least amount of marshaling overhead, and the strongly typed fields of the DTO ensure that type errors are caught at compile time rather than at run time. The downside to this approach is that a new class is created for each DTO. If a solution requires a large number of DTOs, the effort associated with writing and maintaining these classes can be significant.

A second technique for creating a DTO is to use a generic container class for holding the data. A common implementation of this approach is to use something like the ADO.NET **DataSet** as the generic container class. This approach requires two extra translations. The first translation on the sending side converts the application data into a form that is suitable for use by the **DataSet**. The second translation happens on the receiving side when the data is extracted from the **DataSet** for use in the client application. These extra translations can impede performance in some applications. Lack of type safety is another disadvantage of this approach. If a customer object is put into a **DataSet** on the sending side, attempting to extract an order object on the receiving side results in a run-time error. The main advantage to this approach is that no extra classes must be written, tested, or maintained.

ADO.NET offers a third alternative, the typed **DataSet**. ADO.NET provides a mechanism that automatically generates a type-safe wrapper around a **DataSet**. This approach has the same potential performance issues as the **DataSet** approach but allows the application to benefit from the advantages of type safety, without requiring the developer to develop, test, and maintain a separate class for each DTO.

Distributed Systems Patterns

Table 5.1 lists the patterns included in the Distributed Systems patterns cluster, along with the problem statements and associated implementations that serve as a roadmap to the patterns.

Table 5.1: Distributed Systems Patterns

Pattern	Problem	Associated implementations
Broker	How can you structure a distributed system so that application developers don't have to concern themselves with the details of remote communication?	*Implementing Broker with .NET Remoting Using Server-Activated Objects* *Implementing Broker with .NET Remoting Using Client-Activated Objects*
Data Transfer Object	How do you preserve the simple semantics of a procedure call interfeace without being subject to the latency issues inherent in remote communication?	*Implementing Data Transfer Object in .NET with a DataSet* *Implementing Data Transfer Object in .NET with a Typed DataSet*
Singleton	How do you make an instance of an object globally available and guarantee that only one instance of the class is created?	*Implementing Singleton in C#*

Note: The scope for this pattern cluster does not currently include message-oriented middleware, integration of multiple applications, or service-oriented architectures. These topics are extremely important and are part of the overall pattern language, but do not appear in this initial release.

Broker

Context

Many complex software systems run on multiple processors or distributed computers. There are a number of reasons to distribute software across computers, for example:

- A distributed system can take advantage of the computing power of multiple CPUs or a cluster of low-cost computers.
- Certain software may only be available on specific computers.
- Parts of the software may have to run on different network segments due to security considerations.
- Some services may be provided by business partners and may only be accessed over the Internet.

However, implementing a distributed system is not easy because you have to deal with issues such as concurrency, cross-platform connectivity, and unreliable network connections.

Problem

How can you structure a distributed system so that application developers don't have to concern themselves with the details of remote communication?

Forces

The following forces must be reconciled as you build a distributed system:

- Although distributed systems provide a lot of advantages, they also tend to introduce significant complexity into the software system. Physical and logic boundaries exist between processes or computers running on the same network. To have objects running on different processes or computers communicating with each other across these boundaries, you have to deal with issues such as communications, encoding, and security. If you mix these implementation details with the application code, a simple change in the communications infrastructure could lead to significant code changes.

- The distribution of the system often occurs after development is complete. For example, software may be distributed across multiple servers to increase processing power. You would not want to change the application code at this late a stage in the life cycle.

- The details of cross-process communication can be quite tedious. You have to deal with TCP/IP sockets, marshaling and unmarshaling, serialization, timeouts, and many other challenges. Therefore, it makes sense to have a special team focus on the infrastructure so that the application developers do not have to learn about remote communications.

- To maintain the flexibility of being able to move components to different locations at deployment time, you must avoid hard-coding the location of specific components.

Solution

Use the *Broker* pattern to hide the implementation details of remote service invocation by encapsulating them into a layer other than the business component itself [Buschmann96].

This layer provides an interface to the client that allows it to invoke methods just as it would invoke any local interface. However, the methods inside the client interface trigger services to be performed on remote objects. This is transparent to the client because the remote service object implements the same interface. This pattern refers to the business component that initiates the remote service invocation as the *client*, and the component that responds to the remote service invocation as the *server*.

Figure 5.2 shows the static structure of a simple example without any distribution. The client invokes the **performFunctionA** method on the server directly. This is possible only if the server objects reside on the same computer as the client objects.

Figure 5.2
Structure with no distribution

Figure 5.3 shows the static structure when distribution is implemented.

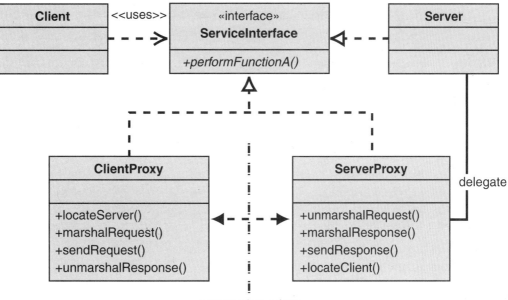

Figure 5.3
Structure with distribution

The **ServiceInterface** is a necessary abstraction that makes distribution possible by providing the contract about the service that the server is going to provide without exposing the implementation details on the server side. When implementing the distribution, client and server proxies would be added to handle all the "plumbing" for sending a method invocation and its parameters across the network to the server and then sending the response back to the client. The proxies would do all the marshaling and unmarshaling of data, security control, transfer channel config- uration, and any other additional work. The client would simply invoke the **performFunctionA** method on the client proxy as if it were a local call because the client proxy actually implements the **ServerInterface**. The code change to the client would be minimal and thus you could develop your whole business domain model without any knowledge about the distribution nature of the system. Any change to the way remote service invocation is implemented would be limited to within the proxy classes, and would not have any impact on the domain model. Figure 5.4 shows one scenario of the interactions between these components.

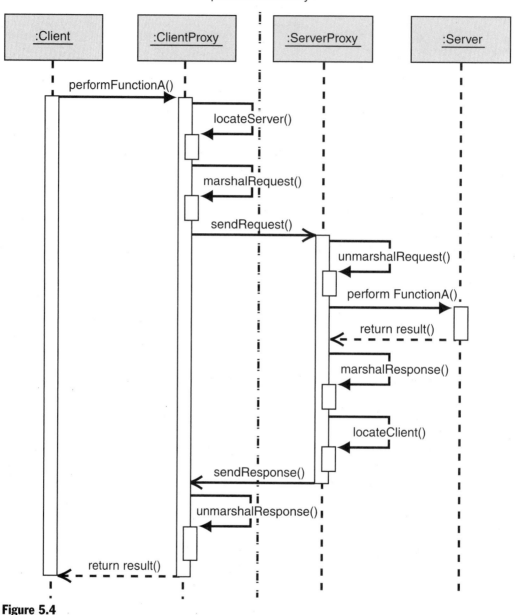

Figure 5.4
Behavior with distribution

Server Look-Up

The *Broker* solution addresses most of the problems described previously. However, because the client proxy communicates with the server proxy directly, the client must be able to find the location of the server at compile time. This means that you cannot change or move the server to a different location at run time. To overcome this limitation, you need to avoid exposing the exact location of the server. Instead, you deploy a new component, the broker component, at a well-known location and then expose that location to the client. The broker component is then responsible for locating the server for the client. The broker component also implements a repository for adding and removing server components, which makes it possible to add, remove, or exchange server components at run time. Figure 5.5 shows the static structure with the broker component involved.

This type of function is often called a *naming service*. Looking up remote objects is a common requirement in enterprise computing. Therefore, a number of platforms implement a naming service, for example, Microsoft uses the Active Directory® directory service.

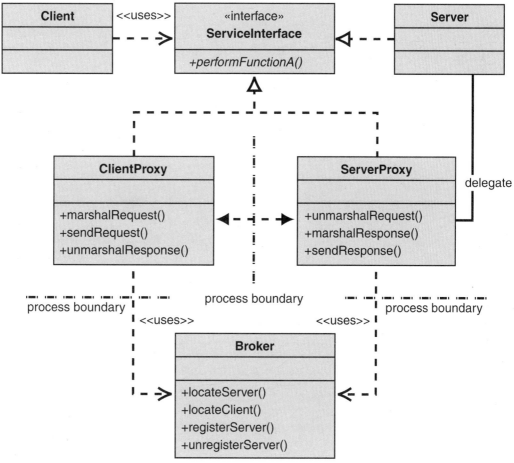

Figure 5.5
Broker structure with server look-up

The broker is hosted at a well-known location that should not change very often. Any server that is activated and ready to receive requests would register itself with the broker so that the next time a client asks the broker for this type of server, the broker would be able to use it. This could also increase the performance and availability of the system, because it enables you to have multiple identical server components that run and serve multiple clients at the same time. This mechanism is sometimes called load balancing. Figure 5.6 shows a sample interaction scenario between these components.

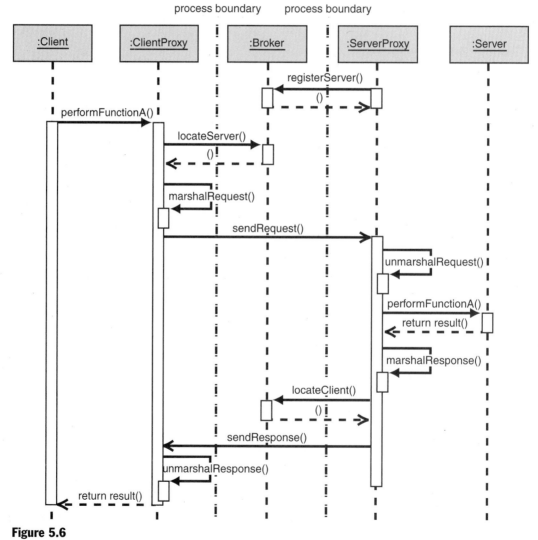

Figure 5.6
Broker behavior with server look-up

Broker as Intermediary

In the previous scenario, the broker is only responsible for locating the server for the client. The client obtains the location of the server from the broker and then communicates with the server directly without any involvement of the broker. In some situations, however, direct communication between client and server is not desirable. For example, for security reasons, you may want to host all the servers in your company's private network, which is behind a firewall, and only allow access to them from the broker. In this case, you must have the broker forward all the requests and responses between the server and the client instead of having them talk to each other directly. Figure 5.7 shows a revised static structure of this model.

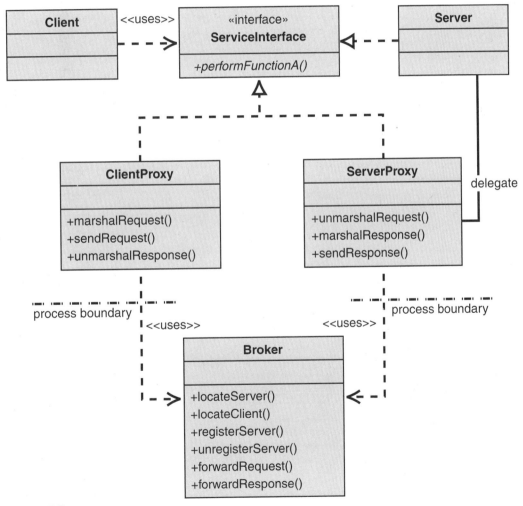

Figure 5.7
Structure of Broker serving as intermediary

Figure 5.8 shows the interaction diagram with the broker serving as a messenger between the client and the server. This example also shows how the communication between the client and the server can be asynchronous (note the open arrowhead on the **sendRequest** call).

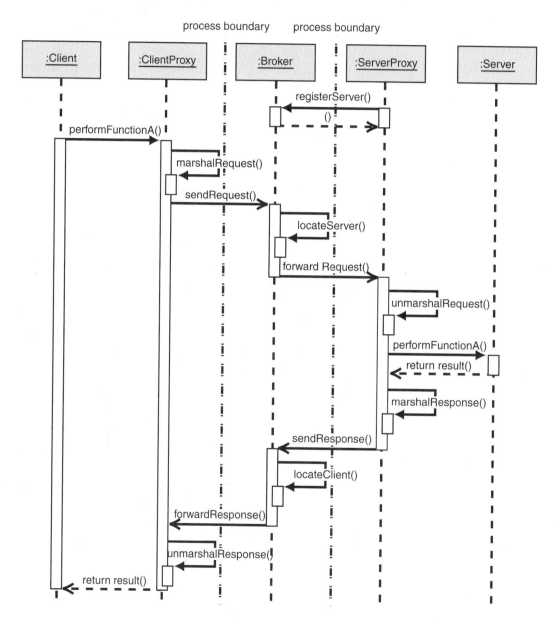

Figure 5.8

Behavior of Broker serving as intermediary

There are also situations when the client must make a series of method invocations on the same server to complete one long and complex business transaction. In these cases, the server must maintain the state between client calls. The broker must then make sure that all server calls that a client makes inside an atomic session are routed to the exact same server component.

Example

The *Broker* pattern and its variants are implemented in many distributed system frameworks. See *Implementing Broker in .NET Remoting Using Server-Activated Objects* and *Implementing Broker in .NET Remoting Using Client-Activated Objects*.

Resulting Context

The *Broker* pattern has many of the benefits and liabilities of the *Layered Application* pattern.

Benefits

Broker provides the following benefits:

- **Isolation**. Separating all the communication-related code into its own layer isolates it from the application. You can decide to run the application distributed or all on one computer without having to change any application code.

- **Simplicity**. Encapsulating complex communication logic into a separate layer breaks down the problem space. The engineers coding the broker do not have to concern themselves with arcane user requirements and business logic, and the application developers do not have to concern themselves with multicast protocols and TCP/IP routing.

- **Flexibility**. Encapsulating functions in a layer allows you to swap this layer with a different implementation. For example, you can switch from DCOM to .NET remoting to standard Web services without affecting the application code.

Liabilities

Unfortunately, layers of abstraction can harm performance. The basic rule is that the more information you have, the better you can optimize. Using a separate broker layer may hide details about how the application uses the lower layer, which may in turn prevent the lower layer from performing specific optimizations. For example, when you use TCP/IP, the routing protocol has no idea what is being routed. Therefore, it is hard to decide that a packet containing a video stream, for instance, should have routing priority over a packet containing a junk e-mail.

Security Considerations

Server components that contain sensitive business data are often located in a company's private network, protected behind a firewall. The broker component then sits in a perimeter network (also known as demilitarized zone, DMZ, or screened subnet), which is a small network inserted as a neutral zone between a company's private network and the outside public network. Access to the server components is only allowed from the perimeter network and not from the outside public network. This extra layer prevents outside users from getting direct access to a server.

Related Patterns

For more information about *Broker*, see the following related patterns:

- *Implementing Broker with .NET Remoting Using Server-Activated Objects* and *Implementing Broker with .NET Remoting Using Client-Activated Objects* describe two implementation strategies for the *Broker* pattern.
- *Data Transfer Object*
- *Remote Proxy*. The ClientProxy object described in this pattern follows a variant of the *Proxy* pattern described in [Gamma95, Buschmann96], which is called *Remote Proxy*.

Acknowledgments

[Buschmann96] Buschmann, Frank, et al. *Pattern-Oriented Software Architecture.* John Wiley & Sons Ltd, 1996.

[Fowler03] Fowler, Martin. *Patterns of Enterprise Application Architecture.* Addison-Wesley, 2003.

[Gamma95] Gamma, Helm, Johnson, and Vlissides. *Design Patterns: Elements of Reusable Object-Oriented Software.* Addison-Wesley, 1995.

Implementing Broker with .NET Remoting Using Server-Activated Objects

Context

You are using the Microsoft® .NET Framework to build an application that requires the use of distributed objects. Your requirements include the ability to pass objects by value or reference, whether those objects reside on the same computer, on different computers in the same local area network (LAN), or on different computers in a wide area network (WAN). Your application does not require you to control the lifetime of the remote objects explicitly.

Background on .NET Remoting

Remoting uses object references to communicate between the client and the server. In the server-activated scenario, your client retrieves a reference to an existing server object using the remoting infrastructure (**Activator.GetObject**). After you have a reference to the object, you can call its methods as though the object were in your process rather than running on a separate computer. The following underlying mechanism is used to implement this functionality:

- The client retrieves an instance of the remote type.

- The remoting infrastructure creates a proxy object that acts as a surrogate for the remote type.

- The client calls a method on that proxy. The remoting system receives the call, routes it to the server process, invokes the server object, and then returns a result to the client proxy, which passes the result to the client object.

The calls themselves have to be sent in some fashion between the client and server. The remoting infrastructure refers to this mechanism as a transport channel. Channels transport messages between applications across remoting boundaries, whether between application domains, processes, or computers. A channel can listen on an endpoint for inbound messages; send outbound messages to another endpoint, or both. This enables you to plug in a wide range of protocols, even if the common language runtime is not at the other end of the channel.

Although the server process knows everything about each unique object, the client knows only that it wants a reference to an object in another application domain, perhaps on another computer. From the world outside the server application domain, the object is located by a URL.

Server Activation

As described in the introduction to the Distributed Systems cluster, the .NET Framework supports two activation models: server activation and client activation. Server-activated objects are objects whose lifetimes are directly controlled by the server. The server application domain creates these objects only when the client makes a method call on the object, not when the client calls **new** or **Activator.GetObject()**; this saves a network round-trip solely for the purpose of instance creation. Only a proxy is created in the client application domain when a client requests an instance of a server-activated type. This also means, however, that only default constructors are allowed for server-activated types. To publish a type whose instances will be created with specific constructors that take arguments, you can use client activation.

To create an instance of a server-activated type, clients typically use **Activator.GetObject()**.

Choosing a Protocol and Serialization Mechanism

The type of protocol you choose to use has an impact on the how your application performs. For some criteria for choosing the correct type of channel for your application, see "Choosing Communication Options in .NET" from the .NET Framework Developer's Guide, available on the MSDN® developer program Web site at: *http://msdn.microsoft.com/library/*.

In this pattern, you will see an example of HttpChannel/SOAP and TcpChannel/ Binary.

Implementation Strategy

This pattern presents two examples of server-activated objects and the flexibility of the .NET remoting infrastructure. The first example uses **HttpChannel** with its default serialization mechanism, SOAP. The second example uses **TcpChannel** with its default serialization mechanism, which is binary. Before examining the applications themselves, let's first look at the class that must be distributed across the network.

Server Object

The **RecordingsManager** class provides a method named **GetRecordings**, which retrieves a list of recordings from a database and return the result in **DataSet**. Note that a series of considerations is involved in determining the best data types to be transmitted over a remote connection. This example uses **DataSet** because it keeps the sample code short and demonstrates the transfer of complex data types. For a thorough treatment of this topic, see the MSDN article "Designing Data Tier Components and Passing Data Through Tiers" at:

http://msdn.microsoft.com/library/en-us/dnbda/html/BOAGag.asp

RecordingsManager.cs

The following sample shows the **RecordingsManager** class:

```
using System;
using System.Data;
using System.Data.SqlClient;
```

```
public class RecordingsManager
{
   public DataSet GetRecordings()
   {
      String selectCmd = "select * from Recording";

      SqlConnection myConnection = new SqlConnection(
         "server=(local);database=recordings;Trusted_Connection=yes");
      SqlDataAdapter myCommand =
         new SqlDataAdapter(selectCmd, myConnection);

      DataSet ds = new DataSet();
      myCommand.Fill(ds, "Recording");
      return ds;
   }
}
```

This class must be accessed remotely. First, the **RecordingsManager** class must inherit from a class in the remoting infrastructure called **MarshallByRefObject**. **MarshalByRefObject** is the base class for objects that communicate across application domain boundaries by exchanging messages using a proxy. Objects that do not inherit from **MarshalByRefObject** are implicitly marshaled by value. When a remote application references a marshal-by-value object, a copy of the object is passed across remoting boundaries. Because you want to use the proxy method instead of the copy method to communicate, you need to inherit from **MarshallByRefObject**. Second, you need to extract an interface from this class. The interface is necessary to reduce the dependencies between the client and server and also to better deploy the application. For more information, see "Deployment Considerations" later in this pattern.

IRecordingsManager.cs

The following is the code for the extracted **IRecordingsManager** interface:

```
using System;
using System.Data;

public interface IRecordingsManager
{
   DataSet GetRecordings();
}
```

RecordingsManager.cs (Remote-Enabled)

Making the changes to **RecordingsManager** results in the following code:

```
public class RecordingsManager : MarshalByRefObject, IRecordingsManager
{ /* ... */ }
```

HttpChannel: SOAP Serialization

The primary motivations for choosing this channel and serialization mechanism include security and interoperability. **HttpChannel** hosted in Microsoft Internet Information Services (IIS) enables you to take advantage of security functions that are built into IIS and ASP.NET. If you choose any other channel or choose not to host **HttpChannel** in IIS, you have to provide your own security functions. Also, to interoperate between different operating systems, you must use the **HttpChannel** and SOAP serialization. However, **HttpChannel** is not the highest-performing option due to the use of XML serialization and the additional overhead of using the HTTP protocol inside IIS and ASP.NET. For more information, see "Operational Considerations" later in this pattern.

The following solution uses **HttpChannel** with SOAP serialization for the **RecordingsManager** class described earlier (See Figure 5.9).

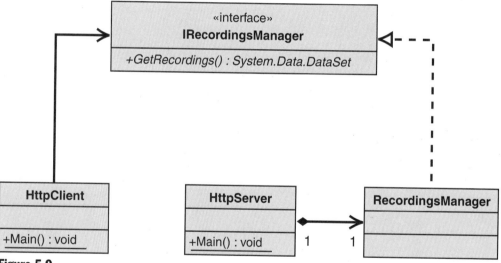

Figure 5.9
HttpChannel implementation

HttpServer.cs

HttpServer is a console application that creates the **HttpChannel** object and assigns port 8100. The code then associates the name "RecordingsManager.soap" with an instance of **RecordingsManager**.

There are two activation modes for server-activated objects: **Singleton** and **SingleCall**.

Singleton types never have more than one instance at any one time. If an instance exists, all client requests are serviced by that instance. If one does not exist, the server creates an instance and all subsequent client requests are serviced by that instance.

SingleCall types always have one instance per client request. The next method invocation will be serviced by a different server instance, even if the previous instance has not yet been recycled by the system.

RecordingsManager uses the **Singleton** activation mode, so that you will have only one instance of **RecordingsManager** running on the server. This works fine, because the object has only a single method that retrieves a predefined set of data. The last line makes sure that the code will not exit until the user presses ENTER. You should note that this is probably not the best way to ensure that the program does not exit. If the program were to do so, clients would not be able to access the server objects.

```
using System;
using System.Runtime.Remoting;
using System.Runtime.Remoting.Channels;
using System.Runtime.Remoting.Channels.Http;


public class HttpServer
{
    static void Main(string[] args)
    {
        HttpChannel channel = new HttpChannel(8100);
        ChannelServices.RegisterChannel(channel);

        RemotingConfiguration.RegisterWellKnownServiceType(
            typeof(RecordingsManager),
            "RecordingsManager.soap",
            WellKnownObjectMode.Singleton);

        Console.ReadLine();
    }
}
```

HttpClient.cs

The client program calls the remoting framework function **Activator.GetObject()**, specifying the URL where the object is located along with the type that should be returned. In this case, you should expect an **IRecordingsManager** object at *http://localhost:8100/RecordingsManager.soap*. After you have the instance, you can call methods on it as if it were in the same application domain.

```
using System;
using System.Data;
using System.Runtime.Remoting;
using System.Runtime.Remoting.Channels;
```

```
using System.Runtime.Remoting.Channels.Http;

public class HttpClient
{
    [STAThread]
    static void Main(string[] args)
    {
        HttpChannel channel = new HttpChannel();
        ChannelServices.RegisterChannel(channel);

        IRecordingsManager mgr = (IRecordingsManager)
            Activator.GetObject(typeof(IRecordingsManager),
            "http://localhost:8100/RecordingsManager.soap");

        Console.WriteLine("Client.main(): Reference acquired");

        DataSet ds = mgr.GetRecordings();
        Console.WriteLine("Recordings Count: {0}",
            ds.Tables["recording"].Rows.Count);
    }
}
```

TcpChannel: Binary Serialization

The primary motivation for choosing this channel and serialization mechanism is performance. In fact, using binary serialization alone increases performance dramatically. (See "Operational Considerations.") If you do not have any security issues (for example, you are building a small application that runs entirely inside a firewall), you should use **TcpChannel** with binary serialization, because it performs the best.

The following solution uses the **TcpChannel** with binary serialization for the **RecordingsManager** class described earlier (See Figure 5.10).

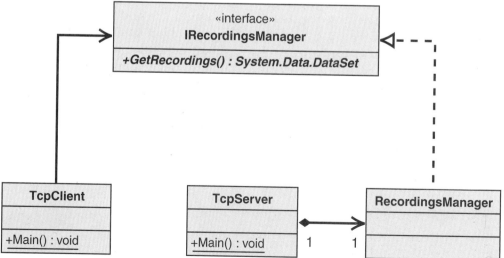

Figure 5.10

TcpChannel/binary serialization implementation

TcpServer.cs

TcpServer is a console application that creates the **TcpChannel** object and assigns port 8100. The code then associates the name "GetRecordingsManager" with an instance of **RecordingsManager**. The activation mode for **RecordingsManager** is a singleton, so you will have only one instance of **RecordingsManager** running on the server. The last line ensures that the code will not exit until the user presses ENTER. You should note that this is probably not best the way to ensure that the program does not exit. If the program were to do so, clients would not be able to access the server objects.

```
using System;
using System.Runtime.Remoting;
using System.Runtime.Remoting.Channels;
using System.Runtime.Remoting.Channels.Tcp;


public class TcpServer
{
    static void Main(string[] args)
    {
        TcpChannel channel = new TcpChannel(8100);
        ChannelServices.RegisterChannel(channel);

        RemotingConfiguration.RegisterWellKnownServiceType(
            typeof(RecordingsManager),
            "GetRecordingsManager",
            WellKnownObjectMode.Singleton);

        Console.ReadLine();
    }
}
```

TcpClient.cs

The client program calls the remoting framework method **Activator.GetObject()** to retrieve a proxy for the **RecordingsManager** object on the server. The method specifies the URL where the object is located along with the type that should be returned. In this case, you should expect an **IRecordingsManager** object at the following location: *http://localhost:8100/GetRecordingsManager*. After you have the instance, you can call methods on it as if it were in the same application domain.

```
using System;
using System.Data;
using System.Runtime.Remoting;
using System.Runtime.Remoting.Channels;
using System.Runtime.Remoting.Channels.Tcp;

class TcpClient
{
    [STAThread]
    static void Main(string[] args)
    {
        TcpChannel channel = new TcpChannel();
        ChannelServices.RegisterChannel(channel);
```

```
IRecordingsManager mgr = (IRecordingsManager)
    Activator.GetObject(typeof(IRecordingsManager),
    "tcp://localhost:8100/GetRecordingsManager");

Console.WriteLine("Client.main(): Reference acquired");

DataSet ds = mgr.GetRecordings();
Console.WriteLine("Recordings Count: {0}",
    ds.Tables["recording"].Rows.Count);
    }
}
```

Deployment Considerations

When using .NET remoting, you must pay careful attention to the deployment of the application into different assemblies. The main goal is to ensure that the code on the server does not have to be shipped to the client. Figure 5.11 on the next page is a UML deployment diagram for the **HttpChannel/SOAP** example.

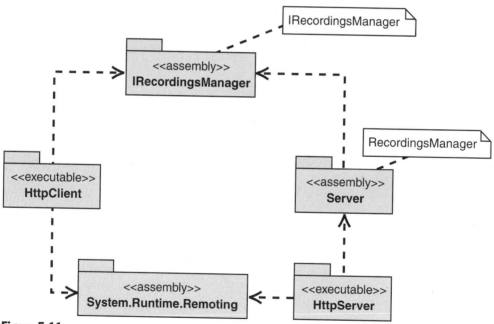

Figure 5.11
Structure for the HttpChannel/SOAP example

This example uses an assembly named **IRecordingsManager**, which is shared between the client and server. This assembly contains the **IRecordingsManager** interface, which defines the interface of the remote object that the client and server are sharing. In the example, the **IRecordingsManager** assembly is downloaded to the client.

Tests

It is relatively simple to write tests for the server in NUnit. You retrieve the object from the server and call methods as if they were local objects. The following class tests the **HttpServer** class:

```
HttpServerFixture.cs
using System;
using System.Data;
using System.Runtime.Remoting;
using System.Runtime.Remoting.Channels;
using System.Runtime.Remoting.Channels.Http;
using NUnit.Framework;

[TestFixture]
public class HttpServerFixture
{
    private IRecordingsManager mgr;
    private HttpChannel channel;
    private DataSet dataSet;

    [SetUp]
    public void LoadDataSet()
    {
        channel = new HttpChannel();
        ChannelServices.RegisterChannel(channel);

        mgr = (IRecordingsManager)
            Activator.GetObject(typeof(IRecordingsManager),
            "http://localhost:8100/RecordingsManager.soap");

        dataSet = mgr.GetRecordings();
    }

    [Test]
    public void RetrieveDataSet()
    {
        DataTable recording = dataSet.Tables["recording"];
        Assertion.AssertEquals(4,recording.Rows.Count);

        DataRow row = recording.Rows[0];
        string title = (string)row["title"];
        Assertion.AssertEquals("Up", title.Trim());
```

```
    }

    [TearDown]
    public void Release()
    {
        ChannelServices.UnregisterChannel(channel);
    }
}
```

Resulting Context

Using server-activated objects to implement *Broker* with .NET remoting results in a number of benefits and liabilities.

Benefits

.NET remoting provides a fully featured distributed object model with full common language runtime semantics running on the client and server. You do not lose any fidelity between client and server. The example demonstrated passing the complicated type, **System.Data.DataSet** between the client and server. This would not be possible without having the common language runtime on both sides of the connection.

Liabilities

Some of the *Broker* benefits are offset by the following potential liabilities:

- **Remote objects**. You cannot forget that these are remote objects. Even though they look like local objects, there is still overhead involved in marshaling data back and forth from the server. Keep in mind that a remote call can be at least 1000 times slower than a local call in the common language runtime. Therefore, you do not want to make more calls than necessary. This desire to minimize round-trips may cause you not to use the finest granularity in regards to the interface.

- **Deployment complexity**. When using server-activated objects as described in the examples, the objects must have been registered prior to the client asking for them. This makes deployment more complex.

- **Limited interoperability**. You can use .NET remoting to build Web services. However, you must pare down your endpoints to the simplest data types. For example, if you want interoperability with other Web service toolkits, you must restrict parameters to built-in simple types and your own data types (don't use .NET Framework types like **DataSet**), and use server-activated objects.

- **More complicated**. Compared to Web services, .NET remoting is more difficult to learn, implement, and debug.

Security Considerations

To use the security features available with Microsoft Internet Information Services (IIS) (for example, standard HTTP authentication schemes include Basic, Digest, digital certificates, and even Microsoft .NET Passport), you must use an HTTP-based application hosted in IIS with ASP.NET. Using any other transport protocol or using the **HttpChannel** outside of IIS requires you to provide a security mechanism.

Operational Considerations

The following is a summary of a performance comparison that appears in the MSDN® article, "Performance Comparison: .NET Remoting vs. ASP.NET Web Services" [Dhawan02]. The article concludes that you can achieve the highest performance by using the TCP channel and binary serialization with a Windows Service host. This configuration transmits binary data over raw TCP sockets, which is more efficient than HTTP. Performance is 60 percent faster than with the slowest approach, which is **HttpChannel** using SOAP serialization hosted in IIS with ASP.NET.

Hosting in IIS is slower because it involves an extra process hop from IIS (Inetinfo.exe) to Aspnet_wp.exe. However, if you choose to host your channel without IIS and ASP.NET, you will need to provide your own mechanisms for authentication, authorization, and privacy.

Related Patterns

For more information, see the following related patterns:

- *Broker*
- *Proxy* [Gamma95]

Acknowledgments

[Dhawan02] Dhawan, Priya. "Performance Comparison: .NET Remoting vs. ASP.NET Web Services." *MSDN Library*, September 2002. Available at: *http://msdn.microsoft.com/library/default.asp?url=/library/en-us/dnbda/html /bdadotnetarch14.asp*.

[Crocker02] Crocker, Olsen, and Jezierski. "Designing Data Tier Components and Passing Data Through Tiers." *MSDN Library*, August 2002. Available at: *http://msdn.microsoft.com/library/default.asp?url=/library/en-us/dnbda/html/boagag.asp*.

Implementing Broker with .NET Remoting Using Client-Activated Objects

Context

You are building an application in .NET that requires the use of distributed objects, the lifetimes of which are controlled by the client. Your requirements include the ability to pass objects by value or reference, whether those objects reside on the same computer, on different computers in the same local area network (LAN), or on different computers in a wide area network (WAN).

Implementation Strategy

This pattern presents two implementations of client-activated objects in .NET remoting. The main difference between client-activated objects (CAO) and server-activated objects (SAO) is what controls the lifetime of the remote object. In the CAO scenario, the client controls the lifetime; in the SAO scenario, the server controls the lifetime. The example used here is similar in functionality to the example used in *Implementing Broker in .NET Using Server-Activated Objects*. The first implementation uses client activation as it is described in the .NET documentation and samples. This implementation demonstrates the capabilities of client-activated objects; however, they do have some drawbacks. The second implementation, known as the hybrid approach, resolves these problems.

Client-Activated Object Implementation

The **RecordingsManager** class has a method named **GetRecordings**, which retrieves a list of recordings from a database and returns the result in **DataSet**. This class extends the **MarshalByRefObject** class to ensure that in a remoting scenario a proxy object is used instead of copying the object from the server to the client. The functionality described here is identical to that of the example described in *Implementing Broker in .NET Using Server-Activated Objects*.

RecordingsManager.cs

The following sample shows the **RecordingsManager** class, which is responsible for retrieving **DataSet** from the database:

```
using System;
using System.Data;
using System.Data.SqlClient;

public class RecordingsManager : MarshalByRefObject
{
```

```
public DataSet GetRecordings()
{
    String selectCmd = "select * from Recording";

    SqlConnection myConnection = new SqlConnection(
        "server=(local);database=recordings;Trusted_Connection=yes");
    SqlDataAdapter myCommand =
        new SqlDataAdapter(selectCmd, myConnection);

    DataSet ds = new DataSet();
    myCommand.Fill(ds, "Recording");
    return ds;
    }
}
```

HttpServer.cs

The following code configures the server to allow for client-activated objects to be created using the **new** operator. Instead of actually registering an instance (as the SAO example demonstrates), this code configures the server with an application name and the type of the object that will be created. The URL for the remote object is *http://localhost:8100/RecordingsServer*. Behind the scenes, an SAO is automatically created by the framework on localhost. This SAO is responsible for accepting requests from clients and creating the objects when the client requests them.

```
using System;
using System.Runtime.Remoting;
using System.Runtime.Remoting.Channels;
using System.Runtime.Remoting.Channels.Http;


public class HttpServer
{
    static void Main(string[] args)
    {
        HttpChannel channel = new HttpChannel(8100);
        ChannelServices.RegisterChannel(channel);

        RemotingConfiguration.ApplicationName = "RecordingsServer";
        RemotingConfiguration.RegisterActivatedServiceType(
            typeof(RecordingsManager));

        Console.WriteLine("Recordings Server Started");
        Console.ReadLine();
    }
}
```

HttpClient.cs

To be able to the use the **new** operator and have the remoting framework create a remote object, as opposed to a local object, you must first associate the type of the remote object with the URL that was specified when the server set the **ApplicationName** property. This example defines **ApplicationName** as **RecordingsServer** and uses port 8100 on localhost.

```
using System;
using System.Data;
using System.Runtime.Remoting;
using System.Runtime.Remoting.Channels;
using System.Runtime.Remoting.Channels.Http;

class HttpClient
{
    [STAThread]
    static void Main(string[] args)
    {
        HttpChannel channel = new HttpChannel();
        ChannelServices.RegisterChannel(channel);

        RemotingConfiguration.RegisterActivatedClientType(
            typeof(RecordingsManager),
            "http://localhost:8100/RecordingsServer");

        RecordingsManager mgr = new RecordingsManager();

        Console.WriteLine("Client.main(): Reference acquired");

        DataSet ds = mgr.GetRecordings();
        Console.WriteLine("Recordings Count: {0}",
            ds.Tables["recording"].Rows.Count);
    }
}
```

Registering the remote object associates the type of the object with the URL. After this occurs, the call to **new** creates a remote object on the server. This object looks like any other object in the code.

This implementation allows for direct creation of remote objects under the control of the client. It also demonstrates that after the client is configured, object creation is identical to local object creation using the **new** operator. However, it has a major flaw. You cannot use the shared interface approach described in the SAO pattern. This means that you must ship the compiled objects to the client. For another alternative that uses SoapSuds, see *Advanced .NET Remoting* [Ingo02].

Note: Shipping compiled server objects violates the general principle of distributed objects. It is also undesirable due to deployment and versioning issues.

To address some of these issues, the following implementation describes a hybrid approach that uses an SAO to create objects. This approach provides the client with the ability to control the lifetime of the object without the server code having to be shipped to the client.

Hybrid Approach

The hybrid approach involves the **RecordingsFactory** SAO, which provides methods to create the **RecordingsManager** CAO. (If you are not familiar with the SAO examples, see *Implementing Broker with .NET Remoting Using Server-Activated Objects*.) The following class diagram describes the overall solution.

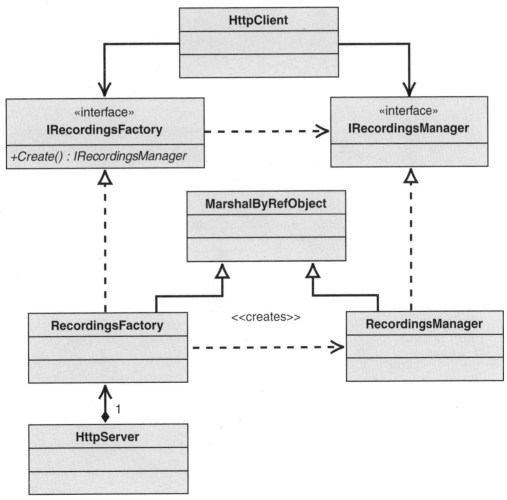

Figure 5.12
Structure of the hybrid approach

This implementation uses the shared interface approach described in the SAO examples. The two interfaces, **IRecordingsManager** and **IRecordingsFactory**, are in an assembly that is shared between the client and the server. **IRecordingsFactory** has a single **Create** method, which returns an object to implement the **IRecordingsManager** interface. This is an example of the *AbstractFactory* [Gamma95] pattern. Because the client only depends on the interfaces, there is no need to ship the server code. When a client needs a **IRecordingsManager** object, it calls the **Create** method on an instance of **IRecordingsFactory**. This allows the client to be in control of the lifetime of the **IRecordingsManager** object without needing its implementation. The two interfaces from the shared assembly are as follows.

IRecordingsManager.cs

The following sample shows the **IRecordingsManager** interface:

```
using System;
using System.Data;

public interface IRecordingsManager
{
    DataSet GetRecordings();
}
```

IRecordingsFactory.cs

The following sample shows the **IRecordingsFactory** interface:

```
using System;

public interface IRecordingsFactory
{
    IRecordingsManager Create();
}
```

The server implementations of these objects, **RecordingsFactory** and **RecordingsManager**, are straightforward and are contained in their own assembly, named **Server**.

RecordingsFactory.cs

This class extends **MarshalByRefObject** and implements the **IRecordingsFactory** interface:

```
using System;

public class RecordingsFactory : MarshalByRefObject, IRecordingsFactory
{
    public IRecordingsManager Create()
    {
        return new RecordingsManager();
    }
}
```

The **RecordingsFactory** object is the server-activated object. This implementation simply calls **new** on the **RecordingsManager** type. This **RecordingsManager** object is created on the server and is returned, not as a **RecordingsManager** object, but as the **IRecordingsManager** interface. This mechanism allows the client to depend on the interface rather than the implementation.

RecordingsManager.cs

The only change required in the **RecordingsManager** class is that it now implements the **IRecordingsManager** interface.

```
using System;
using System.Reflection;
using System.Data;
using System.Data.SqlClient;

public class RecordingsManager : MarshalByRefObject, IRecordingsManager
{
    public DataSet GetRecordings()
    {
        Console.WriteLine("Assembly: {0} - filling a request",
            Assembly.GetEntryAssembly().GetName().Name);

        String selectCmd = "select * from Recording";

        SqlConnection myConnection = new SqlConnection(
            "server=(local);database=recordings;Trusted_Connection=yes");
        SqlDataAdapter myCommand =
            new SqlDataAdapter(selectCmd, myConnection);

        DataSet ds = new DataSet();
        myCommand.Fill(ds, "Recording");
        return ds;
    }
}
```

HttpServer.cs

The server initialization code in the hybrid approach configures the remoting framework for a server-activated **RecordingsFactory** object. The activation scheme is independent of the channel and the protocol used, so they remain the same as before (HTTP protocol on port 8100).

```
using System;
using System.Runtime.Remoting;
using System.Runtime.Remoting.Channels;
using System.Runtime.Remoting.Channels.Http;


public class HttpServer
{
```

```
static void Main(string[] args)
{
    HttpChannel channel = new HttpChannel(8100);
    ChannelServices.RegisterChannel(channel);

    RemotingConfiguration.RegisterWellKnownServiceType(
        typeof(RecordingsFactory),
        "RecordingsFactory.soap",
        WellKnownObjectMode.Singleton);

    Console.ReadLine();
}
}
```

In this code, the **RecordingsFactory** type is associated with the URL:
http://localhost:8100/RecordingsFactory.soap.

HttpClient.cs

The client code demonstrates the hybrid nature of this approach. You first use the
Activator.GetObject method to retrieve the **IRecordingsFactory** object from the
server. Using this server-activated object, you then call the **Create** method to
instantiate an **IRecordingsManager** object. This newly instantiated object is created
on the server but is a remote object.

```
using System;
using System.Data;
using System.Runtime.Remoting;
using System.Runtime.Remoting.Channels;
using System.Runtime.Remoting.Channels.Http;

public class HttpClient
{
    [STAThread]
    static void Main(string[] args)
    {
        HttpChannel channel = new HttpChannel();
        ChannelServices.RegisterChannel(channel);

        IRecordingsFactory factory = (IRecordingsFactory)
            Activator.GetObject(typeof(IRecordingsFactory),
            "http://localhost:8100/RecordingsFactory.soap");

        Console.WriteLine("Client.main(): Factory acquired");

        IRecordingsManager mgr = factory.Create();
        DataSet ds = mgr.GetRecordings();
        Console.WriteLine("Recordings Count: {0}",
            ds.Tables["recording"].Rows.Count);
    }
}
```

Resulting Context

Using client-activated objects to implement *Broker* with .NET remoting results in the following benefits and liabilities:

Benefits

- **Distributed object model**. .NET remoting provides a fully featured distributed object model with full common language runtime semantics running on the client and server. You do not lose any fidelity between client and server. The example demonstrated passing the complicated type, **System.Data.DataSet**, between the client and server. This would not be possible without having the common language runtime on both sides of the connection.

- **Construction parameters**. The objects in both the client-activated and hybrid implementations allow for passing constructor arguments when the objects are created.

Liabilities

- **Remote objects**. You cannot forget that these are remote objects. Even though they look like local objects, there is still overhead involved in marshaling data back and forth from the server. Keep in mind that a remote call can be at least 1000 times slower than a local call in the common language runtime. Therefore, you do not want to make more calls than necessary. This desire to minimize round-trips may cause you not to use the finest granularity in regards to the interface.

- **No shared assembly**. In the CAO approach, you cannot use the shared assembly approach with interfaces. Instead, you must ship the implementation to the client or use SoapSuds to extract the metadata.

- **Deployment complexity**. When using server-activated objects as described in the the hybrid approach, objects must have been registered prior to the client asking for them. This makes deployment more complex.

- **Limited interoperability**. You can use .NET remoting to build Web services. However, you must pare down your endpoints to the simplest data types. For example, if you want interoperability with other Web services toolkits, you must restrict parameters to built-in simple types and your own data types (do not use .NET Framework types such as **DataSet**), and use server-activated objects.

- **More complicated**. Compared to Web services, .NET remoting is more difficult to learn, implement, and debug.

Security Considerations

To use the security features available with Microsoft Internet Information Services (IIS) (for example, standard HTTP authentication schemes include Basic, Digest, digital certificates, and even Microsoft .NET Passport) you must use an HTTP-based application hosted in IIS with ASP.NET. Using any other transport protocol or using the **HttpChannel** outside of IIS requires you to provide a security mechanism.

Operational Considerations

The following is a summary of a performance comparison that appears in the MSDN® article, "Performance Comparison: .NET Remoting vs. ASP.NET Web Services" [Dhawan02]. The article concludes that you can achieve the highest performance by using the TCP channel and binary serialization with a Windows Service host. This configuration transmits binary data over raw TCP sockets, which is more efficient than HTTP. Performance is 60 percent faster than with the slowest approach, which is **HttpChannel** using SOAP serialization hosted in IIS with ASP.NET.

Hosting in IIS is slower because it involves an extra process hop from IIS (Inetinfo.exe) to Aspnet_wp.exe. However, if you choose to host your channel without IIS and ASP.NET, you will need to provide your own mechanisms for authentication, authorization, and privacy.

Related Patterns

For more information, see the following related patterns:
- *Broker*
- *Proxy* [Gamma95]

Acknowledgments

[Ingo02] Rammer, Ingo. *Advanced .NET Remoting*. Apress, 2002.

[Dhawan02] Dhawan, Priya. "Performance Comparison: .NET Remoting vs. ASP.NET Web Services." *MSDN Library*, September 2002. Available at: *http://msdn.microsoft.com/library/default.asp?url=/library/en-us/dnbda/html /bdadotnetarch14.asp*.

Data Transfer Object

Context

You are designing a distributed application, and to satisfy a single client request, you find yourself making multiple calls to a remote interface, which increases the response time beyond acceptable levels.

Problem

How do you preserve the simple semantics of a procedure call interface without being subject to the latency issues inherent in remote communication?

Forces

When communicating with a remote object, consider the following tradeoffs:

- Remote calls (those that have to cross the network) are slow. Although many remote invocation frameworks can hide the complexities of making a remote call, they cannot eliminate the steps that are required for the communication to take place. For example, the remote object location has to be looked up, and a connection to the remote computer has to be made before the data can be serialized into a byte stream, possibly encrypted, and then transmitted to the remote computer.

- When considering the performance of networks, you have to look at both latency and throughput. In simplified terms, *latency* describes the time that passes before the first byte of data reaches the destination. *Throughput* describes how many bytes of data are sent across the network within a certain time period (for example, 1 second). In modern IP routing-based networks (for example, the Internet), latency can be a bigger factor than throughput. That means it may take almost the same amount of time to transmit 10 bytes of data as it takes to transmit 1,000 bytes of data. This effect is particularly pronounced when using connectionless protocols such as HTTP. Faster networks can often increase the throughput, but latency is much more difficult to reduce.

- When designing an object interface, good practices are to hide much of the information inside an object and to provide a set of fine-grained methods for accessing and manipulating that information. *Fine-grained* means that each method should be responsible for a single, fairly small, and atomic piece of functionality. This approach simplifies programming and provides better abstraction from the object internals, thereby increasing potential for reuse. This must be balanced against the fact that using finer-grained methods implies invoking more methods to perform a high-level task. Typically, the overhead of these extra function calls is acceptable when the methods are invoked within the same process; however, the overhead can become severe when these methods are invoked across process and network boundaries.

- The best way to avoid latency issues that are inherent in remote calls is to make fewer calls and to pass more data with each call. One way to accomplish this is to declare the remote method with a long list of parameters. This allows the client to pass more information to the remote component in a single call. Doing so makes programming against this interface error-prone, however, because arguments are likely to call parameters of the external method solely by position in the call statement. For example, if a remote method accepts 10 string parameters, it is easy for the developer to pass arguments in the wrong order. The compiler will not be able to detect such a mistake.

- A long parameter list does not help return more information from the remote call to the client because most programming languages limit the return type of a method call to a single parameter. Coincidentally, the return is often when the most data is transmitted. For example, many user interfaces transmit a small amount of information but expect a large result set in return.

Solution

Create a data transfer object (DTO) that holds all data that is required for the remote call. Modify the remote method signature to accept the DTO as the single parameter and to return a single DTO parameter to the client. After the calling application receives the DTO and stores it as a local object, the application can make a series of individual procedure calls to the DTO without incurring the overhead of remote calls. Martin Fowler describes this pattern in *Patterns of Enterprise Application Architecture* [Fowler03].

The following figure shows how a client application makes a sequence of remote calls to retrieve the various elements of a customer name.

process boundary

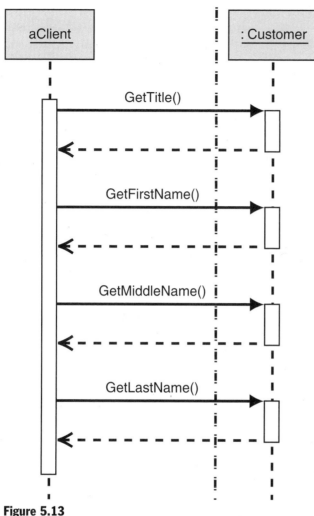

Figure 5.13
Remote calls without a DTO

A DTO allows the remote object to return the whole customer name to the client in a single remote call. In this example, doing so would reduce the number of calls from four to one. Instead of making multiple remote calls, the client makes a single call and then interacts with the DTO locally (see Figure 5.14 on the next page).

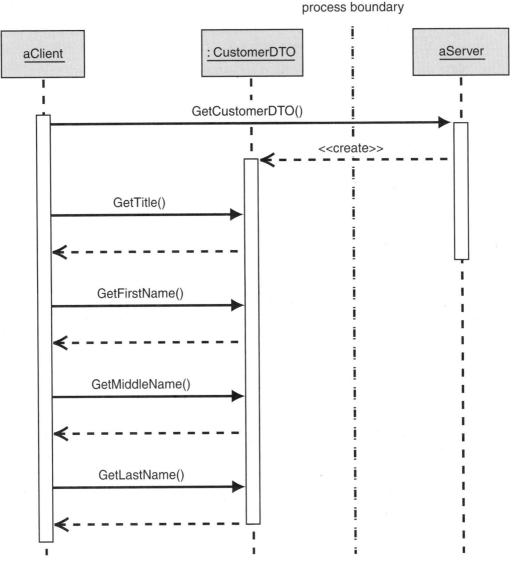

Figure 5.14
Reducing the number of calls by using a DTO

A DTO is a simple container for a set of aggregated data that needs to be transferred across a process or network boundary. It should contain no business logic and limit its behavior to activities such as internal consistency checking and basic validation. Be careful not to make the DTO depend on any new classes as a result of implementing these methods.

When designing a data transfer object, you have two primary choices: use a generic collection or create a custom object with explicit getter and setter methods.

A generic collection has the advantage that you only need a single class to fit any data transfer purpose throughout the whole application. Furthermore, collection classes (for example, simple arrays or hashmaps) are built into almost all language libraries, so you do not have to code new classes at all. The main drawback of using collection objects for DTOs is that the client has to access fields inside the collection either by position index (in the case of a simple array) or by element name (in the case of a keyed collection). Also, collections store items of the same type (usually the most generic **Object** type), which can lead to subtle but fatal coding errors that cannot be detected at compile time.

Creating custom classes for each DTO provides strongly-typed objects that the client application can access exactly like any other object, so they provide compile-time checking and support code editor features such as Microsoft® IntelliSense® technology. The main drawback is that you could end up having to code a large number of these classes if your application makes a lot of remote calls.

A number of options try to combine the benefits of the two approaches. The first is code generation that generates the source code for custom DTO classes off existing metadata, such as an Extensible Markup Language (XML) schema. The second approach is to provide a more powerful collection that is generic but stores relationship and data type information along with the raw data. The Microsoft ADO.NET **DataSet** supports both approaches (see *Implementing Data Transfer Object in .NET with a DataSet*).

Now that you have a DTO class, you need to populate it with data. In most instances, data inside a DTO is derived from more than one domain object. Because the DTO has no behavior, it cannot extract the data from the domain objects. This is fine, because keeping the DTO unaware of the domain objects enables you to reuse the DTO in different contexts. Likewise, you do not want the domain objects to know about the DTO because that may mean that changing the DTO would require changing code in the domain logic, which would lead to a maintenance nightmare.

The best solution is to use the *Assembler* pattern [Fowler03], which creates DTOs from business objects and vice versa. *Assembler* is a specialized instance of the *Mapper* pattern also mentioned in *Patterns of Enterprise Application Architecture* [Fowler03].

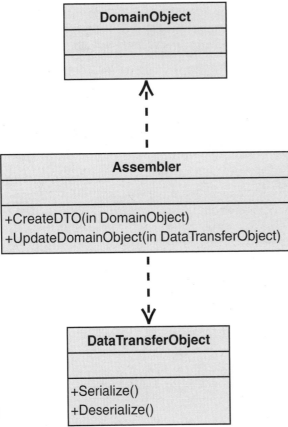

Figure 5.15
Using an Assembler *to load data into the DTO*

The key characteristic of *Assembler* is that the DTO and the domain object do not depend upon each other. This decouples the two objects. The downside is that **Assembler** depends on both the DTO and the domain object. Any change to these classes may result in having to change the **Assembler** class.

Example

See *Implementing Data Transfer Object in .NET with a DataSet*

Testing Considerations

DTOs are simple objects that should not contain any business logic that would require testing. You do, however, need to test data aggregation for each DTO. Depending on your serialization mechanism, testing may or may not be required for each DTO. If serialization is part of the framework, you need to test only one DTO. If not, use a generic reflection mechanism so that you do not need to test the serialization of each DTO.

DTOs also contribute to the testability of remote functions. Having the results of a remote method available in an object instance makes it easy to pass this data to a test module or to compare it with the desired outcome.

Security Considerations

Ideally, data obtained from untrusted sources, such as user input from a Web page, should be cleansed and validated before being placed into a DTO. Doing so enables you to consider the data in the DTO relatively safe, which simplifies future interactions with the DTO.

The security credentials of the processes and associated users receiving the DTO are also important to consider. DTOs often contain a large amount of information that is assembled from many different sources. Are all users of the DTO authorized to access all the information contained within it? The best way to ensure that users are authorized is to populate the DTO with only the specific data that is authorized by the users' security credentials. Try to avoid making the DTO responsible for its own security. This increases the number of dependences the DTO has on other classes, which means these classes must be deployed to all nodes on which the DTO is used. It also spreads the security functionality across more classes, which increases security risk and negatively affects flexibility and maintainability.

Resulting Context

Data Transfer Object results in the following benefits and liabilities:

Benefits

- **Reduced number of remote calls**. By transmitting more data in a single remote call, the application can reduce the number of remote calls.

- **Improved performance**. Remote calls can slow an application drastically. Reducing the number of calls is one of the best ways to improve performance. In most scenarios, a remote call carrying a larger amount of data takes virtually the same time as a call that carries only a small amount of data.

- **Hidden internals**. Passing more data back and forth in a single call also more effectively hides the internals of a remote application behind a coarse-grained interface. This is the main motivation behind the *Remote Facade* pattern [Fowler03].

- **Discovery of business objects**. In some cases, defining a DTO can help in the discovery of meaningful business objects. When creating custom classes to serve as DTOs, you often notice groupings of elements that are presented to a user or another system as a cohesive set of information. Often these groupings serve as useful prototypes for objects that describe the business domain that the application deals with.

- **Testability**. Encapsulating all parameters in a serializable object can improve testability. For example, you could read DTOs from an XML file and call remote functions to test them. Likewise, it would be easy to serialize the results back into XML format and compare the XML document to the desired outcome without having to create lengthy comparison scripts.

Liabilities

- **Possible class explosion**. If you chose to use strongly-typed DTOs, you may have to create one (or two, if you consider the return value) DTO for each remote method. Even in a coarse-grained interface, this could lead to a large number of classes. It can be hard to code and manage this number of classes. Using automatic code generation can alleviate some of this problem.

- **Additional computation**. The act of translating from one data format on the server to a byte stream that can be transported across the network and back into an object format inside the client application can introduce a fair amount of overhead. Typically, you aggregate the data from multiple sources into the single DTO on the server. To improve efficiency of remote calls across the network, you have to perform additional computation on either end to aggregate and serialize information.

- **Additional coding effort**. Passing parameters to a method can be done in a single line. Using a DTO requires instantiating a new object and calling setters and getters for each parameter. This code can be tedious to write.

Related Patterns

For more information, see the following related patterns:

- *Remote Facade*. The *Data Transfer Object* pattern is typically used in conjunction with a coarse-grained *Remote Facade* to reduce the number of remote calls.

- *Mapper* [Fowler03]. A *Mapper* is the recommended technique to load the DTO with data elements from the domain objects.

- *Value Object*. Some books refer to *Data Transfer Object* as *Value Object*. This usage is no longer considered correct. For more information, see *Patterns of Enterprise Application Architecture* [Fowler03].

Acknowledgments

[Fowler03] Fowler, Martin. *Patterns of Enterprise Application Architecture*. Addison-Wesley, 2003.

Implementing Data Transfer Object in .NET with a DataSet

Context

You are implementing a distributed application in the .NET Framework. The client application displays a form that requires making multiple calls to an ASP.NET Web service to satisfy a single user request. Based on performance measurements, you have found that making multiple calls degrades application performance. To increase performance, you would like to retrieve all the data that the user request requires in a single call to the Web service.

Background

Note: The following is the same sample application that is described in *Implementing Data Transfer Object in .NET with a Typed DataSet*.

The following is a simplified Web application that communicates with an ASP.NET Web service to deliver recording and track information to the user. The Web service in turn calls a database to provide the data that the client requests. The following sequence diagram depicts the interaction among the application, the Web service, and the database for a typical page.

Figure 5.16 illustrates the sequence of calls needed to fulfill the entire user request. The first call retrieves the recording information, and the second call retrieves the track information for the specified recording. In addition, the Web service must make separate calls to the database to retrieve the required information.

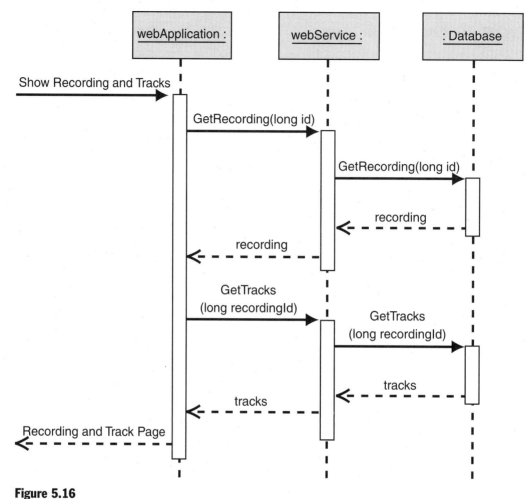

Figure 5.16
Behavior of a typical user request

Database Schema

The schema that is used in the example shown in Figure 5.17 depicts a **recording** record that has a one-to-many relationship with a **track** record.

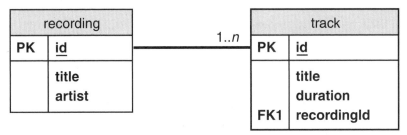

Figure 5.17
Schema for sample application

Implementing a DTO

One way to improve the performance of this user request is to package all the required data into a data transfer object (DTO) that can be sent with a single call to the Web service. This reduces the overhead associated with two separate calls and allows you to use a single connection with the database to retrieve both the recording and the track information. For a detailed description of how this improves performance, see the *Data Transfer Object* pattern.

Implementation Strategy

There are a number of possible implementations for *Data Transfer Object* in the .NET Framework. To use a DTO, you have to complete the following four steps. The good news is that the **DataSet** class that is built into the .NET Framework already takes care of three (actually, more like three and one-half) of the following steps:

1. Design the DTO class. One step in this process is to decide what data types and structures to support. The **DataSet** is generic enough to use for any DTO purpose; therefore, you do not need to design a new class for each DTO.

2. Write or generate the code for the data transfer class. **DataSet** is part of the .NET library, so you do not have to code it.

3. Create an instance of the DTO, and fill it with data. This is the only step that you have to program. **DataSet** provides convenient functions to load the DTO with data from a database or Extensible Markup Language (XML) document, greatly simplifying this task.

4. Serialize the DTO into a byte or character stream (and back) so that the content of the object can be sent over the network. The DTO has built-in serialization functions.

A **DataSet** holds a collection of **DataTable** objects. Each **DataTable** object represents the data that was retrieved using a SELECT statement or stored procedure execution. The data in a **DataSet** can be written out or read as XML. A **DataSet** also stores schema information, constraints, and relationships among multiple **DataTable** objects. Through a **DataSet**, you can add, edit, and delete data; therefore, a **DataSet** makes an ideal data transfer object in the .NET Framework, especially when you add the requirement to display the **DataSet** in controls on a form.

Because the .NET Framework already implements the **DataSet**, the remainder of this implementation strategy focuses on how to fill a **DataSet** from a data source and how to use the resulting **DataSet** in the Web Form.

Filling a DataSet from the Database

This example demonstrates how to fill the **DataSet** with the data that the sample application requires by using a database query. This includes the **recording** record as well as all the **track** records that are associated by the **recordingId**.

Assembler.cs

The **Assembler** class is a specialized instance of the *Mapper* pattern [Fowler03]. Its purpose is to isolate the DTO from the rest of the system. The following code example shows how the DTO is created from the database:

```
using System;
using System.Data;
using System.Data.SqlClient;

public class Assembler
{
    public static DataSet CreateRecordingDto(long id)
    {
        string selectCmd =
            String.Format(
            "select * from recording where id = {0}",
            id);

        SqlConnection myConnection =
            new SqlConnection(
            "server=(local);database=recordings;Trusted_Connection=yes");
        SqlDataAdapter myCommand = new SqlDataAdapter(selectCmd,
            myConnection);

        DataSet ds = new DataSet();
        myCommand.Fill(ds, "recording");

        String trackSelect =
            String.Format(
            "select * from Track where recordingId = {0} order by Id",
            id);
```

```
        SqlDataAdapter trackCommand =
            new SqlDataAdapter(trackSelect, myConnection);
        trackCommand.Fill(ds, "track");

        ds.Relations.Add("RecordingTracks",
            ds.Tables["recording"].Columns["id"],
            ds.Tables["track"].Columns["recordingId"]);

        return ds;
    }
}
```

This code has some interesting aspects. You need to execute queries to fill both the recording and track tables. You must also explicitly define the relationship between the two tables even though the relationship is defined in the database.

Note: The example shown here does not describe the only way to fill the **DataSet**. There are many ways to retrieve this data from the database. For example, you could use a stored procedure.

Using a DataSet in an ASP.NET Page

When using the .NET user interface controls (Web Forms or Windows Forms) a **DataSet** is a natural choice. For example, the sample application page uses two **DataGrid** controls, **RecordingGrid** and **TrackGrid**. Because you need to retrieve both the recording and the tracks for the recording, it makes sense to use a single **DataSet** that contains multiple tables.

Given the **DataSet** that was built by the **Assembler** class, this code displays how to assign a **DataSet** to the **DataSource** property of the two grid controls:

```
using System;
using System.Data;

public class RetrieveForm : System.Web.UI.Page
{
    private RecordingCatalog catalog = new RecordingCatalog();

    // …

    protected void Button1_Click(object sender, System.EventArgs e)
    {
        string stringId = TextBox1.Text;
        long id = Convert.ToInt64(stringId);

        DataSet ds = catalog.Get(id);
        RecordingGrid.DataSource = ds.Tables["recording"];
        RecordingGrid.DataBind();

        TrackGrid.DataSource = ds.Tables["track"];
        TrackGrid.DataBind();
    }
}
```

Tests

Because the **DataSet** is provided by the .NET Framework, you do not need to write tests to verify that it functions correctly. You could argue this point, but you should assume that classes provided by the Framework are innocent until proven guilty; therefore, what you need to test is the code that assembles the **DataSet**, which in this case is the **Assembler** class.

RecordingAssemblerFixture.cs

This fixture tests that the contents of the **DataSet** are filled and that the relationship between recording and track is defined correctly:

```
using NUnit.Framework;
using System.Data;

[TestFixture]
public class RecordingAssemblerFixture
{
    private DataSet ds;
    private DataTable recordingTable;
    private DataRelation relationship;
    private DataRow[] trackRows;

    [SetUp]
    public void Init()
    {
        ds = Assembler.CreateRecordingDto(1234);
        recordingTable = ds.Tables["recording"];
        relationship = recordingTable.ChildRelations[0];
        trackRows = recordingTable.Rows[0].GetChildRows(relationship);
    }

    [Test]
    public void RecordingCount()
    {
        Assert.Equals(1, recordingTable.Rows.Count);
    }

    [Test]
    public void RecordingTitle()
    {
        DataRow recording = recordingTable.Rows[0];
        string title = (string)recording["title"];
        Assert.Equals("Up", title.Trim());
    }


    [Test]
    public void RecordingTrackRelationship()
    {
        Assert.Equals(10, trackRows.Length);
    }
```

```
[Test]
public void TrackContent()
{
    DataRow track = trackRows[0];

    string title = (string)track["title"];
    Assert.Equals("Darkness", title.Trim());
}

[Test]
public void InvalidRecording()
{
    DataSet ds = Assembler.CreateRecordingDto(-1);
    Assert.Equals(0, ds.Tables["recording"].Rows.Count);
    Assert.Equals(0, ds.Tables["track"].Rows.Count);
}
}
```

These tests describe how to access the individual elements of the **DataSet**. The tests themselves demonstrate some of the issues, in that you need to know the column names as well as the types of the objects. Because of this direct dependency, this code must change if the database schema changes. These types of issues are mitigated when you use a typed DataSet. For more information, see *Implementing Data Transfer Object in .NET with a Typed DataSet*.

Resulting Context

The following are the benefits and liabilities related to using a **DataSet** as a data transfer object:

Benefits

- **Development tool support**. The **DataSet** class is implemented in ADO.NET, so there is no need to design and implement the data transfer object. There is also extensive support in the Microsoft Visual Studio® version 6.0 development system for automating the creation and filling of **DataSet** objects.

- **Integration with controls**. A **DataSet** works directly with the built-in controls in Windows Forms and Web Forms, making it a logical choice as a data transfer object.

- **Serialization**. The **DataSet** comes with the ability to serialize itself into XML. Not only is the content serialized but the schema for the content is also present in the serialization.

- **Disconnected database model**. The **DataSet** is a snapshot of the current contents of the database. This means that you can alter the contents of the **DataSet** and subsequently use the **DataSet** as the means to update the database.

Liabilities

- **Interoperability**. Because the **DataSet** class is part of ADO.NET, it is not the best choice for a data transfer object in cases requiring interoperability with clients that are not running the .NET Framework. You can still use **DataSet**, however, the client will be forced to parse the XML and build its own representation. If interoperability is a requirement, see *Implementing Data Transfer Object in .NET with Serialized Objects*.

- **Stale data**. The **DataSet**, as stated previously, is disconnected from the database. It is filled with a snapshot of the data in the database when it is constructed. This implies that the actual data in the database may be different from what is contained in the **DataSet**. For reading primarily static data, this is not a major issue. If the data is constantly changing, however, using a **DataSet** is not recommended.

- **Dependency on database schema**. Because the **DataSet** is most often filled from the database, any code that references the column names depends on the database schema. Also, because the programmer must explicitly code the relationships between tables, if a relationship changes in the database, the code also has to be modified.

- **Potential for performance degradation**. Instantiating and filling a **DataSet** can be expensive. Serializing and deserializing a **DataSet** can also be very time consuming. A good rule of thumb for using a **DataSet** is that a **DataSet** is a good choice when you are using more than one table or relying on the capability of the **DataSet** to update the database. If you are displaying the results from a single table and do not require the capabilities that a **DataSet** provides, you could consider using a **DataReader** to load strongly-typed objects, which may offer better performance.

- **Not type-safe**. The values that you receive from the **DataSet** may have to be cast to the correct data type. This requires you to determine what the types are supposed to be. This can be tedious and error-prone because you have to inspect the **DataSet** type information explicitly. A typed DataSet, as described in "Working with a Typed DataSet" [Microsoft02], alleviates this issue by generating a strongly-typed **DataSet** subclass that inherits from the generic **DataSet** class.

- **Proliferation of two-tiered architecture**. The convenience of using a **DataSet** can become a liability when it tempts developers to pass **DataSets** from the database directly to the user interface. This can couple the user interface tightly to the physical database schema. A number of mechanisms can help avoid this issue. For example, a **DataSet** can be filled from a stored procedure so that the **DataSet** structure is abstracted from the physical database schema. Alternatively, **DataSets** can be loaded from XML documents, which can be transformed using Extensible Stylesheet Language (XSL). This provides another level of indirection among user interface, business logic, and data storage.

Related Patterns

For more information, see the following related patterns:

- *Implementing Data Transfer Object in .NET with Serialized Objects.*
- *Implementing Data Transfer Object in .NET with a Typed DataSet.*
- *Assembler.* In *Patterns of Enterprise Application Architecture,* Fowler defines *Assembler* as a specialized instance of the *Mapper* pattern *[Fowler03].*

Acknowledgments

[Fowler03] Fowler, Martin. *Patterns of Enterprise Application Architecture.* Addison-Wesley, 2003.

[Powell03] Powell, Matt. "DataSets, Web Services, DiffGrams, Arrays, and Interoperability." *MSDN Library*, February, 2003. Available at: *http:// www.msdn.microsoft.com/library/default.asp?url=/library/en-us/dnservice/html /service02112003.asp.*

Implementing Data Transfer Object in .NET with a Typed DataSet

Context

You are implementing a distributed application with the .NET Framework. The client application displays a form that requires making multiple calls to an ASP.NET Web service to satisfy a single user request. Based on performance measurements you have found that making multiple calls degrades application performance. To increase performance, you would like to retrieve all the data that the user request requires in a single call to the Web service.

Background

Note: The following is the same sample application that is described in *Implementing Data Transfer Object in .NET with a DataSet*.

The following is a simplified Web application that communicates with an ASP.NET Web service to deliver recording and track information to the user. The Web service in turn calls a database to provide the data that the client requests. The following sequence diagram depicts the interaction among the application, the Web service, and the database for a typical page.

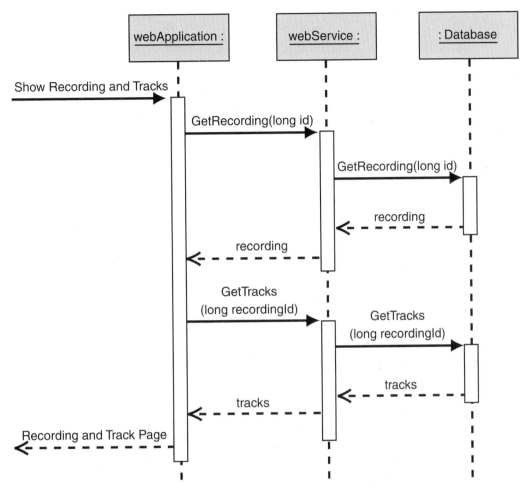

Figure 5.18
Behavior of a typical user request

Figure 5.18 illustrates the sequence of calls needed to fulfill the entire user request. The first call retrieves the recording information, and the second call retrieves the track information for the specified recording. In addition, the Web service must make separate calls to the database to retrieve the required information.

Database Schema

The schema that is used in the example shown in Figure 5.19 on the next page depicts a **recording** record that has a one-to-many relationship with a **track** record.

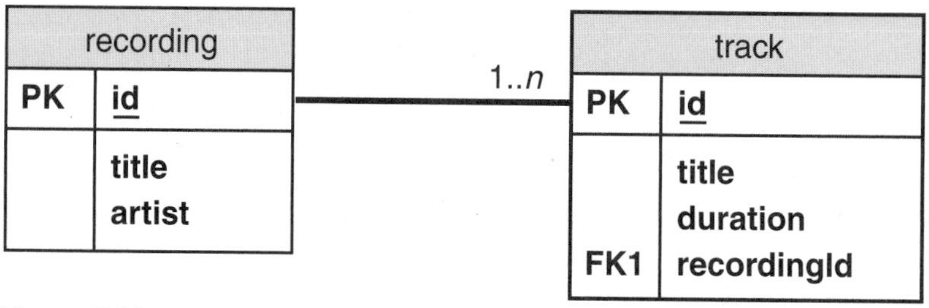

Figure 5.19
Schema for sample application

Implementing a DTO

One way to improve the performance of this user request is to package all the required data into a data transfer object (DTO) that can be sent with a single call to the Web service. This reduces the overhead associated with two separate calls and allows you to use a single connection with the database to retrieve both the recording and the track information. For a detailed description of how this improves performance, see the *Data Transfer Object* pattern.

Implementation Strategy

A typed **DataSet** is a generated subclass of **System.Data.DataSet**. You provide an XML schema file which is then used to generate a strongly-typed wrapper around the **DataSet**. The following two code samples illustrate the differences. The first sample is implemented with an ordinary **DataSet**:

```
DataTable dataTable = dataSet.Tables["recording"];
DataRow row = dataTable.Rows[0];
string artist = (string)row["artist"];
```

This sample indicates that you need to know the table and column names to access the tables and fields contained in the **DataSet**. You also have to know the return type of the Artist field to ensure that the correct cast is done. If you do not use the correct type, you will get a runtime error. The following is the same example implemented with a typed **DataSet**:

```
Recording recording = typedDataSet.Recordings[0];
string artist = recording.Artist;
```

This example demonstrates the benefits that the typed interface provides. You no longer have to refer to table or column by name and you do not have to know that the return type of the Artist column is a string. A typed **DataSet** defines a much more explicit interface that is verifiable at compile time instead of at runtime.

In addition to the strongly-typed interface a typed **DataSet** also can be used in all places a **DataSet** can be used; therefore, it also can be used as a DTO. It is loaded in a similar fashion as a **DataSet** and it can be serialized to and from XML. In comparison to an ordinary **DataSet** you do have to write and maintain an XML schema that describes the typed interface. The Microsoft Visual Studio® .NET development system provides a number of tools that simplify the creation and maintenance of the schema.

The rest of this implementation strategy outlines the steps required in creating a typed DataSet for the sample application just described.

Creating a Typed DataSet

A typed DataSet is generated from an XML schema. Visual Studio .NET provides a drag-and-drop tool which automates the creation of the schema (see Figure 5.20) and the generation of the typed DataSet classes. If you do not use Visual Studio.NET, you can write the XML schema and use a command-line tool called XSD.exe to generate the typed DataSet. For detailed instructions on both of these methods, see "Typed DataSets in ADO.NET" from the May 2001 issue of *.NET Developer* [Wildermuth02].

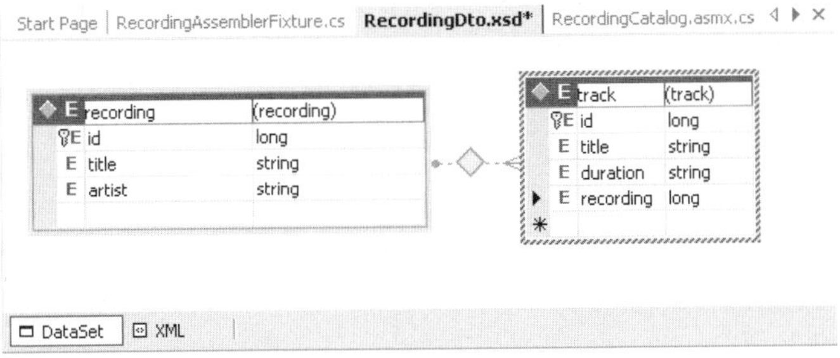

Figure 5.20
Visual Studio .NET DataSet file type

RecordingDto.xsd

The following is the XML schema for the DTO to be used in this example. It combines both the recording table along with its associated track records in a single typed DataSet named **RecordingDto**:

```xml
<?xml version="1.0" encoding="utf-8" ?>
<xs:schema id="RecordingDto" targetNamespace="http://msdn.microsoft.com/practices/
RecordingDto.xsd"
    elementFormDefault="qualified" attributeFormDefault="qualified" xmlns="http://
tempuri.org/RecordingDTO.xsd"
    xmlns:mstns="http://msdn.microsoft.com/practices/RecordingDto.xsd"
xmlns:xs="http://www.w3.org/2001/XMLSchema"
    xmlns:msdata="urn:schemas-microsoft-com:xml-msdata" xmlns:codegen="urn:schemas-
microsoft-com:xml-msprop">
    <xs:element name="RecordingDto" msdata:IsDataSet="true">
```

```
        <xs:complexType>
            <xs:choice maxOccurs="unbounded">
                <xs:element name="recording" codegen:typedName="Recording"
codegen:typedPlural="Recordings"
                    codegen:typedChildren="Track">
                    <xs:complexType>
                        <xs:sequence>
                            <xs:element name="id" type="xs:long" codegen:typedName="Id" /
>
                            <xs:element name="title" type="xs:string"
codegen:typedName="Title" />
                            <xs:element name="artist" type="xs:string"
codegen:typedName="Artist" />
                        </xs:sequence>
                    </xs:complexType>
                </xs:element>
                <xs:element name="track" codegen:typedName="Track"
codegen:typedPlural="Tracks" codegen:typedParent="Recording">
                    <xs:complexType>
                        <xs:sequence>
                            <xs:element name="id" type="xs:long" codegen:typedName="Id" /
>
                            <xs:element name="title" type="xs:string"
codegen:typedName="Title" />
                            <xs:element name="duration" type="xs:string"
codegen:typedName="Duration" />
                            <xs:element name="recordingId" type="xs:long"
codegen:typedName="RecordingId" />
                        </xs:sequence>
                    </xs:complexType>
                </xs:element>
            </xs:choice>
        </xs:complexType>
        <xs:unique name="RecordingDTOKey1" msdata:PrimaryKey="true">
            <xs:selector xpath=".//mstns:recording" />
            <xs:field xpath="mstns:id" />
        </xs:unique>
        <xs:unique name="RecordingDTOKey2" msdata:PrimaryKey="true">
            <xs:selector xpath=".//mstns:track" />
            <xs:field xpath="mstns:id" />
        </xs:unique>
        <xs:keyref name="recordingtrack" refer="mstns:RecordingDTOKey1">
            <xs:selector xpath=".//mstns:track" />
            <xs:field xpath="mstns:recordingId" />
        </xs:keyref>
    </xs:element>
</xs:schema>
```

This schema is not the exact file produced by Visual Studio .NET. It is annotated with a number of attributes that are prefixed from the **codegen** namespace. This modification is desirable because the code that is generated does not adhere to the .NET naming conventions. For example, without the modification, Visual Studio

.NET would generate a **track** class that corresponds to the track table, whereas according to conventions used in the .NET Framework the class should be named **Track**. To change the name of the class that is generated, you must add the codegen:typedName attribute to the element definition in the XML schema:

```
<xs:element name="track" codegen:typedName="Track">
   ...
</element>
```

There are a number of other attributes besides codegen:typedName. For a detailed description of all the attributes, see "Typed DataSets in ADO.NET" from the May 2001 issue of *.NET Developer* [Wildermuth02].

Filling a Typed DataSet from the Database

The following code example demonstrates how to fill a typed **DataSet** with the data that the sample application requires. This includes the specific **recording** record and all of its associated **track** records. The difference between this code and filling an ordinary **DataSet** is that you do not need to explicitly define the relationship between the recording and track records.

Assembler.cs

Just as in *Implementing a Data Transfer Object in .NET with a DataSet*, an **Assembler** class maps the actual database calls into the typed **DataSet**:

```
using System;
using System.Data;
using System.Data.SqlClient;

using Recording;

public class Assembler
{
    public static RecordingDto CreateRecordingDto(long id)
    {
        string selectCmd =
            String.Format(
            "select * from recording where id = {0}",
            id);

        SqlConnection myConnection =
            new SqlConnection(
            "server=(local);database=recordings;Trusted_Connection=yes;");
        SqlDataAdapter myCommand = new SqlDataAdapter(selectCmd,
            myConnection);

        RecordingDto dto = new RecordingDto();
        myCommand.Fill(dto, "recording");

        String trackSelect =
```

```
        String.Format(
        "select * from Track where recordingId = {0} order by Id",
        id);

    SqlDataAdapter trackCommand =
        new SqlDataAdapter(trackSelect, myConnection);
    trackCommand.Fill(dto, "track");

    return dto;
    }
}
```

Note: The example shown here is not meant to describe the only way to fill the typed **DataSet**. There are many ways to retrieve this data from the database. For example, you could use a stored procedure.

Using a Typed DataSet in an ASP.NET Page

As mentioned previously, a typed **DataSet** inherits from **System.Data.DataSet**. This means that it can be substituted for a **DataSet**. For example, when using the .NET user interface controls (Web Forms or Windows Forms) a typed **DataSet** can be used in all places you could use a **DataSet**. The sample application page shown in the following code example uses two **DataGrid** controls, **RecordingGrid** and **TrackGrid**. You can use the typed **DataSet**, **RecordingDto** when setting the **DataSource** properties on the controls because a typed **DataSet** inherits from **DataSet**.

```
using System;
using System.Data;
using RecordingApplication.localhost;

public class RetrieveForm : System.Web.UI.Page
{
    private RecordingCatalog catalog = new RecordingCatalog();

    // ...

    protected void Button1_Click(object sender, System.EventArgs e)
    {
        string stringId = TextBox1.Text;
        long id = Convert.ToInt64(stringId);

        RecordingDTO dto = catalog.Get(id);
        RecordingGrid.DataSource = dto.recording;
        RecordingGrid.DataBind();

        TrackGrid.DataSource = dto.track;
        TrackGrid.DataBind();
    }
}
```

Tests

Because the typed **DataSet** is generated by tools in the .NET Framework, you do not need to write tests to verify that it functions correctly. In the following tests, you are testing that the **Assembler** class loaded the typed **DataSet** correctly.

AssemblerFixture.cs

```
using NUnit.Framework;
using System.Data;
using Recording;

[TestFixture]
public class AssemblerFixture
{
    private RecordingDto dto;
    private RecordingDto.Recording recording;
    private RecordingDto.Track[] tracks;

    [SetUp]
    public void Init()
    {
        dto = Assembler.CreateRecordingDto(1234);
        recording = dto.Recordings[0];
        tracks = recording.GetTracks();
    }

    [Test]
    public void RecordingCount()
    {
        Assert.Equals(1, dto.Recordings.Rows.Count);
    }

    [Test]
    public void RecordingTitle()
    {
        Assert.Equals("Up", recording.Title.Trim());
    }


    [Test]
    public void RecordingChild()
    {
        Assert.Equals(10, tracks.Length);

        foreach(RecordingDto.Track track in tracks)
        {
            Assert.Equals(recording.Id, track.RecordingId);
        }
    }

    [Test]
    public void TrackParent()
```

```
    {
        RecordingDto.Track track = tracks[0];
        RecordingDto.Recording parent = track.Recording;
        Assert.Equals("Up", parent.Title.Trim());
    }

    [Test]
    public void TrackContent()
    {
        RecordingDto.Track track = tracks[0];
        Assert.Equals("Darkness", track.Title.Trim());
    }

    [Test]
    public void InvalidRecording()
    {
        RecordingDto dto = Assembler.CreateRecordingDto(-1);
        Assert.Equals(0, dto.Recordings.Rows.Count);
        Assert.Equals(0, dto.Tracks.Rows.Count);
    }
}
```

These tests describe how to access the individual elements of the **DataSet**. Because of the use of a typed **DataSet**, the test code does not require the actual column names and does not require the return type to be cast. Comparing these tests with the ones described in *Implementing Data Transfer Object in .NET with a DataSet* reveals the differences between using a strongly-typed interface and a generic interface. The strongly-typed interface is easier to use and understand. It also provides the added benefit of compile-time checking on return types.

Resulting Context

Implementing DTO with a typed **DataSet** shares a number of the same benefits and liabilities as implementing DTO with a **DataSet**; however, certain benefits and liabilities are unique to a typed-**DataSet** implementation.

Benefits

The typed **DataSet** shares the following benefits with a **DataSet** when used as a DTO:

- **Development tool support**. Because the **DataSet** class is implemented in ADO.NET, there is no need to design and implement the DTO. There is also extensive support in Visual Studio for automating the creation and filling of **DataSet** and typed-**DataSet** objects.

- **Integration with controls**. A **DataSet** works directly with the built-in controls in Windows Forms and Web Forms, making it a logical choice as a DTO.

- **Serialization**. The **DataSet** comes complete with the ability to serialize itself into XML. Not only is the content serialized, but the schema for the content is also present in the serialization.

- **Disconnected database model**. The **DataSet** represents a snapshot of the current contents of the database. This means that you can alter the contents of the **DataSet** and subsequently use the **DataSet** as the means to update the database.

An additional benefit that might persuade you to use a typed **DataSet** as opposed to an ordinary **DataSet** is the strongly-typed interface of the typed **DataSet**. A typed **DataSet**, as described here, generates classes that can be used to access the contained data. The classes present an interface which defines how the class is to be used in a more explicit manner. This removes the need for casting which was present in the **DataSet** implementation.

Liabilities

The typed **DataSet** shares the following liabilities with a **DataSet** when used in the context of a DTO:

- **Interoperability**. Because the **DataSet** class is part of ADO.NET, it is not the best choice for a DTO in cases requiring interoperability with clients that are not running the .NET Framework.. You can still use **DataSet**, however, the client will be forced to parse the XML and build its own representation. If interoperability is a requirement, see *Implementing Data Transfer Object in .NET with Serialized Objects*.

- **Stale data**. The typed **DataSet**, like a **DataSet**, is disconnected from the database. It is filled with a snapshot of the data in the database when it is constructed. This implies that the actual data in the database may be different from what is contained in the typed **DataSet**. For reading primarily static data, this is not a major issue. If the data is constantly changing, however, using any kind of **DataSet** is not recommended.

- **Potential for performance degradation**. Instantiating and filling a **DataSet** can be an expensive operation. Serializing and deserializing a **DataSet** can also be very time consuming. A good rule of thumb for using a **DataSet** is that a **DataSet** is a good choice when you are using more than one table or relying on the capability of the **DataSet** to update the database. If you are displaying the results from a single table, then using a **DataReader** with strongly-typed objects may offer better performance. For more information, see *Implementing Data Transfer Object in .NET with Serialized Objects*.

The following are additional liabilities when using a typed **DataSet** as opposed to an ordinary **DataSet**:

- **A typed DataSet is still a DataSet.** A typed **DataSet** can be substituted at runtime with a **DataSet**. This means that even though the strongly-typed interface exists, programmers can still access the data without the typed interface. A possible result of doing this is that there could be parts of the code which couple the application tightly to the **DataSet** table and column names.

- **The need for an XML schema**. When using a typed DataSet you have to create and maintain an XML schema to describe the strongly-typed interface. Visual

Studio .NET provides a number of tools to assist in this process, but nevertheless you still have to maintain an additional file.

Related Patterns

For more information, see the following related patterns:

- *Implementing Data Transfer Object in .NET with a DataSet.*
- *Implementing Data Transfer Object in .NET with Serialized Objects.*
- *Assembler.* In *Enterprise Application Architecture Patterns*, Fowler defines *Assembler* as a specialized instance of the *Mapper* pattern *[Fowler03].*

Acknowledgments

[Beau02] Beauchemin, Bob. *Essential ADO.NET.* Addison-Wesley, 2002.

[Fowler03] Fowler, Martin. *Enterprise Application Architecture Patterns.* Addison-Wesley, 2003.

[Wildermuth01] Wildermuth, Shawn. "Typed DataSets in ADO.NET." *.NET Developer.* May 2001.

Singleton

Context

In some situations, a certain type of data needs to be available to all other objects in the application. In most cases, this type of data is also unique in the system. For example, a user interface can have only one mouse pointer that all applications must access. Likewise, an enterprise solution may interface with a single-gateway object that manages the connection to a specific legacy system.

Problem

How do you make an instance of an object globally available and guarantee that only one instance of the class is created?

Note: The definition of singleton used here is intentionally narrower than in *Design Patterns: Elements of Reusable Object-Oriented Software* [Gamma95].

Forces

The following forces act on a system within this context and must be reconciled as you consider a solution to the problem:

- Many programming languages (for example, Microsoft Visual Basic® version 6.0 or C++) support the definition of objects that are global in scope. These objects reside at the root of the namespace and are universally available to all objects in the application. This approach provides a simple solution to the global accessibility problem but does not address the one-instance requirement. It does not stop other objects from creating other instances of the global object. Also, other object-oriented languages, such as Visual Basic .NET or C#, do not directly support global variables.

- To ensure that only a single instance of a class can exist, you must control the instantiation process. This implies that you need to prevent other objects from creating an instance of the class by using the instantiation mechanism inherent in the programming language (for example, by using the **new** operator). The other part of controlling the instantiation is providing a central mechanism by which all objects can obtain a reference to the single instance.

Solution

Singleton provides a global, single instance by:

- Making the class create a single instance of itself.

- Allowing other objects to access this instance through a class method that returns a reference to the instance. A class method is globally accessible.

- Declaring the class constructor as private so that no other object can create a new instance.

Figure 5.21 shows the static structure of this pattern. The UML class diagram is surprisingly simple because *Singleton* consists of a simple class that holds a reference to a single instance of itself.

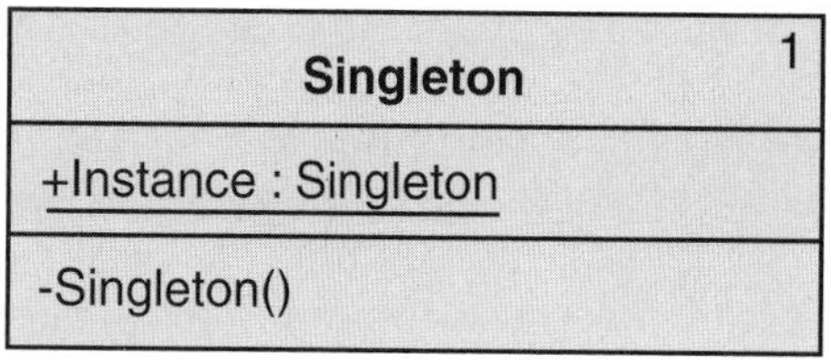

Singleton   1
+Instance : Singleton
-Singleton()

Figure 5.21
Singleton structure

Figure 5.21 shows that the **Singleton** class contains a public class-scope (static) property, which returns a reference to the single instance of the **Singleton** class. (The underline in UML indicates a class-scope property.) Also, the numeral *1* in the upper-right corner indicates that there can only be one instance of this class in the system at any time. Because the default constructor for **Singleton** is private, any other object in the system has to access the **Singleton** object through the **Instance** property.

The *Singleton* pattern is often classified as an idiom rather than a pattern because the solution depends primarily on the features of the programming language you use (for example, class methods and static initializers). Separating the abstract concept from a particular implementation, as this patterns collection does, may make the *Singleton* implementation look surprisingly simple.

Example

For an example, see *Implementing Singleton in C#*.

Resulting Context

Singleton results in the following benefits and liabilities:

Benefits

- **Instance control**. *Singleton* prevents other objects from instantiating their own copies of the **Singleton** object, ensuring that all objects access the single instance.
- **Flexibility**. Because the class controls the instantiation process, the class has the flexibility to change the instantiation process.

Liabilities

- **Overhead**. Although the amount is minuscule, there is some overhead involved in checking whether an instance of the class already exists every time an object requests a reference. This problem can be overcome by using static initialization as described in *Implementing Singleton in C#.*

- **Possible development confusion**. When using a singleton object (especially one defined in a class library), developers must remember that they cannot use the **new** keyword to instantiate the object. Because application developers may not have access to the library source code, they may be surprised to find that they cannot instantiate this class directly.

- **Object lifetime**. *Singleton* does not address the issue of deleting the single object. In languages that provide memory management (for example, languages based on the .NET Framework), only the **Singleton** class could cause the instance to be deallocated because it holds a private reference to the instance. In languages, such as C++, other classes could delete the object instance, but doing so would lead to a dangling reference inside the **Singleton** class.

Related Patterns

For more information, see the following related patterns:

- *Abstract Factory* [Gamma95]. In many cases, *Abstract Factories* are implemented as singletons. Typically, factories should be globally accessible. Restricting the factory to a single instance ensures that the one factory globally controls object creation. This is useful if the factory allocates object instances from a pool of objects.

- *Monostate* [Martin02]. *Monostate* is similar to the *Singleton*, but it focuses on state rather than on identity. Instead of controlling the instances of an object, *Monostate* ensures that only one shared state exists for all instances by declaring all data members static.

- *Implementing Broker with .NET Remoting Using Server-Activated Objects*. This pattern uses a *Singleton* factory to create new objects on the server.

Acknowledgments

[Gamma95] Gamma, Helm, Johnson, and Vlissides. *Design Patterns: Elements of Reusable Object-Oriented Software*. Addison-Wesley, 1995.

[Martin02] Martin, Robert C. *Agile Software Development: Principles, Patterns, and Practices*. Prentice Hall, 2002.

Implementing Singleton in C#

Context

You are building an application in C#. You need a class that has only one instance, and you need to provide a global point of access to the instance. You want to be sure that your solution is efficient and that it takes advantage of the Microsoft® .NET common language runtime features. You may also want to make sure that your solution is thread safe.

Implementation Strategy

Even though *Singleton* is a comparatively simple pattern, there are various tradeoffs and options, depending upon the implementation. The following is a series of implementation strategies with a discussion of their strengths and weaknesses.

Singleton

The following implementation of the *Singleton* design pattern follows the solution presented in *Design Patterns: Elements of Reusable Object-Oriented Software* [Gamma95] but modifies it to take advantage of language features available in C#, such as properties:

```
using System;

public class Singleton
{
    private static Singleton instance;

    private Singleton() {}

    public static Singleton Instance
    {
        get
        {
            if (instance == null)
            {
                instance = new Singleton();
            }
            return instance;
        }
    }
}
```

This implementation has two main advantages:

- Because the instance is created inside the **Instance** property method, the class can exercise additional functionality (for example, instantiating a subclass), even though it may introduce unwelcome dependencies.

- The instantiation is not performed until an object asks for an instance; this approach is referred to as *lazy instantiation*. Lazy instantiation avoids instantiating unnecessary singletons when the application starts.

The main disadvantage of this implementation, however, is that it is not safe for multithreaded environments. If separate threads of execution enter the **Instance** property method at the same time, more that one instance of the **Singleton** object may be created. Each thread could execute the following statement and decide that a new instance has to be created:

```
if (instance == null)
```

Various approaches solve this problem. One approach is to use an idiom referred to as *Double-Check Locking* [Lea99]. However, C# in combination with the common language runtime provides a *static initialization* approach, which circumvents these issues without requiring the developer to explicitly code for thread safety.

Static Initialization

One of the reasons *Design Patterns* [Gamma95] avoided static initialization is because the C++ specification left some ambiguity around the initialization order of static variables. Fortunately, the .NET Framework resolves this ambiguity through its handling of variable initialization:

```
public sealed class Singleton
{
    private static readonly Singleton instance = new Singleton();

    private Singleton(){}

    public static Singleton Instance
    {
        get
        {
            return instance;
        }
    }
}
```

In this strategy, the instance is created the first time any member of the class is referenced. The common language runtime takes care of the variable initialization. The class is marked **sealed** to prevent derivation, which could add instances. For a discussion of the pros and cons of marking a class **sealed**, see [Sells03]. In addition, the variable is marked **readonly**, which means that it can be assigned only during static initialization (which is shown here) or in a class constructor.

This implementation is similar to the preceding example, except that it relies on the common language runtime to initialize the variable. It still addresses the two basic problems that the *Singleton* pattern is trying to solve: global access and instantiation control. The public static property provides a global access point to the instance. Also, because the constructor is private, the **Singleton** class cannot be instantiated outside of the class itself; therefore, the variable refers to the only instance that can exist in the system.

Because the **Singleton** instance is referenced by a private static member variable, the instantiation does not occur until the class is first referenced by a call to the **Instance** property. This solution therefore implements a form of the lazy instantiation property, as in the *Design Patterns* form of *Singleton*.

The only potential downside of this approach is that you have less control over the mechanics of the instantiation. In the *Design Patterns* form, you were able to use a nondefault constructor or perform other tasks before the instantiation. Because the .NET Framework performs the initialization in this solution, you do not have these options. In most cases, static initialization is the preferred approach for implementing a *Singleton* in .NET.

Multithreaded Singleton

Static initialization is suitable for most situations. When your application must delay the instantiation, use a non-default constructor or perform other tasks before the instantiation, and work in a multithreaded environment, you need a different solution. Cases do exist, however, in which you cannot rely on the common language runtime to ensure thread safety, as in the Static Initialization example. In such cases, you must use specific language capabilities to ensure that only one instance of the object is created in the presence of multiple threads. One of the more common solutions is to use the *Double-Check Locking* [Lea99] idiom to keep separate threads from creating new instances of the singleton at the same time.

Note: The common language runtime resolves issues related to using *Double-Check Locking* that are common in other environments. For more information about these issues, see "The 'Double-Checked Locking Is Broken' Declaration," on the University of Maryland, Department of Computer Science Web site, at *http://www.cs.umd.edu/~pugh/java/memoryModel /DoubleCheckedLocking.html*.

The following implementation allows only a single thread to enter the critical area, which the **lock** block identifies, when no instance of **Singleton** has yet been created:

```
using System;

public sealed class Singleton
{
    private static volatile Singleton instance;
    private static object syncRoot = new Object();
```

```
   private Singleton() {}

   public static Singleton Instance
   {
      get
      {
         if (instance == null)
         {
            lock (syncRoot)
            {
               if (instance == null)
                  instance = new Singleton();
            }
         }

         return instance;
      }
   }
}
```

This approach ensures that only one instance is created and only when the instance is needed. Also, the variable is declared to be **volatile** to ensure that assignment to the instance variable completes before the instance variable can be accessed. Lastly, this approach uses a **syncRoot** instance to lock on, rather than locking on the type itself, to avoid deadlocks.

This double-check locking approach solves the thread concurrency problems while avoiding an exclusive lock in every call to the **Instance** property method. It also allows you to delay instantiation until the object is first accessed. In practice, an application rarely requires this type of implementation. In most cases, the static initialization approach is sufficient.

Resulting Context

Implementing *Singleton* in C# results in the following benefits and liabilities:

Benefits

- The static initialization approach is possible because the .NET Framework explicitly defines how and when static variable initialization occurs.
- The *Double-Check Locking* idiom described earlier in "Multithreaded Singleton" is implemented correctly in the common language runtime.

Liabilities

If your multithreaded application requires explicit initialization, you have to take precautions to avoid threading issues.

Acknowledgments

[Gamma95] Gamma, Helm, Johnson, and Vlissides. *Design Patterns: Elements of Reusable Object-Oriented Software*. Addison-Wesley, 1995.

[Lea99] Lea, Doug. *Concurrent Programming in Java*, Second Edition. Addison-Wesley, 1999.

[Sells03] Sells, Chris. "Sealed Sucks." *sellsbrothers.com News*. Available at: *http://www.sellsbrothers.com/news/showTopic.aspx?ixTopic=411*.

Note: Despite its title, the "Sealed Sucks" article is actually a balanced discussion of the pros and cons of marking a class **sealed**.

6

Services Patterns

Abstractions enable us to assign behavior and data to discrete chunks of software that interact at runtime. In well-architected systems, the sum of these interactions forms a coherent executable intelligence, which provides tangible business value to the enterprise.

The previous chapter introduced patterns for distributing a single application across multiple processing nodes using instance-based collaboration and systems separated by near links. *Near links*, as you may recall, are reliable links that connect distributed systems residing in the same trust zone and within the same enterprise; near links do not require interoperability. *Far links* are all other links, including links that span the Internet. This chapter is primarily concerned with systems that are connected by far links and that use service-based collaboration.

When building distributed systems characterized by near links and instance based collaboration, the developing organization usually has full control over all components involved in the solution. However, many large enterprise applications contain systems separated by far links and have to interact with preexisting systems that are usually not under control of the developing organization. For example, an order management system may use credit scoring functionality implemented in a preexisting system or a sales tax calculation service provided by an external service provider. As a result, complex solutions are likely to have to interact with functions that are controlled by outside organizations and must be used as is.

This chapter focuses on collaboration between applications and external services. To describe how Web services provide an interoperable environment that facilitates such collaboration, the chapter overview addresses the following topics:

- Basic collaboration concepts
- Web services
- Patterns for service-based collaboration using Web services

Collaboration Concepts

Classes, objects, components, and interfaces are the basic building blocks of modern software. Some of these elements encapsulate problem domains, while others provide system infrastructure and technical architecture. Each building block provides a useful function, but the real power lies in the composition of individual elements into a collaborative solution that provides tangible business value to an enterprise (or a web of connected enterprises). To enable this level of collaboration, software elements must adhere to agreed-upon organizing principles and must expose standard interfaces to each other. Where components are dissimilar, one element must be adapted to the other, or both must be adapted to an agreed upon standard.

Service-Based Collaboration

Chapter 5 introduced the notion of instance-based and service-based collaboration, highlighting the strengths and weaknesses of each approach. Service-based collaboration works well in scenarios where the consuming application does not have any control over the remote services or has to interoperate with solutions developed on top of different programming languages or platforms.

Service-based interfaces expose a single instance of an interface that provides a service to potential consumers. In the context of Web services, Microsoft defines a software service as a "discrete unit of application logic that exposes message-based interfaces suitable for being accessed across a network." [Microsoft02-2]

A service does not depend on the process that invokes it; it is self-contained and context-independent. This allows any potential consumer on the network to access the service. Services are well-defined by means of a *contract* that specifies the format for requests to the service and the format of the associated replies.

Although not necessarily message based, the notion of creating a set of logically grouped services was used in application development before the advent of distributed applications. For example, operating systems provide services to all applications running on the operating system. The Microsoft Windows® GDI library, for instance, provides graphical services, and the Open Database Connectivity (ODBC) API exposes database access services. And just as abstracting some of the core capabilities of an operating system in to a set of services helped simplify application programming models, identifying core business capabilities of an enterprise and encapsulating them as a set of interoperable services helps to simplify collaborations with partners outside the corporate firewall.

Service-Oriented Architecture

Service-oriented architectures (SOAs) apply the concept of a service to distributed enterprise applications. In an SOA, each application exposes high-level business functions as services to be consumed by other applications. Because of the expanded scope and complexity of these service-oriented solutions, a service-oriented architecture must provide additional functions beyond the capability to invoke a remote service. The most important of these functions include:

- **Making services locatable at runtime**. It is easy for a stand-alone application to locate an operating system service such as a GDI call; it is implemented in a local dynamic-link library named gdi32.dll. However, enterprise services can be distributed across many computers, networks, or facilities. Some of these services may change locations because they are tied to existing applications. Therefore, locating a service in a distributed, service-oriented architecture can be a complex task.

- **Making service and consumer agree on a common format**. After the correct service is found, the consuming application must be able to dynamically determine which protocol to use to access the service, how to format a request, and what type of response to expect. Because services can be implemented in a variety of languages and platforms, getting the service and the consumer to agree on a common format can also be a challenging task.

Service Contracts

When one method calls another inside an application, the method signature defines the "understanding" between the method and the caller, for example the number and types of parameters passed into the method and returned on its completion. Method calls can embody their understanding in a simple method signature because the caller and the method make a number of implicit assumptions; for example, that both methods execute inside the same process and share the same memory space; that both methods use the same programming language; and that execution returns to the calling method once the called method is complete. In the world of distributed SOAs, many of these assumptions are no longer valid and need to be spelled out explicitly in a service contract.

The *service contract* must specify the implementation of the communication channel connecting the Service Consumers with the Service Provider Applications, such as the network protocol. The service contract must also specify what kinds of messages the service can consume or produce, described by means of a detailed schema for each message involved in the interaction.

Figure 6.1 shows the elements of a service-oriented architecture.

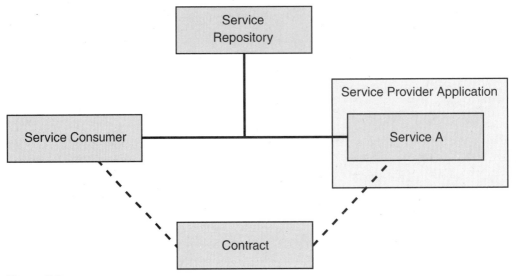

Figure 6.1
Invocation of a service in an SOA

A single service may need to support multiple contracts. For instance, service consumers within the same organization may want to interact with the service through a series of relatively fine-grained messages and may be granted access to sensitive functionality. Service consumers external to the organization may want to interact with the service in a more coarse-grained manner for performance reasons, and will not be granted access to sensitive functionality.

The following steps are required to invoke a remote service:

1. **Discovery**: A service consumer (any application wanting to access a service) queries the service repository, which provides the location of the desired service.

2. **Negotiation**: The service consumer and the service provider agree on a communications format specified by the service contract.

3. **Invocation**: The service consumer invokes the service.

Web Services

Web services provide a standards-based implementation of an SOA. Web services define a suite of technologies and protocols that greatly simplify creating solutions based on a set of collaborating applications. Among the many technologies and principles associated with Web services, two features are key:

- A communication contract between the service provider and service consumer
- Interoperability

Communication Contract

A protocol stack is commonly used as a metaphor for communication between systems, the most well-known incarnation being the Open Systems Interconnect (OSI) layer model. A protocol stack describes communication as a set of layered services on both sides of the communication, with "higher" layers using the services of the lower layers. For example, an application protocol such as FTP or HTTP can use a TCP/IP transport protocol, which in turn uses an Ethernet card to move bits and bytes over the connection.

A communication contract defines all layers of this protocol stack in detail. As an example, the telephone system provides the hardware layer as voice communication in a certain frequency range (400 – 4000 Hz) and MTDF dialing. However, it does two participants little good if they use compatible telephony hardware but speak different languages. If you have ever received a phone call from a confused international caller or a fax machine, you know that the communication can fail even if the communication layer works beautifully.

The Web services contract works similarly. It needs to address two primary aspects of the communication:

- A common communications channel
- Data representation and message schemas

Common Communications Channel

In order for the applications to communicate, they must use compatible protocols. TCP/IP has become the default core communication protocol stack. Most, if not all, operating systems provide built-in TCP/IP functionality. Any application that uses a properly configured TCP/IP stack can communicate with other applications that use TCP/IP stacks on the same local network.

Figure 6.2 shows the communication channel between two applications with compatible protocol stacks.

Figure 6.2
Communication channel and TCP/IP protocol stacks

As an example, Application A may make a request for a Web service exposed by Application B. Application A's protocol stack breaks down the application-level request into one or more low-level data packets to be streamed across the network.

Application B's protocol stack translates the packets back into an application-level call to the service. The service reply undergoes an equivalent process.

The ubiquity of the TCP/IP protocol stack makes it the ideal foundation for inter-operable communications. However, TCP/IP is a low-level protocol and does not define the content of any messages between the applications. Like a phone line, it provides a channel for communication but does not specify a common language to be spoken.

HTTP is a protocol layered on top of TCP/IP that provides the most basic conventions for making a request to an external resource. The simplicity of HTTP has helped it gain wide support as the protocol used to transport information across the Internet and across corporate firewalls. Thus, HTTP has become both a blessing and a curse. Its universal use makes it ideal for routing messages, but its capability to permeate most corporate firewalls concerns many IT security administrators.

With the addition of HTTP, the resulting protocol stack now appears as shown in Figure 6.3.

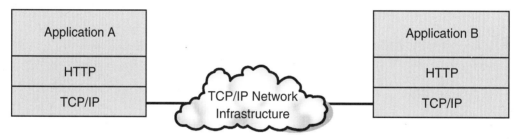

Figure 6.3
Communication protocol stacks with addition of HTTP

Data Representation and Message Schemas

The second part of the communication contract deals with what is being passed across the communications channel, comparable to the language spoken across a telephone line. This part of the contract needs to define three things:

- The data representation format
- The message schema
- The binding of messages to services

Data Representation Format

If applications are to successfully communicate with each other, they must all agree to a common set of data definitions for data passed over the connection. The Web services protocol stack already constrains the data passed back and forth to be in a textual format. But what does that textual data represent? Does it represent a serialized object? An array of integers? Or an XML document?

There are basically two ways to provide information about what the data represents: provide an external description or use self-describing data.

An external description defines the schema of the data in some form external to the data itself. The interface definition languages (IDL) used by Distributed RPC, DCOM, or CORBA technologies are examples of languages designed to write external descriptions. This external approach to data description limits interoperability because all computers involved in the collaboration must have access to the external description.

Self-describing data includes an embedded description of the data with the data itself. Using this approach enhances interoperability because the data can be parsed without having to consult an external description of the data.

Web services use XML as the data representation format. XML provides the following advantages:

- It is text based and therefore compatible with the communication channel
- It is an industry standard with broad industry and user support
- It is self-describing
- It is interoperable
- XML parsers exist for virtually all platforms, and many development tools are available to ease the development of XML applications

Message Schema

The message is the fundamental unit of communication in Web services and therefore it is imperative that all collaborating parties have a precise understanding of the message contents.

The communication contract must specify all the request messages associated with a service and any associated response messages. Then the contents for each message must be specified. This task typically involves identifying the data elements of each message, specifying the data type of the elements, and specifying any constraints associated with the types or between types.

SOAP divides a message into two sections: an optional header and a mandatory body. The header contains information associated with the communication and services infrastructure. The body contains the business-oriented content of the message while the header contains metadata.

Message Binding

After the messages have been defined, they must be associated with a communication channel. In addition to HTTP, SOAP can work with other text-based communication protocols such as SMTP. As a result, a service may support more than one communication protocol.

Web services use Web Services Description Language (WSDL) to provide a detailed specification of all the messages supported by a service. In turn, WSDL uses the XML Schema Definition (XSD) standard to document the internal structure of each message and any constraints on any of the message elements.

WSDL groups messages into operations. An operation is the logical unit of interaction with a service, which is defined as a request message and any associated response messages.

Finally, WSDL binds operations to one or more protocols, such as HTTP and SMTP, and then groups these bound operation together in a service. In addition to specifying the operations associated with a service, the WSDL service specification also documents the communication channel-specific address of the service. For instance, the service specification would document the URL to identify a service that is exposed through SOAP over HTTP.

Interoperability

Interoperability was a major factor in the previous discussion of communication channels and message descriptions. Several other features of Web services significantly aid interoperability.

Open Standards

One of the key disadvantages of using a traditional approach to distributed communication is that applications are dependent on proprietary communication technology, protocols, and data formats.

Web services are entirely based on a set of widely-supported, platform-independent, open standards. As a result, virtually every major platform has one or more implementations of the Web services protocol stack. This significantly reduces the effort and cost associated with implementing and deploying solutions based on collaborating applications.

Service Repository

The final piece of the Web services puzzle is service discovery. How does a service consumer application find the services it needs to collaborate with? The answer is to provide a federated service repository that contains descriptions of the services and associate these descriptions with various metadata elements that are useful for identifying particular services. For instance, the service repository should return pointers to services based on several different criteria such as developing organization, hosting organization, industry type, and business process supported.

Using a service repository significantly reduces coupling between the service provider and service consumer. The reduction results from the consumer only needing a reference to the service, rather than hard-coding all the details needed to access the service within the service consumer. This allows the service provider to change many pieces of the communications contract without requiring any changes to the service consumer. The provider only needs to update the registry. Applications that make full use of the UDDI specification will automatically use the new settings the next time they access the service.

UDDI

The Universal Discovery, Description, and Integration (UDDI) specification solves the service discovery problem for Web services. Interoperability was one of the primary goals of UDDI, so it is not surprising that UDDI uses many of the technologies and protocols already discussed in this chapter.

At its core, UDDI is simply a repository containing links to WSDL service descriptions. UDDI defines several XML descriptions of various metadata that may be associated with a service. These descriptions include, information about the organization providing the service, the business process supported by the service, and the service type. Finally, UDDI exposes its functionality as a set of SOAP services.

Patterns Overview

The patterns in this chapter describe how to structure a custom-developed solution in a service-oriented environment. Specifically, these patterns enable you to:

- Expose application functionality as a service
- Encapsulate the details of consuming services that are exposed by other applications

Figure 6.4 shows the relationship between a service gateway, a service interface, and the implementation of the service.

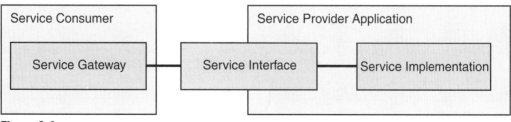

Figure 6.4
Service elements

As you design service oriented systems, it is helpful to separate the elements that are responsible for application business logic from those elements responsible for communicating with services and participating in service contracts. Separating these elements furthers the general design objective of separation of concerns, and improves maintainability, flexibility, and testability.

The *Service Interface* pattern provides guidance on structuring the service provider portion of the contract. It discusses using a service interface component that encapsulates the details of communicating with a particular set of service consumers and invokes a service implementation component that performs the actual business logic associated with the service *Implementing Service Interface in .NET* then provides a concrete example of creating a service interface component using the .NET framework.

The *Service Gateway* design pattern provides guidance for implementing the service consumer portion of the contract. It discusses using a service agent component that encapsulates all the low-level details of communicating with the service and exposes an interface that is optimized for the use of the other components within the service consumer application. *Implementing Service Gateway in .NET* then provides a concrete example of creating a Service Gateway component using the .NET Framework.

Services Patterns

Table 6.1 lists the patterns in the Services patterns cluster, along with the problem statements and associated implementations that serve as a roadmap to the patterns.

Table 6.1: Service Patterns

Pattern	Problem	Associated implementations
Service Interface	How do you make pieces of your application's functionality available to other applications, while ensuring that the interface mechanics are decoupled from the application logic?	*Implementing Service Interface in .NET*
Service Gateway	How do you decouple the details of fulfilling the contract responsibilities defined by the service from the rest of your application?	*Implementing Service Gateway in .NET*

Service Interface

Context

You are designing an enterprise application, and you need to make some of its functionality available across a network. This functionality needs to be accessible to various types of systems, so interoperability is a key aspect of the design. In addition to interoperability, you also may need to support different types of communications protocols and accommodate varying operational requirements.

Problem

How do you make pieces of your application's functionality available to other applications, while ensuring that the interface mechanics are decoupled from the application logic?

Forces

While designing your application, you must address the following forces:

- It is desirable to separate elements that are responsible for the application's business logic from the elements responsible for communication protocols, data transformation, and fulfillment of service contracts. Doing so furthers the general design objective of separation of concerns.

- Consumers of your application may want responses optimized for particular usage scenarios. For example, some consumers may want responses optimized for direct display to users, while others may want responses optimized for software processing.

- Consumers of your application may want to communicate with the application using different technologies. For instance, consumers that are external to your company may want to access the application through SOAP over the Internet, while consumers that are internal to your company may want to access the application through .NET remoting.

- The application itself may impose different operational requirements on different consumers. For example, your application may have security requirements that authorize consumers internal to your company to perform update and delete operations, while consumers that are external to your company are only authorized to perform read-only operations. Or, for example, different consumers may need different transactional support from the application. To some clients, the context in which specific transactions occur is not important while other clients may need precise control of the transactional context. A handle to this context might then be passed to other elements of the application as needed.

- The application's ability to respond to changes in the business environment in a timely manner is greatly enhanced if changes to the business logic are isolated from the mechanisms used by consumers to interact with the application. For example, the fact that a particular set of business logic was implemented in a custom built component and then later implemented as a wrapper around a packaged solution should ideally have no impact on the consumers of the application.

Solution

Design your application as a collection of software services, each with a service interface through which consumers of the application may interact with the service.

A software service is a discrete unit of application logic that exposes a message-based interface that is suitable for being accessed by other applications. [Microsoft02-2] Each software service has an associated interface that it presents to the consumers. This interface defines and implements a contract between the consumers of the service and the provider of the service. This contract and its associated implementation are referred to as a service interface.

Figure 6.5 shows a service gateway consuming a service provided by a service interface. The collaboration between these two elements is governed by a contract.

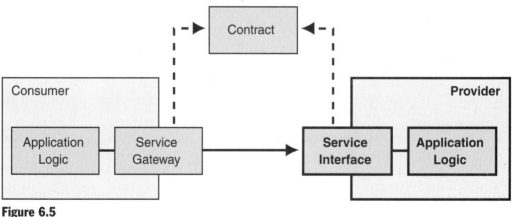

Figure 6.5
Service elements

Service Interface

As Figure 6.5 shows, *Service Interface* provides an entry point that consumers use to access the functionality exposed by the application. The *Service Interface* is usually network addressable, meaning that it is capable of being accessed by the consumer over some sort of communication network. The network address can be a well-known location or it can be obtained from a service directory such as UDDI.

A key aspect of the design of a service interface is to decouple the implementation needed to communicate with other systems from the application's business logic.

The service interface provides a much more coarse-grained interface while preserving the semantics and finer granularity of the application logic. It also provides a barrier that enables the application logic to change without affecting the consumers of the interface.

The service interface implements the contract between the consumer and provider. This contract allows them to exchange information even if they are on different systems. The service interface is responsible for all of the implementation details needed to perform this communication. Such details include but are not limited to:

- **Network protocol**. The service interface should encapsulate all aspects of the network protocol used for communication between the consumer and service. For example, suppose that a service is exposed to consumers through HTTP over a TCP/IP network. You can implement the service interface as an ASP.NET component published to a well-known URL. The ASP.NET component receives the HTTP request, extracts the information needed by the service to process the request, invokes the service implementation, packages the service response, and sends the response back to the consumer as an HTTP response. From the service perspective, the only component that understands HTTP is the service interface. The service implementation has its own contract with the service interface and should have no dependencies on the specifics of the technology that consumers use to communicate with the service interface.

- **Data formats**. The service interface translates between consumer data formats and the data formats that the service expects. For example, consumers external to the company may supply data and expect reply data to be in an XML format that conforms to an industry-standard XML schema. Consumers internal to the company may want to use an XML format optimized for this particular service. The service interface is responsible for transforming and mapping both data formats in a format that the service can use. The service implementation does not have any knowledge of the specific data formats the service interface might use to communicate with the consumers.

- **Security**. The service interface should be considered its own trust boundary. Different consumers may have different security requirements, so it is up to the service interface to implement these consumer-specific requirements. For instance, consumers external to the company will generally have more restrictive security requirements than consumers internal to the company. External consumers may have strong authentication requirements and may only be authorized to perform a very limited subset of the operations authorized for internal consumers. Internal consumer may be implicitly trusted for most operations and only require authorization for the most sensitive operations.

- **Service level agreements**. The service interface has a significant role in ensuring that the service meets its service level commitments to a specific set of consumers. Service interfaces may implement caching to increase response time and reduce bandwidth consumption. Multiple instances of a service interface may be deployed across a load-balanced set of processing nodes to achieve scalability, availability, and fault-tolerance requirements.

Minimizing the Number of Service Interfaces

In general, you will need one service interface for each unique usage scenario, technology stack, service level agreement, or operational requirement. However, the more service interfaces supported by your application, the more work is involved in building and maintaining the implementation. Therefore, you should try to minimize the number of service interfaces that an application needs to support. For example, an application may offer two service interfaces for accessing its functionality. The first service interface may be optimized for consumers that are external to the company. It may specify a few very coarse-grained sets of request–and-response pairs using SOAP over HTTP communication technology and mandate very strict security requirements. The second service interface may be optimized for consumers that are internal to the company. It may specify a somewhat larger number of request-and-response pairs that are not quite as coarse-grained as those specified in the first service interface, and emphasize performance requirements over security concerns.

Example

See *Implementing Service Interface in .NET*.

Testing Considerations

Service Interface encapsulates all the details of providing a service and decouples it from the application logic. This separation enables you to replace the application logic with mock [Mackinnon00] implementations. These mock implementations replace the real application code with dummy implementations that emulate the real code. Using mock implementations allows you to write tests that verify that the code works without having to depend on the actual application code. You can also extend the mock implementations to simulate error conditions that might be difficult or impossible to simulate with the real code.

Resulting Context

Using the *Service Interface* pattern results in the following benefits and liabilities:

Benefits

- The service interface mechanics are decoupled from the application logic. This separation allows you to easily add new interfaces and to change the implementation of the underlying application with minimal impact on consumers.

- Decoupling the service interface code from the service implementation code enables you to deploy the two code bases on separate tiers, potentially increasing the deployment flexibility of the solution.

Liabilities

- Many platforms make exposing the application functionality simple. However, this can lead to a poor decision in terms of granularity. If the interface is too fine-grained, you can end up making too many calls to the service to perform a specific action. You need to design your service interfaces to be appropriate for network or out–of–process communication.

- Each additional service interface provided by a service increases the amount of work required to make a change to the functionality exposed by a service.

- The *Service Interface* pattern adds complexity and performance overhead that may not be justified for very simple service-oriented applications.

Related Patterns

For more information, see the following related patterns:

- *Service Gateway. Service Gateway* performs the role of the consumer of a service interface.

- *Remote Facade* [Fowler03]: *Service Interface* is a specific type of *Remote Facade* adapted for use in service-oriented architectures. A remote facade is similar to a remote proxy, but sometimes uses encapsulation to make the remote interface more coarse-grained.

- *Service Layer* [Fowler03]: As the number and complexity of service interfaces increase, it may make sense to pool the common pieces of functionality into its own software layer.

Acknowledgments

[Fowler03] Fowler, Martin. *Patterns of Enterprise Application Architecture*. Addison-Wesley, 2003.

[Mackinnon00] Mackinnon, Tim, et al. "Endo-Testing: Unit Testing with Mock Objects." *eXtreme Programming and Flexible Processes in Software Engineering—XP2000* conference.

[Microsoft02-2] Microsoft Corporation. "Application Architecture: Conceptual View." *.NET Architecture Center*. Available from MSDN at: *http://msdn.microsoft.com /architecture/default.aspx?pull=/library/en-us/dnea/html/eaappconland.asp.*

Implementing Service Interface in .NET

Context

Your application is deployed on the Microsoft Windows® operating system. You have decided to expose a piece of your application's functionality as an ASP.NET Web Service. Interoperability is a key issue so you cannot use complex data types that are present only in the Microsoft .NET Framework.

Background

When you insert an audio compact disc (CD) into your computer often the program that you use to play the CD informs you of various pieces of information regarding the recording. This information might include track information, cover art, reviews, and so on. To demonstrate an implementation of the *Service Interface* pattern, this is implemented as an ASP.NET Web service.

Implementation Strategy

Service Interface describes a separation of interface mechanics and application logic. The interface is responsible for implementing and enforcing the contract for a service that is being exposed and the application logic is responsible for the business functionality that the interface uses in a particular way. This example uses an ASP.NET Web service to implement the service interface.

Note: The application logic that is shown here is an example of the *Table Data Gateway* pattern. In a typical application, there would be some additional business functionality that the implementation would provide. To focus on Service Interface, such additional business functionality is omitted from this example.

Service Interface Implementation

An ASP.NET Web Service is used to implement *Service Interface*. Implementing this as a Web Service makes this piece of functionality accessible to any number of disparate systems using Internet standards, such as XML, SOAP, and HTTP. Web services depend heavily upon the acceptance of XML and other Internet standards to create an infrastructure that supports application interoperability.

Because the focus is on interoperability between the consumer and the provider you cannot rely on complex types that may or may not be present on different platforms. This leads you to define a contract that provides interoperability. The approach described below involves defining a data transfer object using an XML schema, generating the data transfer object using platform specific tools and then relying on the platform to implement the service interface code that uses the data transfer object. This is not the only approach that will work. The .NET Framework generates all the pieces of functionality for you. However, there are cases in which it generates service interfaces that are not easily interoperable. On the other hand, you could specify the interface using Web Services Description Language (WSDL) and XML schema and then use the wsdl.exe utility to generate service interfaces for your application..

Contract

As described in *Service Interface* a contract exists which allows providers of a service and consumers to interoperate. There are three aspects to this contract when implementing it as an ASP.NET Web service:

- **Specify XML schema**. The definition of the data that is transferred between the consumer and the provider is specified using an XML schema. The input to the service is a simple variable of the type **long**; therefore a schema is not needed for this scenario because simple types are built into the SOAP specification. However, the return type of the Web service is not a simple type, so the type must be specified using an XML schema. In this example, the schema is contained in the Recording.xsd file.

- **Data transfer object**. The .NET framework has a tool called **xsd.exe** which, given an XML schema, can generate a data transfer object to be used by the code that implements the Web service. In this example, the name of the data transfer object is **Recording** and it is contained in the Recording.cs file.

- **Service Interface implementation**. A class that inherits from **System.Web.Services.WebService** and specifies at least one method that is marked with the **[WebMethod]** attribute. In this example, the class is called **RecordingCatalog** and it is contained in the RecordingCatalog.asmx.cs file. This class is responsible for making the call to the service implementation and also for translating the output of the service implementation into the format that the Web service will use. The functionality to translate the data is encapsulated in a class called **RecordingAssembler** and contained in the RecordingAssembler.cs file. This class is an example of an assembler, which is a variant of the *Mapper* pattern. [Fowler03]

The diagram on the next page depicts the relationship of the classes that implement the service interface.

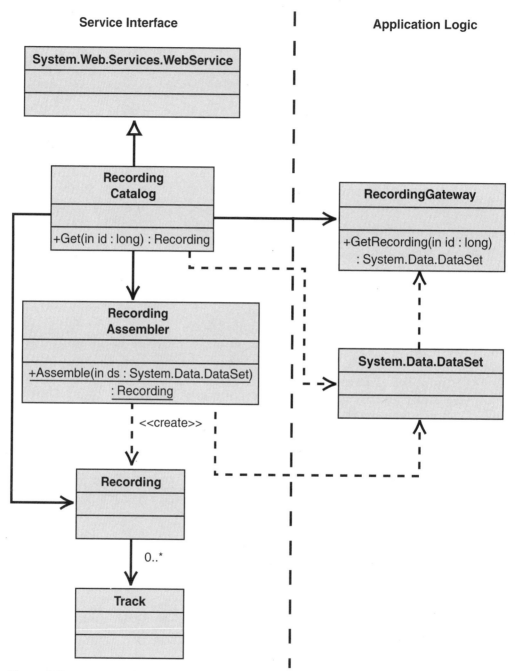

Figure 6.6
Service Interface class diagram

Recording.xsd

The definition of the information that will be transferred to the client is specified using an XML schema. The following schema defines two complex types; **Recording** and **Track**.

```xml
<?xml version="1.0" encoding="utf-8" ?>
<xs:schema xmlns:tns="http://msdn.microsoft.com/practices"
elementFormDefault="qualified" targetNamespace="http://msdn.microsoft.com/pat-
terns" xmlns:xs="http://www.w3.org/2001/XMLSchema">
    <xs:element name="Recording" type="tns:Recording" />
    <xs:complexType name="Recording">
        <xs:sequence>
            <xs:element minOccurs="1" maxOccurs="1" name="id" type="xs:long" />
            <xs:element minOccurs="1" maxOccurs="1" name="title" type="xs:string" />
            <xs:element minOccurs="1" maxOccurs="1" name="artist" type="xs:string" />
            <xs:element minOccurs="0" maxOccurs="unbounded" name="Track"
type="tns:Track" />
        </xs:sequence>
    </xs:complexType>
    <xs:complexType name="Track">
        <xs:sequence>
            <xs:element minOccurs="1" maxOccurs="1" name="id" type="xs:long" />
            <xs:element minOccurs="1" maxOccurs="1" name="title" type="xs:string" />
            <xs:element minOccurs="1" maxOccurs="1" name="duration" type="xs:string" />
        </xs:sequence>
    </xs:complexType>
</xs:schema>
```

The Recording type has an ID, artist, title, and an unbounded number of Track types. A Track type also has ID, title, and duration elements.

Recording.cs

As mentioned earlier, the .NET Framework has a xsd.exe command-line tool, which takes as input an XML schema and outputs a class that can be used in your program. The generated class is used as the return value of the Web service. The command that was used to generate the **Recording.cs** class is as follows:

```
xsd /classes Recording.xsd
```

```
The output that was produced by running this command is shown below:
//------------------------------------------
// <autogenerated>
//      This code was generated by a tool.
//      Runtime Version: 1.0.3705.288
//
//      Changes to this file may cause incorrect behavior and will be lost if
//      the code is regenerated.
// </autogenerated>
//------------------------------------------
```

```csharp
//
// This source code was auto-generated by xsd, Version=1.0.3705.288.
//
using System.Xml.Serialization;


/// <remarks/>
[System.Xml.Serialization.XmlTypeAttribute(Namespace="http://msdn.microsoft.com/
practices")]
[System.Xml.Serialization.XmlRootAttribute(Namespace="http://msdn.microsoft.com/
practices", IsNullable=false)]
public class Recording {

    /// <remarks/>
    public long id;

    /// <remarks/>
    public string title;

    /// <remarks/>
    public string artist;

    /// <remarks/>
    [System.Xml.Serialization.XmlElementAttribute("Track")]
    public Track[] Track;
}

/// <remarks/>
[System.Xml.Serialization.XmlTypeAttribute(Namespace="http://msdn.microsoft.com/
practices")]
public class Track {

    /// <remarks/>
    public long id;

    /// <remarks/>
    public string title;

    /// <remarks/>
    public string duration;
}
```

RecordingCatalog.asmx.cs

After the types are defined, you need to implement the actual Web service implementation. This class encapsulates all of the *Service Interface* behavior. The service that is being exposed is defined explicitly by using the **[WebMethod]** attribute.

```csharp
[WebMethod]
public Recording Get(long id)
{ /* … */ }
```

The **Get** method takes as input an **id** and returns a **Recording** object. As described in the XML schema a **Recording** may also include a number of **Track** objects.

The following is the implementation.

```csharp
using System.ComponentModel;
using System.Data;
using System.Web.Services;

namespace ServiceInterface
{
    [WebService(Namespace="http://msdn.microsoft.com/practices")]
    public class RecordingCatalog : System.Web.Services.WebService
    {
        private RecordingGateway gateway;

        public RecordingCatalog()
        {
            gateway = new RecordingGateway();
                InitializeComponent();
        }

        #region Component Designer generated code
        // ...
        #endregion

        [WebMethod]
        public Recording Get(long id)
        {
            DataSet ds = RecordingGateway.GetRecording(id);
            return RecordingAssembler.Assemble(ds);
        }
    }
}
```

The **Get** method makes a call to the **RecordingGateway** to retrieve a **DataSet**. It then makes a call to the **RecordingAssembler.Assemble** method to translate the **DataSet** into the generated **Recording** and **Track** objects.

RecordingAssembler.cs

The reason this class is part of the service interface is because of the need to translate the output of the application logic into the objects that are being sent out over the Web service. The **RecordingAssembler** class is responsible for translating the return type of the service implementation, in this case an ADO.NET **DataSet**, into the **Recording** and **Track** types that were generated in a previous step.

```csharp
using System;
using System.Collections;
using System.Data;

public class RecordingAssembler
{
    public static Recording Assemble(DataSet ds)
    {
        DataTable recordingTable = ds.Tables["recording"];
```

```
        if(recordingTable.Rows.Count == 0) return null;

        DataRow row = recordingTable.Rows[0];

        Recording recording = new Recording();
        recording.id = (long)row["id"];
        string artist = (string)row["artist"];
        recording.artist = artist.Trim();
        string title = (string)row["title"];
        recording.title = title.Trim();

        ArrayList tracks = new ArrayList();
        DataTable trackTable = ds.Tables["track"];
        foreach(DataRow trackRow in trackTable.Rows)
        {
            Track track = new Track();
            track.id = (long)trackRow["id"];
            string trackTitle = (string)trackRow["title"];
            track.title = trackTitle.Trim();
            string duration = (string)trackRow["duration"];
            track.duration = duration.Trim();
            tracks.Add(track);
        }
        recording.Track = (Track[])tracks.ToArray(typeof(Track));

        return recording;
    }
}
```

Assembler classes in general are somewhat ugly. Their job is to translate from one representation to another so they are usually straightforward but always depend on both representations. These dependencies make them susceptible to changes from both representations.

Although assemblers are useful, you may not always want to create one yourself if there are readily available alternatives that meet your needs. As an alternative in this case, you could use XML serialization to create an instance of an XMLDataDocument, associate it with the **DataSet** and return the XML instead. For details on this approach, see the "DataSets, Web Services, DiffGrams, Arrays, and Interoperability" article on MSDN®: *http://msdn.microsoft.com/library/default.asp?url= /library/en-us/dnservice/html/service02112003.asp?frame=true*

Application Logic

The application logic in this example is probably too simple for most enterprise applications. The reasoning for this that the pattern focuses on the *Service Interface* so the implementation portion is shown more for completeness instead of being a representative example. This implementation uses a *Table Data Gateway* to retrieve data from a database. The *Table Data Gateway* class, called **RecordingGateway**, retrieves the recording record and the track records associated with the recording. The result is returned in a single **DataSet**. For a detailed discussion of the database schema used and of **DataSet**, see *Implementing Data Transfer Object in .NET with a DataSet.*

RecordingGateway.cs

This class fills a **DataSet** with two results sets: recording and track. The client passes in the ID of the recording record that is desired. The class performs two queries against the database to fill the **DataSet**. The last thing it does is to define the relationship between the recording and its track records.

```
using System;
using System.Collections;
using System.Data;
using System.Data.SqlClient;

public class RecordingGateway
{
    public static DataSet GetRecording(long id)
    {
        String selectCmd =
            String.Format(
            "select * from recording where id = {0}",
            id);

        SqlConnection myConnection =
            new SqlConnection(
"server=(local);database=recordings;Trusted_Connection=yes");
        SqlDataAdapter myCommand =
new SqlDataAdapter(selectCmd, myConnection);

        DataSet ds = new DataSet();
        myCommand.Fill(ds, "recording");

        String trackSelect =
            String.Format(
            "select * from Track where recordingId = {0} order by Id",
            id);

        SqlDataAdapter trackCommand =
new SqlDataAdapter(trackSelect, myConnection);
        trackCommand.Fill(ds, "track");

        ds.Relations.Add("RecordingTracks",
            ds.Tables["recording"].Columns["id"],
            ds.Tables["track"].Columns["recordingId"]);

        return ds;
    }
}
```

Note: The example shown here is not meant to describe the only way to fill a **DataSet**. There are many ways to retrieve this data from the database. For example, you could use a stored procedure.

Tests

The unit tests focus on testing the internal aspects of the implementation. One unit test tests the retrieval of information from the database (**RecordingGatewayFixture**) and the other tests the conversion of a **DataSet** into **Recording** and **Track** objects (**RecordingAssemblerFixture**).

RecordingGatewayFixture

The **RecordingGatewayFixture** class tests the output of the **RecordingGateway**, which is a **DataSet**. This verifies that, given an ID, a proper DataSet is retrieved from the database with both recording and track information.

```
using NUnit.Framework;
using System.Data;

[TestFixture]
public class RecordingGatewayFixture
{
    private DataSet ds;
    private DataTable recordingTable;
    private DataRelation relationship;
    private DataRow[] trackRows;

    [SetUp]
    public void Init()
    {
        ds = RecordingGateway.GetRecording(1234);
        recordingTable = ds.Tables["recording"];
        relationship = recordingTable.ChildRelations[0];
        trackRows = recordingTable.Rows[0].GetChildRows(relationship);
    }

    [Test]
    public void RecordingCount()
    {
        Assertion.AssertEquals(1, recordingTable.Rows.Count);
    }

    [Test]
    public void RecordingTitle()
    {
        DataRow recording = recordingTable.Rows[0];
        string title = (string)recording["title"];
        Assertion.AssertEquals("Up", title.Trim());
    }


    [Test]
    public void RecordingTrackRelationship()
    {
        Assertion.AssertEquals(10, trackRows.Length);
    }
```

```
[Test]
public void TrackContent()
{
    DataRow track = trackRows[0];

    string title = (string)track["title"];
    Assertion.AssertEquals("Darkness", title.Trim());
}

[Test]
public void InvalidRecording()
{
    DataSet ds = RecordingGateway.GetRecording(-1);
    Assertion.AssertEquals(0, ds.Tables["recording"].Rows.Count);
    Assertion.AssertEquals(0, ds.Tables["track"].Rows.Count);
}
}
```

RecordingAssemblerFixture

The second fixture tests the **RecordingAssembler** class by testing the conversion of a **DataSet** into **Recording** and **Track** objects:

```
using NUnit.Framework;
using System.Data;
using System.IO;
using System.Xml;

[TestFixture]
public class RecordingAssemblerFixture
{
    private static readonly long testId = 1234;
    private Recording recording;

    [SetUp]
    public void Init()
    {
        DataSet ds = RecordingGateway.GetRecording(1234);
        recording = RecordingAssembler.Assemble(ds);
    }

    [Test]
    public void Id()
    {
        Assertion.AssertEquals(testId, recording.id);
    }

    [Test]
    public void Title()
    {
        Assertion.AssertEquals("Up", recording.title);
    }
```

```
[Test]
public void Artist()
{
    Assertion.AssertEquals("Peter Gabriel", recording.artist);
}


[Test]
public void TrackCount()
{
    Assertion.AssertEquals(10, recording.Track.Length);
}

[Test]
public void TrackTitle()
{
    Track track = recording.Track[0];
    Assertion.AssertEquals("Darkness", track.title);
}

[Test]
public void TrackDuration()
{
    Track track = recording.Track[0];
    Assertion.AssertEquals("6:51", track.duration);
}

[Test]
public void InvalidRecording()
{
    DataSet ds = RecordingGateway.GetRecording(-1);
    Recording recording = RecordingAssembler.Assemble(ds);
    Assertion.AssertNull(recording);
}
}
```

After running these tests you have confidence that the retrieval of information from the database works correctly and you can translate the database output into the data transfer objects. However, the tests do not address end-to-end functionality nor do they test all of the service interface code. The following example tests the full functionality. It is referred to as a functional or acceptance test since it verifies that the whole interface works as expected. The approach described below retrieves a **DataSet** from the **RecordingGateway**. It then makes a call using the web service to retrieve the exact same Recording. After it is received it simply compares the two results. If they are the equal then Service Interface works correctly.

Note: Only a sample of possible acceptance tests are shown here. You should also note that there are also other ways to do this type of testing. This is just one way of performing the tests.

AcceptanceTest.cs

The following are some sample acceptance tests for the service interface:

```csharp
using System;
using System.Data;
using NUnit.Framework;
using ServiceInterface.TestCatalog;

[TestFixture]
public class AcceptanceTest
{
    private static readonly long id = 1234;
    private DataSet localData;
    private DataTable recordingTable;

    private RecordingCatalog catalog = new RecordingCatalog();
    private ServiceInterface.TestCatalog.Recording recording;

    [SetUp]
    public void Init()
    {
        // get the recording from the database
        localData = RecordingGateway.GetRecording(id);
        recordingTable = localData.Tables["recording"];

        // get the same recording from the web service
        recording = catalog.Get(id);
    }


    [Test]
    public void Title()
    {
        DataRow recordingRow = recordingTable.Rows[0];
        string title = (string)recordingRow["title"];
        Assertion.AssertEquals(title.Trim(), recording.title);
    }

    [Test]
    public void Artist()
    {
        DataRow recordingRow = recordingTable.Rows[0];
        string title = (string)recordingRow["artist"];
        Assertion.AssertEquals(title.Trim(), recording.artist);
    }

    // continued
}
```

Resulting Context

The following are the benefits and liabilities related to using an ASP.NET Web service as an implementation of *Service Interface*:

Benefits

- **Separation of concerns**. The separation of the service interface and application logic is important because they are likely to vary independently. Implementing the interface portion as an ASP.NET Web service facilitates the separation.

- **Interoperability**. Basing the interface on Internet standards, such as XML and SOAP, allow for different clients to access the Web service, no matter which operating system they are using.

- **ASP.NET Web services and Microsoft Visual Studio.NET**. The environment makes working with Web services very straightforward. The xsd.exe tool demonstrated in this example provides a tool to translate an XML schema into a C# or Microsoft Visual Basic® .NET class. To create the Web service, this example used a predefined template in the Microsoft Visual Studio® .NET development system and generated the majority of the RecordingCatalog.asmx.cs file.

Liabilities

- **Data Transformation**. In many cases, there must be a data transformation from the application logic representation to the representation that is being used by the service interface. This transformation is always problematic due to the dependencies introduced by having a class that depends on both representations. In this example, the **RecordingAssembler** class depends on the **DataSet** returned by the **RecordingGateway** as well as the generated **Recording** and **Track** classes.

- **Synchronization**. Keeping the schema and the generated code both updated is not automatic. Therefore, any change to the schema requires that you rerun the xsd.exe tool to regenerate the **Recording.cs** class.

Related Patterns

- *Table Data Gateway* [Fowler03]. The **RecordingGateway** shown here is an example of this pattern.

- *Mapper* [Fowler03] The RecordingAssembler shown here is a variant of the *Mapper* pattern, which is often referred to as an assembler.

- *Implementing Data Transfer Object in .NET with a DataSet*. This pattern describes the database schema that is used in this example.

Acknowledgments

[Microsoft02-1] Microsoft Corporation. "XML Web Services Overview." *.NET Framework Developer's Guide*. Available from the MSDN Library at: *http://msdn.microsoft.com /library/default.asp?url=/library/en-us/cpguide/html/cpconwebservicesoverview.asp*.

[Fowler03] Fowler, Martin. *Enterprise Application Architecture Patterns*. Addison-Wesley, 2003.

Service Gateway

Context

You are designing an enterprise application that consumes a service provided by another application. The service defines a contract that all service consumers must conform to in order to access the service. The contract defines such things as the technology, communications protocols, and message definitions needed to communicate with the service. To communicate with the service, your application needs to fulfill its responsibilities as detailed in the contract.

Problem

How do you decouple the details of fulfilling the contract responsibilities defined by the service from the rest of your application?

Forces

When designing an application that consumes services provided by other applications, you must address the following forces:

- Implementing the consumer's contract responsibilities requires you to implement security and communication mechanisms such as authentication, marshaling, encryption, and message routing. These mechanisms often change at a different rate and for different reasons than the application's business logic.

- The contract may specify data formats that are different from your application's internal representation. If so, the data must be translated. Sometimes this translation is a simple as renaming a field or converting a data type, but other times this conversion involves complex structural and semantic transformations. For example, most services expose coarse-grained type-based interfaces to optimize their use in distributed environments. Therefore, when an operation is invoked on a service from an object-oriented application, information from several of your applications' fine-grained objects will often need to be aggregated and transformed into the format specified by the contract. Likewise, the response from the operation will usually need to be broken apart and mapped back to fine-grained objects.

- Your organization may not control the contract specified by the service. If the contract changes, you will want to minimize the impact on the application code.

- The communications channel that provides connectivity between your application and the services typically exposes a generic, low-level application programming interface (API) to the application. This API may include generic functions such as **SendData**. In most situations, you want your application to deal with a more semantically rich interface, through methods such as **ValidateCreditCard** or **GetCustomerAddress**.

- Some contracts may specify asynchronous messaging; that is, they may not return a result immediately. Instead, the service consumer must be prepared to receive a separate result message from the service. The event-driven programming needed to handle such incoming messages from a service can complicate an application significantly.

Solution

Encapsulate the code that implements the consumer portion of the contract into its own *Service Gateway* component. Service gateways play a similar role when accessing services as data access components do for access to the application's database. They act as proxies to other services, encapsulating the details of connecting to the source and performing any necessary translation.

Service Gateway is a specific type of Martin Fowler's *Gateway* pattern [Fowler03] that is adapted for use in service-oriented architectures, and as such, its major concern is encapsulating a consuming application's access to external systems. *Service Gateway* often interacts with *Remote Facade* [Fowler03] instead of interacting with an external system directly. *Remote Facade* encapsulates complex functionality in provider applications and exposes that functionality as a single simple interface to consumer applications. *Service Interface* is a specific type of *Remote Facade* adapted for use in service-oriented architectures. In service-oriented architectures, it is common for a consuming application's service gateway to collaborate with a service interface exposed by a provider application. The following figure illustrates this relationship.

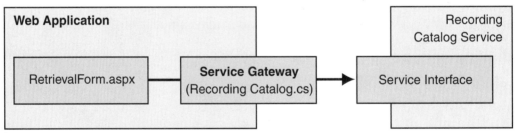

Figure 6.7
Service Gateway consuming the service of a service interface

The *Service Gateway* component encapsulates the low-level details of communicating with a service. Such details include but are not limited to:

- **Communications channel**. *Service Gateway* encapsulates all the low-level network communications functionality needed to communicate with the service. For example, *Service Gateway* hides all the details of using SOAP over HTTP for communicating with a Web service.

- **Data formats**. *Service Gateway* maps between the internal organization of information in your application and the format mandated by the service's communication contract. For example, your application may be composed of a collaborating set of fine-grained objects; however a Web service it consumes may require an XML document as input and provide an XML document as a result. The gateway is responsible for translating between the fine-grained object interfaces and XML documents.

- **Service discovery**. For simple to moderately complex scenarios, *Service Gateway* should encapsulate the process of finding the proper service. This may involve looking up the network address of the service in a configuration file or using a service repository such as UDDI. For complex scenarios, such as those that require dynamic determination of the proper service to call based on changing data, the service discovery functionality may be encapsulated in its own *Service Gateway* component.

- **Process adapter**. *Service Gateway* should adapt the application's business process to work with the service. For example, a single call to the service gateway may result in multiple invocations to one or more service operations. Therefore, the interface that the service gateway presents to the application should be in terms of the application's processes, rather than in terms of communication and security protocols..

- **Asynchronous vs. synchronous calling semantics**. *Service Gateway* adapts the consuming application's calling semantics (asynchronous or synchronous) to the calling semantics specified by the contract. For instance, a consuming application's design may not support the asynchronous calling semantics specified in the contract. The consuming application's service gateway would then be required to convert the application's synchronous calls to the asynchronous protocol specified in the contract.

You do not have to implement *Service Gateway* as a single object. In fact, it may be advantageous to separate some of the functions into separate objects. For example, using separate objects may make it easier to use code generation to create some portions of the gateway. The code that implements the mapping data between the internal application format and the format expected by the service is an ideal candidate for this mapping, provided that the service provider publishes metadata describing the required data format (for example, in the form of WSDL or an XML schema). This metadata can be used to generate a strongly typed class that encapsulates this mapping.

Example

See *Implementing Service Gateway in .NET*.

Testing Considerations

Service Gateway can significantly improve the testability of the system. A service gateway encapsulates all the details of accessing the service into a single component and hides the component behind an interface that has no direct dependencies on the underlying communications channel. This allows you to replace the gateway with a

Service Stub [Fowler03] during testing. This stub does not access the external system at all, but returns results that simulate the external system directly to the application logic. *Service Stub* can also be used to simulate error conditions, such as the external service being unavailable.

Resulting Context

Using a *Service Gateway* component to isolate the application from the details of communicating with the service provides the following benefits and liabilities:

Benefits

- Decoupling the service access logic from the rest of the application makes it easy to change the service the application accesses. For example, you may want to switch to a new version of the same service, or you may want to use a service with better service-level guarantees from another vendor. Switching to another service is much easier if you can automatically generate the code that does the data mapping.

- *Service Gateway* hides the complexities of accessing a service from the application. This improves reuse of both the application components and the service access components. The application has no direct reference to the service, so it is independent of any implementation details and the location of the service. Encapsulating the service access logic in a separate layer also improves the reuse of the access logic because it can now be used across multiple service calls as long as the same transport and authentication mechanism is used.

- *Service Gateway* provides an ideal location for providing common features such as asynchronous invocation, caching, and error handling.

Liabilities

- *Service Gateway* adds an additional level of complexity that may be unnecessary for simple solutions. In particular, the effort and infrastructure needed to support the automatic generation of mapping components may not be needed if your organization will only be accessing a few relatively static services.

- A particular service gateway is responsible for interacting with a single service. Coordination among multiple services must he handled by an additional component such as the business process component specified in *Three-Layered Services Application.*

- The service gateway is often contained within a single application. Therefore, code duplication can result: if multiple applications access the same service, both applications may duplicate the gateway functionality. Developing a reusable service gateway component is one alternative. Another solution is to extract the common functionality into its own service that is deployed locally within your organization. Some of distributed computing solutions discussed in the previous chapter, such as *Remote Facade*, can also be useful in this situation.

Related Patterns

For more information, see the following related patterns:

- Three-Layered Services Application. The *Service Gateway* component specified in *Three-Layered Services Application* is an implementation of the *Service Gateway* pattern.

- *Service Interface. Service Interface* plays a role in provider applications that is similar to the role *Service Gateway* plays in consumer applications.

- *Mapper* [Fowler03]. *Mapper* provides translation between two or more fixed interfaces without either object being aware of the other. Service gateways may incorporate *Mapper* to translate between application and service data formats.

- *Remote Facade* [Fowler03]. *Service Interface* is a specific type of *Remote Facade* adapted for use in service-oriented architectures. A remote facade is similar to a remote proxy but sometimes uses encapsulation to make the remote interface more coarse-grained.

- *Gateway* [Fowler03]. *Gateway* is an object that encapsulates access to an external system or resource. *Service Gateway* is a specific instance of *Gateway*.

- *Assembler*: Similar to *Mapper*, this pattern assembles an object from many objects. Communication between two interfaces in a mapper is bidirectional, whereas it tends to be unidirectional in assemblers.

Acknowledgments

[Fowler03] Fowler, Martin. *Patterns of Enterprise Application Architecture*. Addison-Wesley, 2003.

[Schmidt00] Schmidt, Douglas, *Pattern-Oriented Software Architecture Vol.2*, Wiley & Sons, 2000.

Implementing Service Gateway in .NET

Context

You are implementing *Service Gateway* in an application that will be deployed on the Microsoft Windows® operating system. The service to be consumed is a Web service that uses SOAP over HTTP for communications and is fully described by means of Web Services Description Language (WSDL).

Implementation Strategy

Service Gateway recommends encapsulating the code that implements the low-level details of communicating with a service into its own component. The component is responsible for implementing the consumer portion of the communications contract between the consumer and the service provider.

Web services document the service provider portion of the communications contract using WSDL. The wsdl.exe tool in the .NET Framework SDK processes a WSDL description of a Web service and generates a class that encapsulates all the details of communicating with the service through SOAP. For many applications, this proxy class can be used as the service gateway. Some advanced scenarios require the service gateway to have responsibilities beyond basic communication, such as transactions and security; in these scenarios, you may need to wrap the generated class to provide this additional functionality.

Example Overview

This example shows how you could use the implementation strategy described to develop a Web application that displays recording information. The recording catalog service discussed in *Implementing Service Interface in .NET* provides the recording information.

Figure 6.8 shows the overall structure of the application.

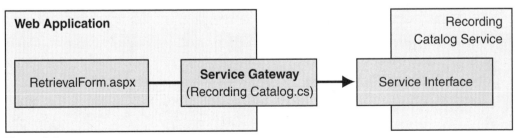

Figure 6.8
Application structure

Figure 6.9 shows the user interface of the example Web application.

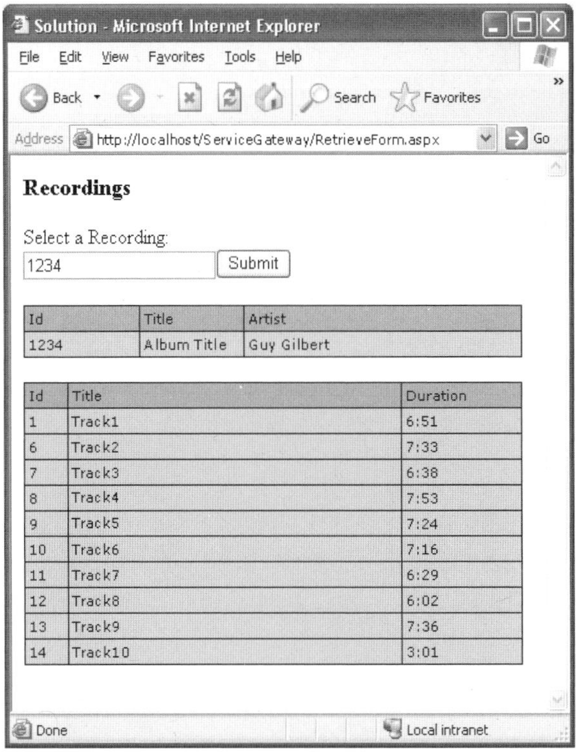

Figure 6.9
Example Web application

This is a very simple Web application. The user enters a recording ID in the **Select a Recording** text box and clicks **Submit**. The Web application queries the recording catalog service and displays the result.

Figure 6.10 on the next page shows a detailed class diagram of the application.

The **RecordingCatalog** class is the *Service Gateway* component. It is the class that is generated by the wsdl.exe utility. Further details are discussed later in the pattern.

The **RetrievalForm** class derives from **WebForm** class and provides the Web-based user interface for the application.

The **Recording** and **Track** classes are defined in the WSDL description of the service and therefore are generated by the wsdl.exe utility. These classes are purely data containers and contain no methods. Their primary role is to act as data transfer objects in interactions with the service.

The **RecordingDisplayAdapter** and **TrackDisplayAdapter** classes are wrappers around **Recording** and **Track** that adapt their interfaces for ease of use by the user interface controls.

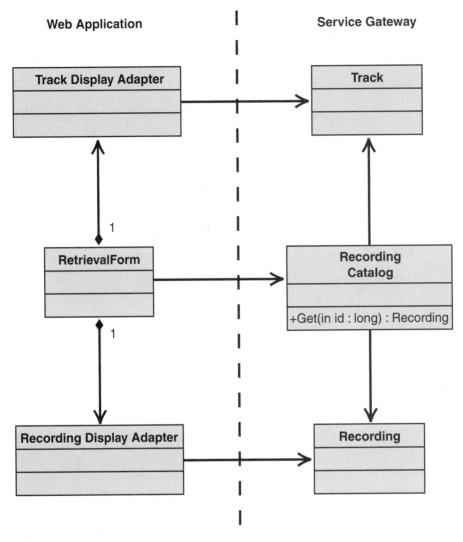

Figure 6.10
Structural view of example Web application

WSDL Description

You need to obtain the WSDL description for the service to be able to generate the service gateway. The WSDL describes the contract that the service gateway and service interface agree on. The service used in this example was developed in ASP.NET. ASP.NET-based Web services have a built-in mechanism for obtaining the WSDL description of the service. In the URL text box of a Web browser, you type the URL of the service with **?WSDL** appended to the end.

For example, if the URL of the service is:

http://localhost/ServiceInterface/RecordingCatalog.asmx

you would type the following to display the WSDL description for the service:

http://localhost/ServiceInterface/RecordingCatalog.asmx?WSDL

The WSDL description for the service gateway in the Web application example defines a service named RecordingCatalog as follows. For the implementation in this discussion, only the SOAP port is of interest. This section of the description specifies the URL for the service and references the RecordingCatalogSoap binding.

Note: The full WSDL description is not shown here. However, key excerpts that have an impact on the generated service gateway classes are shown.

```
<service name="RecordingCatalog">
  <port name="RecordingCatalogSoap" binding="s0:RecordingCatalogSoap">
    <soap:address location="http://localhost/ServiceInterface/
RecordingCatalog.asmx" />
  </port>
  ...
  Description of other ports.
  ...
</service>
The following is the binding definition for RecordingCatalog:
<binding name="RecordingCatalogSoap" type="s0:RecordingCatalogSoap">
  ...
</binding>
```

The next section specifies that the service has one operation, which is named "Get". It also describes the type of message that the service expects and the type of message that the service will respond with:

```
<portType name="RecordingCatalogSoap">
  <operation name="Get">
   <input message="s0:GetSoapIn" />
   <output message="s0:GetSoapOut" />
  </operation>
</portType>
```

The following section defines the parameters associated with calling the service and the type of what is returned to the user:

```
<message name="GetSoapIn">
  <part name="parameters" element="s0:Get" />
</message>
<message name="GetSoapOut">
  <part name="parameters" element="s0:GetResponse" />
</message>
```

Lastly, the WSDL description specifies, in the form of an XML schema, the Get message to have one element, which is a long value. The response message returns a type, named Recording, which is composed of the recording ID, title, artist, and list of tracks.

```
<types>
  <s:schema elementFormDefault="qualified"targetNamespace="http://
msdn.microsoft.com/patterns">
    <s:element name="Get">
      <s:complexType>
        <s:sequence>
      <s:element minOccurs="1" maxOccurs="1" name="id" type="s:long" />
  </s:sequence>
        </s:complexType>
      </s:element>
      <s:element name="GetResponse">
        <s:complexType>
          <s:sequence>
      <s:element minOccurs="0" maxOccurs="1" name="GetResult" type="s0:Recording" />
  </s:sequence>
        </s:complexType>
      </s:element>
      <s:complexType name="Recording">
        <s:sequence>
          <s:element minOccurs="1" maxOccurs="1" name="id" type="s:long" />
          <s:element minOccurs="0" maxOccurs="1" name="title" type="s:string" />
          <s:element minOccurs="0" maxOccurs="1" name="artist" type="s:string" />
          <s:element minOccurs="0" maxOccurs="unbounded" name="Track"
type="s0:Track" />
        </s:sequence>
      </s:complexType>
      <s:complexType name="Track">
        <s:sequence>
          <s:element minOccurs="1" maxOccurs="1" name="id" type="s:long" />
          <s:element minOccurs="0" maxOccurs="1" name="title" type="s:string" />
          <s:element minOccurs="0" maxOccurs="1" name="duration" type="s:string" />
        </s:sequence>
      </s:complexType>
      <s:element name="Recording" type="s0:Recording" />
        </s:schema>
        </types>
```

Service Gateway Implementation

To generate the class and the data transfer classes, you need to execute the following command:

wsdl http://localhost/ServiceInterface/RecordingCatalog.aspx

The name of the output file is based on the service name given in the WSDL description; in this example, the file name is RecordingCatalog.cs. This file contains the source code for three class definitions: **RecordingCatalog**, **Recording**, and **Track**.

For more information on wsdl.exe, see .NET Framework Tools on MSDN®:

*http://msdn.microsoft.com/library/default.asp?url=/library/en-us/cptools/html
/cpgrfwebservicesdescriptionlanguagetoolwsdlexe.asp*

RecordingCatalog.cs

RecordingCatalog is the class that encapsulates the details of SOAP messaging and
HTTP communications. This class exposes a public Get method that is responsible
for calling the "Get" operation on the service. Notice the correspondence between
the types defined in the XML schema definition and the C# types. The sample
application uses this method to obtain the catalog data that will be displayed to
the user.

```
public class RecordingCatalog :
System.Web.Services.Protocols.SoapHttpClientProtocol {

    /// <remarks/>
    public RecordingCatalog() {
        this.Url = "http://localhost/ServiceInterface/RecordingCatalog.asmx";
    }

    /// <remarks/>
    [System.Web.Services.Protocols.SoapDocumentMethodAttribute("http://
microsoft.com/pag/patterns/Get", RequestNamespace="http://microsoft.com/pag/
patterns", ResponseNamespace="http://microsoft.com/pag/patterns",
Use=System.Web.Services.Description.SoapBindingUse.Literal,
ParameterStyle=System.Web.Services.Protocols.SoapParameterStyle.Wrapped)]
    public Recording Get(long id) {
        object[] results = this.Invoke("Get", new object[] {
                    id});
        return ((Recording)(results[0]));
    }

    // …
}
```

Recording Data Transfer Object

The following is the implementation of the **Recording** type specified in the XML
schema section of the WSDL description and generated in C# by the wsdl.exe tool:

```
public class Recording {

    /// <remarks/>
    public long id;

    /// <remarks/>
    public string title;

    /// <remarks/>
    public string artist;
```

```
    /// <remarks/>
    [System.Xml.Serialization.XmlElementAttribute("Track")]
    public Track[] Track;
}
```

Track Data Transfer Object

One of the fields defined in the Recording class refers to the Track type. Track is also specified in the XML schema section of the WSDL file. Its representation as a C# class is defined as follows:

```
public class Track {

    /// <remarks/>
    public long id;

    /// <remarks/>
    public string title;

    /// <remarks/>
    public string duration;
}
```

Application Implementation

The remaining three classes, RetrievalForm, RecordingDisplayAdapter, and TrackDisplayAdapter, are used to create a Web page that displays the catalog information.

RetrievalForm.aspx

The RetrievalForm is an ASP.NET page that provides a basic user interface for displaying the data retrieved from the Recording Catalog Web service. It has a text box for entering a recording ID, a button control to initiate the data lookup, and two repeater controls for displaying the returned information. The code for this class is as follows:

```
<%@ Page language="c#" Codebehind="RetrievalForm.aspx.cs" AutoEventWireup="false"
Inherits="RetrieveForm" %>
<HTML>
  <HEAD>
    <title>Solution</title>
  </HEAD>
  <body>
    <form id="start" method="post" runat="server">
      <h3>Recordings</h3>
      Select a Recording:<br>
      <asp:textbox id="TextBox1" runat="server"></asp:textbox><asp:button
id="Button1" onclick="Button1_Click" runat="server" text="Submit"></asp:button>
      <p><asp:repeater id="RecordingRepeater" runat="server">
        <HeaderTemplate>
```

```
                     <table cellpadding="3" cellspacing="0" bordercolor="black" border="1"
style="background-color:#CCCCFF;border-color:Black;font-family:Verdana;font-
size:8pt;width:400px;border-collapse:collapse;">
                          <tr bgcolor="#aaaadd">
                            <td>Id</td>
                            <td>Title</td>
                            <td>Artist</td>
                          </tr>
                    </HeaderTemplate>
                    <ItemTemplate>
                      <tr>
                        <td><%# DataBinder.Eval(Container.DataItem, "Id") %></td>
                        <td><%# DataBinder.Eval(Container.DataItem, "Title") %></td>
                        <td><%# DataBinder.Eval(Container.DataItem, "Artist") %></td>
                      </tr>
                    </ItemTemplate>
                    <FooterTemplate>
                      </table>
                    </FooterTemplate>
                 </asp:repeater></p>
            <p>
                <asp:Repeater id="TrackRepeater" runat="server">
                  <HeaderTemplate>
                     <table cellpadding="3" cellspacing="0" bordercolor="black" border="1"
style="background-color:#CCCCFF;border-color:Black;font-family:Verdana;font-
size:8pt;width:400px;border-collapse:collapse;">
                          <tr bgcolor="#aaaadd">
                            <td>Id</td>
                            <td>Title</td>
                            <td>Duration</td>
                          </tr>
                    </HeaderTemplate>
                    <ItemTemplate>
                      <tr>
                        <td><%# DataBinder.Eval(Container.DataItem, "Id") %></td>
                        <td><%# DataBinder.Eval(Container.DataItem, "Title") %></td>
                        <td><%# DataBinder.Eval(Container.DataItem, "Duration") %></td>
                      </tr>
                    </ItemTemplate>
                    <FooterTemplate>
                      </table>
                    </FooterTemplate>
                 </asp:Repeater></p>
          </form>
          <P></P>
        </body>
      </HTML>
```

RetrievalForm.apsx.cs

RetrevalForm.apsx.cs is the code-behind class for the RetrievalForm page. Its responsibility is to map the results of the call to the Web service to the user interface components. This class uses the RecordingCatalog class to access the Web service. The code is as follows:

```
using System;
using System.Collections;
using System.Data;

public class RetrievalForm : System.Web.UI.Page
{
        private RecordingCatalog catalog = new RecordingCatalog();

        protected System.Web.UI.WebControls.Button Button1;
        protected System.Web.UI.WebControls.Repeater RecordingRepeater;
        protected System.Web.UI.WebControls.Repeater TrackRepeater;
        protected System.Web.UI.WebControls.TextBox TextBox1;

        private void Page_Load(object sender, System.EventArgs e)
        {
                // Put user code to initialize the page here
        }

        #region Web Form Designer generated code
        ...
        #endregion

        protected void Button1_Click(object sender, System.EventArgs e)
        {
                string stringId = TextBox1.Text;
                long id = Convert.ToInt32(stringId);

                Recording recording = catalog.Get(id);
                if(recording != null)
                {
                        ArrayList recordingAdapters = new ArrayList();
                        recordingAdapters.Add(new
RecordingDisplayAdapter(recording));
                        RecordingRepeater.DataSource = recordingAdapters;
                        RecordingRepeater.DataBind();

                        ArrayList trackAdapters = new ArrayList();
                        foreach(Track track in recording.Track)
                        {
                                trackAdapters.Add(new TrackDisplayAdapter(track));
                        }

                        TrackRepeater.DataSource = trackAdapters;
                        TrackRepeater.DataBind();
                }
                else
                {
```

```
                                RecordingRepeater.DataSource = null;
                                RecordingRepeater.DataBind();

                                TrackRepeater.DataSource = null;
                                TrackRepeater.DataBind();
                        }
                }
        }
```

RecordingDisplayAdapter.cs

The RecordingDisplayAdapter class performs two functions. First, it isolates the user interface from changes made to the types defined in the XML schema section of the WSDL description. Second, because the data binding functionality of the repeater control only works with properties and not public fields, the adapter provides a property interface for the fields defined in the Recording class. The code is as follows:

```
using System;

public class RecordingDisplayAdapter
{
private Recording recording;

    public RecordingDisplayAdapter(Recording recording)
    {
        this.recording = recording;
    }

    public long Id
    {
        get { return recording.id; }
    }

    public string Artist
    {
        get { return recording.artist; }
    }

    public string Title
    {
        get { return recording.title; }
    }
}
```

TrackDisplayAdapter.cs

The TrackDisplayAdapter class performs the same function for the Track class as the RecordingDisplayAdapter does for the Recording class, as shown in the following code:

```csharp
using System;

public class TrackDisplayAdapter
{
  private Track track;

  public TrackDisplayAdapter(Track track)
  {
    this.track = track;
  }

  public long Id
  {
    get { return track.id; }
  }

  public string Duration
  {
    get { return track.duration; }
  }

  public string Title
  {
    get { return track.title; }
  }
}
```

Tests

The example application consists mostly of generated code, which does not generally require unit tests. The type of testing it requires is referred to as acceptance testing. Acceptance tests exercise the system entirely to ensure that it performs the functions necessary for completion.

Resulting Context

Benefits

- **Ease of development**. Using this implementation approach incurs very little development cost because the tools generate much of the code for you.
- **Support for both synchronous and asynchronous invocation**. The proxy generated by wsdl.exe provides support for both synchronous and asynchronous invocation. Synchronous invocation is simple and easy to work with. Asynchronous invocation can have a very positive impact on performance.

Liabilities

- **Limited flexibility**. You will need to add any functionality the generating class does not provide by developing a custom wrapper class that implements the new functionality and then forwards the request to the class generated by wsdl.exe.

Related Patterns

For more information, see the following related patterns:

- *Adapter* [Gamma95]. *Service Gateway* is an example of an adapter class. It translates from its own interface into the calls needed to invoke the Web service.

- *Service Interface*. *Service Gateway* consumes services that are provided by implementations of *Service Interface*.

Acknowledgments

[Microsoft02-1] Microsoft Corporation. "XML Web Services Overview." *.NET Framework Developer's Guide*. Available from the MSDN Library at: *http://msdn.microsoft.com/library/default.asp?url=/library/en-us/cpguide/html/cpconwebservicesoverview.asp*.

[Fowler03] Fowler, Martin. *Enterprise Application Architecture Patterns*. Addison-Wesley, 2003.

[Gamma95] Gamma, Helm, Johnson, and Vlissides. *Design Patterns: Elements of Reusable Object-Oriented Software*. Addison-Wesley, 1995.

7

Performance and Reliability Patterns

Performance, scalability, and reliability are important attributes of any enterprise application. Although there are many ways to increase performance and improve reliability, this patterns cluster focuses how to combine multiple systems that serve any number of applications or users for greater scalability and improved availability. The patterns in this chapter provide a basis to effectively adapt to changes in load and peak traffic, and to increase availability.

Meeting Operational Requirements

Today's enterprise applications have to meet ever-increasing operational demands, including higher availability, improved performance, and the ability to maintain these demands as the load on applications increases. This creates the need for application and supporting infrastructure designs that maximize scalability and availability.

Scalability

Scalability is the ability of a system or systems to handle increasing demands while maintaining acceptable performance levels. To scale a system effectively, you must identify the nature of the increasing demand and understand its impact on the various system components. After you identify the limiting component, you can either *scale up* or *scale out*.

Scaling Up

Scaling up is a strategy that increases the capacity of a resource (for example, processor, memory, or storage) in a single server to handle load. For example, you can scale up a database cluster that is built on a multiprocessor operating system by increasing the number of processors or memory.

Scaling Out

Scaling out is the strategy that increases the capacity of an infrastructure tier to handle load by adding servers, thereby increasing the aggregate capacity of those servers.

Availability

Availability is the measurable run time of a server, the software running on a server, or an application and depends on careful design and operational discipline, including change controls, rigorous testing, and quick upgrade and fallback mechanisms. To achieve the highest levels of availability, it is important to isolate all single points of failure in the design. A highly available design process should analyze each component of the architecture to verify that overall system performance does not depend on any single piece of hardware or software performing a specific function or providing access to a specific piece of information.

Patterns Overview

This patterns cluster starts off with *Server Clustering*, which focuses on using server clusters to design an infrastructure tier that meets specific availability and scalability requirements. A *server cluster* is two or more servers that are interconnected to form a unified virtual computing resource.

Clustering servers increases the availability of a system by ensuring that if a server becomes unavailable because of failure or planned downtime, another server in the cluster can assume the workload, ensuring that the application remains available to users. Clustering also enhances scalability by supporting more users at the current level of performance or by improving application performance for the current users. Clustering servers for scalability adds server redundancy, helping to increase system availability, as mentioned earlier.

The *Server Clustering* pattern focuses on clustering as a general design technique, which is applied to two additional design patterns: *Load-Balanced Cluster* and *Failover Cluster*. Figure 7.1 shows the Performance and Reliability patterns cluster.

Design

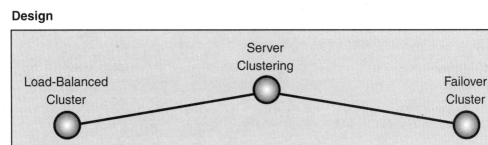

Figure 7.1
Performance and Reliability patterns cluster

Load-Balanced Cluster

The *Load-Balanced Cluster* pattern addresses how to maintain acceptable performance through the design and implementation of a scalable infrastructure tier. This pattern describes the common ways to balance incoming Internet Protocol (IP) traffic across a set, or farm, of read-only or application servers.

Load balancing enhances the performance, availability, and scalability of infrastructure tiers, which contain servers such as Web servers, streaming media servers, and virtual private network (VPN) servers, by distributing requests across all of the healthy servers in the server farm (see *Server Farm*). Load-balanced servers also serve a failover function by redistributing load to the remaining servers when a server in the load-balanced cluster fails.

Failover Cluster

The *Failover Cluster* pattern helps you design a highly available application infra-structure tier that protects against loss of service due to the failure of a single server or the software that it hosts. The pattern describes failover clusters and how they provide high availability for read/write stores such as databases, messaging systems, and file and print services.

In a failover cluster, if one of the servers becomes unavailable, another server takes over and continues to provide the service to the end-user, a process known as *failover*. When failover occurs, users continue to use the application and are unaware that a different server is providing it.

Performance and Reliability Patterns

Table 7.1 lists the patterns in the Performance and Reliability patterns cluster. The patterns are arranged so that later patterns build on earlier patterns. This implies a progression from more general patterns (such as *Server Clustering*) to more specific patterns (such as *Failover Cluster*).

Table 7.1: Performance and Reliability Patterns

Pattern	Problem
Server Clustering	How do you provide an infrastructure for your application that meets specific operational requirements, such as availability and scalability?
Load-Balanced Cluster	How should you design a scalable infrastructure tier that accounts for changes in load while maintaining an acceptable level of performance?
Failover Cluster	How should you design a highly available infrastructure tier that protects against loss of service due to the failure of a single server or the software that it hosts?

Server Clustering

Context

You are designing an infrastructure tier upon which an application will be deployed. Your operational requirements include availability or performance capabilities that cannot be met because either performance bottlenecks or single points of failure exist in your infrastructure.

Problem

How do you provide an infrastructure for your application that meets specific operational requirements such as availability and scalability?

Forces

As you are designing your infrastructure, consider the following forces:

- Users expect applications to be available and responsive when they use them.
- Continuous uptime in a production environment, whether it is a database powering a critical client/server application or an e-commerce Web site, is becoming a common business requirement.
- There is a potential for high monetary loss when an application fails. For example, a high-volume online store bringing in $25,000 per hour goes down due to a single server that fails in the infrastructure. The monetary impact can become quite severe if the outage lasts for several hours.
- All systems within an application infrastructure require maintenance. Individual systems must be able to accommodate both hardware and software upgrades without incurring application downtime. For example, a patch is released to repair a security issue associated with a component running on a server that delivers the application. If this is the only server, the application will experience downtime. If it is one of a series of servers, only the server will experience downtime, not the application.
- Adding hardware can increase the cost and complexity of the solution. For example, new or more capable hardware requires additional development and testing to enable an application to take full advantage of the more capable environment. Additional maintenance and training costs are also associated with managing a more complex environment.

Solution

Design your application infrastructure so that your servers appear to users and applications as virtual unified computing resources. One means by which to achieve this virtualization is by using a server cluster. A *server cluster* is the combination of two or more servers that are interconnected to appear as one, thus creating a virtual resource that enhances availability, scalability, or both.

Clustering servers might include the goal of increasing availability by ensuring that if a server becomes unavailable due to failure or planned downtime, another server in the cluster can assume the workload (see the *Failover Cluster* pattern). This type of clustering avoids loss of service to the users or applications that access the cluster and can occur transparently, without the users' knowledge.

You can also use clustering to enhance scalability. Server clusters can support more users at the current level of performance or improve application performance for the current number of users by sharing the workload across multiple servers. A byproduct of clustering servers for scalability is that the additional redundancy of the multiple servers helps increase system availability, as mentioned earlier (see the *Load-Balanced Cluster* pattern).

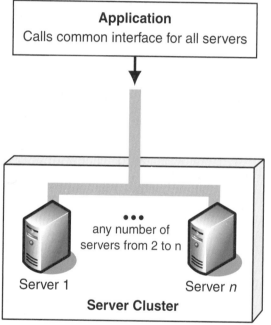

Figure 7.2
Basic clustering concepts

Figure 7.2 illustrates how server clustering can make two or more servers (Server 1 through Server *n*) appear as one virtual resource to a dependent application.

Asymmetric Clusters

In *asymmetric clusters*, a standby server exists only to take over for another server in the event of failure. This type of cluster is usually used to provide high availability and scalability for read/write stores such as databases, messaging systems, and file and print services. If one of the nodes in a cluster becomes unavailable, due to either planned downtime for maintenance or unplanned downtime due to failure, another node takes over the function of the failed node.

The standby server performs no other useful work and is either as capable as or less capable than a primary server. A less capable, less expensive standby server is often used when primary servers are configured for high availability and fault tolerance with multiple redundant subsystems. One common type of asymmetric cluster is known as a *failover cluster* (see the *Failover Cluster* pattern).

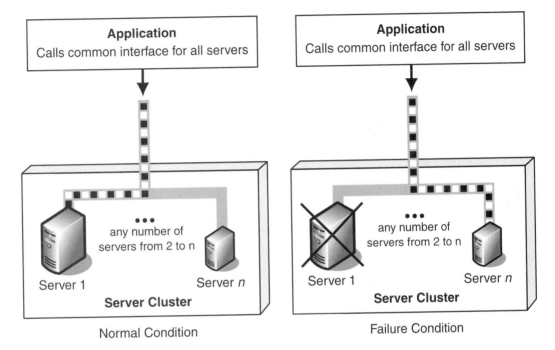

Figure 7.3
Asymmetric cluster

Figure 7.3 illustrates how an asymmetric cluster presents a virtual resource to an application. Under normal conditions, the primary server handles all requests. In the event of a failure, the standby server takes over handling all requests.

Symmetric Clusters

In *symmetric clusters*, every server in the cluster performs useful work. Typically, each server is the primary server for a particular set of applications. If one server fails, the remaining server continues to process its assigned set of applications as well as the applications on the failed server. Symmetric clusters are more cost-effective because they use more of the cluster's resources more often; however, in the event of a failure, the additional load on the remaining servers could cause them to fail as well.

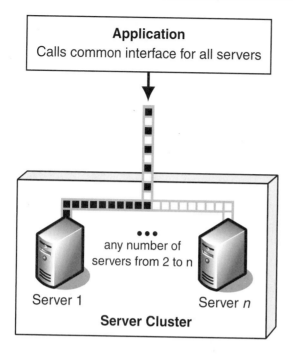

Figure 7.4
Symmetric cluster

Figure 7.4 illustrates how a symmetric cluster presents a virtual resource to an application. Requests are divided among healthy servers to distribute load and increase scalability.

One common type of symmetric cluster is a load-balanced cluster (see the *Load-Balanced Cluster* pattern). Load-balanced clusters enhance the performance, availability, and scalability of services such as Web servers, media servers, VPN servers, and read-only stores by distributing requests across all of the healthy servers in the server cluster.

Example

See the *Load Balanced Cluster* and *Failover Cluster* patterns.

Resulting Context

Server Clustering results in the following benefits and liabilities:

Benefits

- **Improved scalability**. *Server Clustering* enables applications to handle more load.
- **Higher availability**. *Server Clustering* helps applications avoid interruptions in service.

- **Greater flexibility**. The ability of clustering to present a virtual unified computing resource provides IT personnel with more options for configuring the infrastructure to support application performance, availability, and scalability requirements.

Liabilities

- **Increased infrastructure complexity**. Some clustering designs significantly increase the complexity of your solution, which may affect operational and support requirements. For example, clustering can increase the numbers of servers to manage, storage devices to maintain, and network connections to configure and monitor.

- **Additional design and code requirements**. Applications may require specific design and coding changes to function properly when used in an infrastructure that uses clustering. For example, the need to manage session state can become more difficult across multiple servers and could require coding changes to accommodate maintaining state so that session information is not lost if a server fails.

- **Incompatibility**. An existing application or application component may not be able to support clustering technologies. For example, a limitation in the technology used to develop the application or component may not support clustering even through code changes.

Related Patterns

For more information, see the following related patterns:

- *Tiered Distribution. Tiered Distribution* organizes the system infrastructure into a set of physical tiers to optimize server environments for specific operational requirements and system resource usage.

- *Load-Balanced Cluster.* Load-balanced clusters can improve application performance for the current number of users by sharing the workload across multiple servers.

- *Failover Cluster*. Failover clusters can increase availability by creating redundancy in the infrastructure.

Acknowledgments

[Microsoft03] Microsoft Corporation. "Technical Overview of Windows Server 2003 Clustering Services." Available on the Microsoft Windows Server 2003 Web site at: *http://www.microsoft.com/windowsserver2003/techinfo/overview/clustering.mspx.*

[Marcus00] Marcus, Evan, and Hal Stern. *Blueprints for High Availability: Designing Resilient Distributed Systems.* John Wiley & Sons, 2000.

Load-Balanced Cluster

Context

You have decided to use clustering in designing or modifying an infrastructure tier to maintain performance requirements while supporting the ability to adapt to changing demands.

Problem

How should you design a scalable infrastructure tier that accounts for changes in load while maintaining an acceptable level of performance?

Forces

When designing your scalable infrastructure tier, consider the following forces:

- Individual servers have a maximum amount of load capacity for any given application. For example, if a single server provides Web pages as part of a Web-based application and the user or transaction load increases beyond the limitation of the server, the application will either fall below performance expectations or, in the worst case, become unavailable.

- Individual servers have maximum physical performance limitations, including limitations to the bus speed, the amount of memory, the number of processors, and the number of peripherals that any one server can use. For example, if the server is capable of housing only four processors, you cannot add a fifth processor to enhance performance.

- Certain applications have limitations on the number of CPUs that they can use.

- Servers, as individual entities, are single points of failure within a solution. If only one server is responsible for delivering the functionality of a component within an application, its failure results in an application failure.

- Adding servers can increase the complexity of managing and monitoring the server hardware and its associated software.

Solution

Install your service or application onto multiple servers that are configured to share the workload. This type of configuration is a *load-balanced cluster*. Load balancing scales the performance of server-based programs, such as a Web server, by distributing client requests across multiple servers. Load balancing technologies, commonly referred to as *load balancers*, receive incoming requests and redirect them to a specific host if necessary. The load-balanced hosts concurrently respond to different client requests, even multiple requests from the same client. For example, a Web browser may obtain the multiple images within a single Web page from different hosts in the cluster. This distributes the load, speeds up processing, and shortens the response time to clients.

Load balancers use different algorithms to control traffic. The goal of these algorithms is to intelligently distribute load and/or maximize the utilization of all servers within the cluster. Some examples of these algorithms include:

- **Round-robin.** A *round-robin algorithm* distributes the load equally to each server, regardless of the current number of connections or the response time. Round-robin is suitable when the servers in the cluster have equal processing capabilities; otherwise, some servers may receive more requests than they can process while others are using only part of their resources.

- **Weighted round-robin.** A *weighted round-robin algorithm* accounts for the different processing capabilities of each server. Administrators manually assign a performance weight to each server, and a scheduling sequence is automatically generated according to the server weight. Requests are then directed to the different servers according to a round-robin scheduling sequence.

- **Least-connection.** A *least-connection algorithm* sends requests to servers in a cluster, based on which server is currently serving the fewest connections.

- **Load-based.** A *load-based algorithm* sends requests to servers in a cluster, based on which server currently has the lowest load.

Additionally, some load balancers incorporate failure detection. The balancer keeps track of the server or the application running on the server and stops sending requests to a server after a failure. Figure 7.5 on the next page shows the basic components of load balancing.

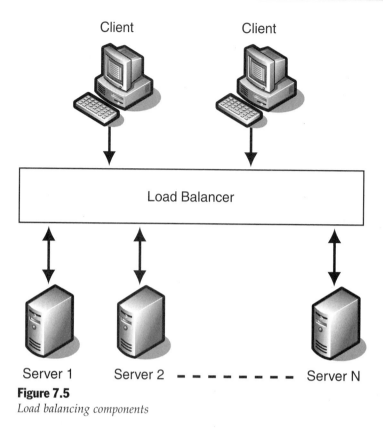

Figure 7.5

Load balancing components

When the load balancer receives a request from the client, one of the servers in the group processes the request. Every server is capable of handling the request independently. If any server is unavailable due to error or maintenance, other servers can still serve requests without being affected. Thus, the overall availability of the service is much higher than if a single server were serving all the requests. Using a single physical load balancer or a single network switch in front of a set of software load-balanced servers introduces another single point failure, however. You can use redundant load balancing devices and/or switches to mitigate this risk.

Session State Management

Applications often require user interaction among the individual steps in a complete use case. Each response the user makes during the interaction affects the choices available to the user and the state of the application as it progresses toward the user's goal. The term *session state* is often used to describe this use-case-focused state. A portion of this session state is needed only to track progress through the task and is discarded when the use case is complete; other parts of the session state are saved in long-term storage in the database if the use case concludes successfully. For example, a customer using an online shopping cart is rarely asked for payment or shipping information until he or she has selected a checkout button, which is not enabled until there is at least one item in the shopping cart.

Distributed applications typically call software components on remote servers over a network connection. The application must track the changes in session state that occur between the individual steps to provide continuity between them. Application designers typically maintain session state in one of three basic places:

- **Client**. Application designers store each user's session state on the user's computer.

- **Intermediate server**. Application designers store session state on a computer that serves as an intermediary between client computers and the database servers on which the user's information is permanently stored.

- **Database server**. Application designers store session state in the database server along with other long-term application and user data.

Only the intermediate server approach affects this pattern. Each approach and its advantages and disadvantages are described in detail in Chapter 2, "Designing for Scalability," of *Designing for Scalability with Microsoft Windows DNA* [Sundblad00].

A simple solution such as the one shown in Figure 7.5 is good enough when all the servers are stateless; that is, after a server serves a request, the state of the server is restored to the default value. There are two scenarios in which the server can be stateless. In one, the client does not need a session; that is, each request is a single unit of work, and no temporary values persist between requests. In the other scenario, known as *client session management*, the client itself keeps the state of a session and sends the session state information within the request so that any server can pick up the request and keep processing it.

In *server session management* scenarios, the server maintains the state of a user session. Server session management requires the load balancer to direct all requests from one client within the same user session to the same server instance. This mechanism is often called *server affinity*.

One inherent concern to session management is that if the server goes offline due to error or maintenance, the client's work could be lost and the client would have to resend all the previous requests from the lost session. In some cases, occasional session loss is not a major problem for the user. For example, in an online map search application, if the server loses an address that the user has just typed, it's not too much trouble for the user to retype the address. In other cases, however, session loss could be extremely inconvenient. For example, in an online leasing application with a stateless client, it may take the user 10 minutes to type several pages worth of information into a contract form. You certainly do not want the user spend another 10 minutes retyping all of the information if one of the servers in the load balancing group goes offline. To avoid session loss due to server failure in a load balancing group, there are two approaches: centralized state management and asynchronous session state management. Figure 7.6 shows centralized state management.

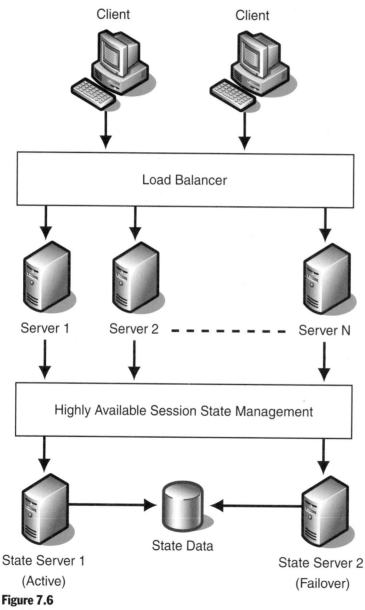

Figure 7.6
Load balancing and centralized state management

The centralized state management approach stores the session state information on a centralized server in a different tier from the application servers. Each time the application server receives a request that is part of a session, it fetches the session state from the session management server before processing the request. The session management service can be a database or another type of application that runs on a server that stores shared resources and is configured for high reliability. For more information about how to improve fault-tolerance on shared resources, see the *Failover Cluster* pattern.

Figure 7.7 shows asynchronous session state management.

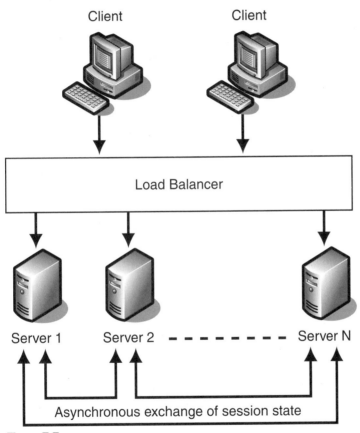

Figure 7.7
Load balancing and asynchronous session state management

Using the asynchronous session state management approach, every server broadcasts its session state to all other servers whenever the session state is changed; therefore, every server contains the state information for all sessions, and any server can process a request that is part of a session. Session state also survives individual server failures. This solution is cheaper because no extra equipment is required but harder to configure and maintain because it involves asynchronous calls. Storing the state for all sessions on every server can also be less efficient.

Implementation

The two major categories of load balancing implementations are:

- **Software-based load balancing.** *Software-based load balancing* consists of special software that is installed on the servers in a load-balanced cluster. The software dispatches or accepts requests from the client to the servers, based on different algorithms. The algorithms can be a simple round-robin algorithm or a much more complicated algorithm that considers server affinity. For example, Microsoft® Network Load Balancing is a load balancing software for Web farms, and Microsoft Component Load Balancing is a load balancing software for application farms.

- **Hardware-based load balancing.** *Hardware-based load balancing* consists of a specialized switch or router with software to give it load balancing functionality. This solution integrates switching and load balancing into a single device, which reduces the amount of extra hardware that is required to implement load balancing. Combining the two functions, however, also makes the device more difficult to troubleshoot.

Example

To help you better understand how to use load balancing to achieve scalability, the following discussion compares an existing non-load-balanced solution, which contains a single system (single point of failure) in the application tier, to a highly scalable solution that maintains performance and increases availability.

Non-Load-Balanced Tier

Initially, an organization might start with a solution architecture such as the one outlined in Figure 7.8, which might meet initial performance expectations. As the load increases, however, the application tier must adapt to the increased load to maintain acceptable performance.

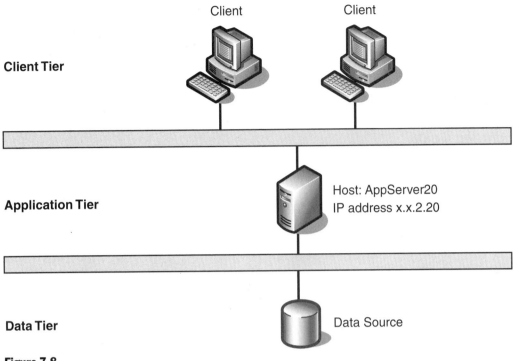

Figure 7.8
Basic solution with a single application server

In Figure 7.8, the application tier contains only one application server (AppServer20), which serves client requests. If the server becomes overloaded, the solution will either fall below acceptable performance levels or become unavailable.

Load-Balanced Tier

To increase the scalability and to maintain performance, the organization might use a load balancer to extend the application tier. The following example, shown in Figure 7.9 on the next page, adds two servers to the application tier to create a load-balanced cluster, which accesses data from the data tier and provides application access to the clients in the client tier.

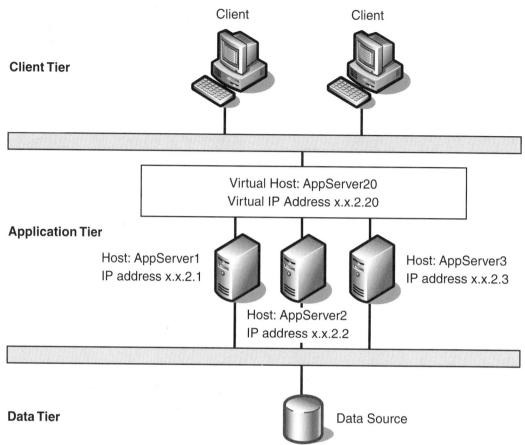

Figure 7.9
Solution with a scalable application tier

The result is a standard load-balanced design. Either a hardware device or software that is running on the host machines assigns a virtual host name (AppServer20) and an IP address to AppServer1, AppServer2, and AppServer3. The load-balanced cluster exposes this virtual IP address and host name to the network and balances the load of the incoming requests evenly across healthy servers within the group. If AppServer1 fails, the request is simply directed to AppServer2 or AppServer3. Depending upon the technology used to provide this functionality, a certain number of additional servers can be added to the load-balanced cluster to maximize scalability and stay ahead of increasing demand.

Resulting Context

The *Load-Balanced Cluster* pattern results in the following benefits and liabilities:

Benefits

- **Improved scalability**. Scalable load-balanced tiers enable the system to maintain acceptable performance levels while enhancing availability.

- **Higher availability**. Load balancing enables you to take a server offline for maintenance without loss of application availability.

- **Potential cost savings**. Multiple low-cost servers often provide a cost savings over higher-cost multiprocessor systems.

Liabilities

- **Development complexity**. A load-balanced solution can be difficult to develop if the solution must maintain state for individual transactions or users.

- **Doesn't account for network failure**. If a server or network failure occurs during a client session, a new logon may be required to reauthenticate the client and to reestablish session state.

Related Patterns

For more information, see the following related patterns:

- *Server Clustering*. *Server Clustering* discusses the use of virtual computing resources to enhance the scalability and eliminate the single points of failure that affect availability.

- *Failover Cluster*. Failover clusters can create redundancy in the infrastructure to increase availability.

- *Tiered Distribution*. *Tiered Distribution* organizes the system infrastructure into a set of physical tiers to optimize server environments for specific operational requirements and system resource usage.

Acknowledgments

[Microsoft03] Microsoft Corporation. "Technical Overview of Windows Server 2003 Clustering Services." Available on the Microsoft Windows Server 2003 Web site at: *http://www.microsoft.com/windowsserver2003/techinfo/overview/clustering.mspx*.

[Sundblad00] Sundblad, Sten and Per. *Designing for Scalability with Microsoft Windows DNA*. Microsoft Press, 2000.

Failover Cluster

Context

You have decided to use clustering in designing or modifying an infrastructure tier to provide highly available services.

Problem

How should you design a highly available infrastructure tier that protects against loss of service due to the failure of a single server or the software that it hosts?

Forces

As you design a highly available infrastructure tier, consider the following forces:

- The failure of hardware components, applications, or services can render an application unusable or unavailable. For example, imagine if a server that is delivering an application experiences a power supply failure. If this is the only server or only power supply in the server, a single point of failure exists and the application will be unavailable.

- Planned server downtime can affect the application availability. For example, if you want to update the operating system on a database server for which there is no standby server, you might have to bring down the application to patch the server.

- Monitoring and maintaining multiserver tiers increases demand on system and network resources.

- An application using a failover cluster may need special coding to ensure that when a failure occurs, the failover process is transparent to the user and the application remains available. For example, placing timeouts and retries in code that saves data to a database ensures that a transaction will complete if a failover occurs.

Solution

Install your application or service on multiple servers that are configured to take over for one another when a failure occurs. The process of one server taking over for a failed server is commonly known as *failover*. A failover cluster is a set of servers that are configured so that if one server becomes unavailable, another server automatically takes over for the failed server and continues processing. Each server in the cluster has at least one other server in the cluster identified as its standby server.

Detecting Failure

For a standby server to become the active server, it must somehow determine that the active server no longer functions. The system usually uses one of the following general types of heartbeat mechanisms to accomplish this:

- **Push heartbeats**. For *push heartbeats*, the active server sends specified signals to the standby server at a well-defined interval. If the standby server does not receive a heartbeat signal over a certain time interval, it determines that the active server failed and takes the active role. For example, the active server sends a status message to the standby server every 30 seconds. Due to a memory leak, the active server eventually runs out of memory and then crashes. The standby server notes that it has not received any status messages for 90 seconds (three intervals) and takes over as the active server.

- **Pull heartbeats**. For *pull heartbeats*, the standby server sends a request to the active server. If the active server does not respond, the standby server repeats the request a specific number of times. If the active server still does not respond, the standby server takes over as the active server. For example, the standby server may send a getCustomerDetails message to the active server every minute. Due to a memory leak, the active server eventually crashes. The standby server sends the getCustomerDetails request three times without receiving a response. At this time, the standby server takes over as the active server.

A cluster can use multiple levels of heartbeats. For example, a cluster can use push heartbeats at the server level and a set of pull heartbeats at the application level. In this configuration, the active server sends heartbeat messages to the standby server any time the server is up and connected to the network. These heartbeat messages are sent at relatively frequent intervals (for example every 5 seconds) and the standby server may be programmed to take over as active server if only two heartbeats are missed. This means that no more than 10 seconds will elapse before the standby server will detect the failure of the active server and initiate the standby process.

Quite often, heartbeats are sent over dedicated communication channels so that network congestion and general network problems do not cause spurious failovers. Additionally, the standby server might send query messages to one or more key applications running on the active server and wait for a response within a specified timeout interval. If the standby server receives the correct response, it takes no further action. To minimize the performance impact on the active server, application-level querying is usually conducted over a relatively long period, such as every minute or longer. The standby server may be programmed to wait until it has sent at least five requests without a response before taking over as the active server. This means that up to 5 minutes could elapse before the standby server initiates the failover process.

Synchronizing State

Before the standby server can start processing transactions, it must synchronize its state with the state of the failed server. There are basically three different approaches to synchronization:

- **Transaction log**. In *transaction log*, the active server maintains a log of all changes to its state. Periodically, a synchronization utility processes this log to update the standby server's state to match the state of the active server. When the active server fails, the standby server must use the synchronization utility to process any additions to the transaction log since the last update. After the state is synchronized, the standby server becomes the active server and begins processing.

- **Hot standby**. In *hot standby*, updates to the internal state of the active server are immediately copied to the standby server. Because the standby server's state is a clone of the active server's, the standby server can immediately become the active server and start processing transactions.

- **Shared storage**. In *shared storage*, both servers maintain their state on a shared storage device such as a Storage Area Network or a dual-hosted disk array. Again, the failover can happen immediately because no state synchronization is required.

Determining the Active Server

It is extremely important that only one active server exists for a given set of applications. If multiple servers behave as if they are the active server, data corruption and deadlock often result. The usual way to address this issue is by using some variant of the *active token* concept. The token, at its simplest level, is a flag that identifies a server as the active server for an application. Only one active token exists for each set of applications; therefore, only one server can own the token. When a server starts, it verifies that its partner owns the active token. If it does, the server starts as the standby server. If it does not detect the active token, it takes ownership of the active token and starts as the active server. The failover process transfers the active token to the standby server when the standby server becomes active.

In most cases, when a standby server becomes active, it is transparent to the application or user that it is supporting. When a failure does occur during a transaction, the transaction may have to be retried for it to complete successfully. This raises the importance of coding the application in such a way that the failover process remains transparent. One example of doing so is including timeouts with retries when committing data to a database.

Additionally, most servers use Internet Protocol (IP) addresses to communicate; therefore, for a failover to succeed, the infrastructure must be able to support the transferring of an IP address from one server to another. An example of this is having network switches that can support the IP address transfer. If your systems infrastructure cannot support this, you may want to use a load-balanced cluster instead of a failover cluster. For more information, see the *Load-Balanced Cluster* pattern.

Scaling Failover Cluster Servers

Scalability in failover clusters is typically achieved by scaling up, or adding more capability, to an individual server within the cluster. It is important to understand that a failover cluster must be designed to handle the expected load and that individual servers should be sized so that they can accommodate expected growth in CPU, memory, and disk usage. *Failover Cluster* servers are typically high-end multiprocessor servers that are configured for high availability by using multiple redundant subsystems. If the resource requirements of your solution are greater than the limitations of the servers in the cluster, the cluster will be extremely difficult to scale.

Example

To help you better understand how to use failover clustering to achieve high availability, the following discussion walks through refactoring an already implemented basic solution, which contains a single system (single point of failure), into a highly available solution.

Non-Failover Solution

Initially, an organization might start with a basic solution architecture such as the one outlined in Figure 7.10 on the next page. Although the solution might meet initial availability expectations, certain factors such as an increase in the number of users or a need for less application downtime may force changes in the design.

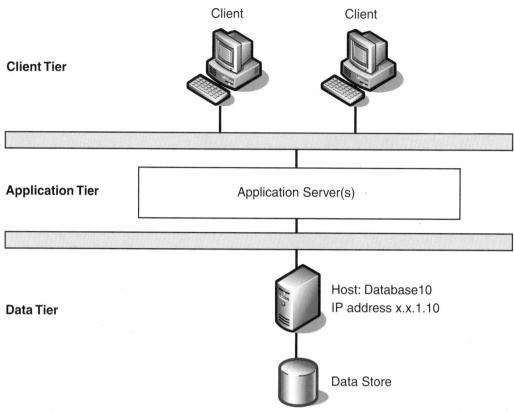

Figure 7.10
Non-failover solution with single point of failure

In Figure 7.10, the data tier contains only a single database server (Database10) that services the application tier. If the database server or the software that it hosts fails, the application server will no longer be able to access the data it needs to service the client. This will make the application unavailable to the client.

Failover Cluster Solution

To increase the availability of the solution, the organization might decide to eliminate the potential single point of failure presented by the single database server in the data tier. You could do this by adding a server to the data tier and creating a failover cluster from the existing database server, the new server, and a shared storage device. In Figure 7.11, which illustrates this change, the cluster consists of the two servers connected to a shared storage array.

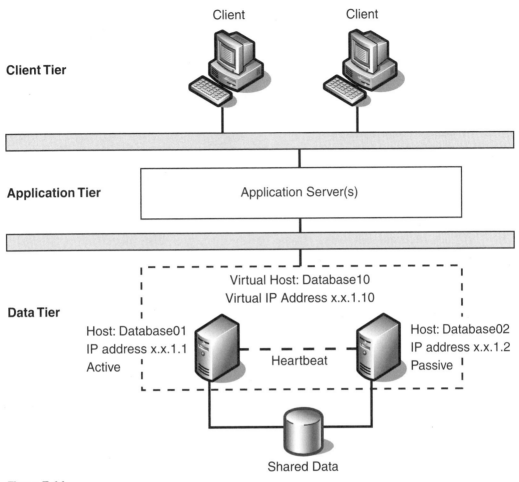

Figure 7.11
Solution with failover data tier

The first server (Database01) is the active server that handles all of the transactions. The second server (Database02), which is sitting idle, will handle transactions only if Database01 fails. The cluster exposes a virtual IP address and host name (Database10) to the network that clients and applications use.

Note: You can extend this design to include multiple active servers (more than the one shown) either with a single standby server shared among them or with each active server configured as a standby server for another active server.

Resulting Context

The *Failover Cluster* pattern results in the following benefits and liabilities:

Benefits

- **Accommodates planned downtime**. Failover clusters can allow for system downtime without affecting availability. This accommodates routine maintenance and upgrades.
- **Reduces unplanned downtime**. Failover clusters reduce application downtime related to server and software failure by eliminating single points of failure at the system and application levels.

Liabilities

- **Can increase response times**. Failover cluster designs can increase response times due to the increased load on the standby server or the need to update state information on or from multiple servers.
- **Increases equipment costs**. The additional hardware that failover clusters require can easily double the cost of an infrastructure tier.

Related Patterns

For more information, see the following related patterns:

- *Server Clustering*. *Server Clustering* presents the concept of using virtual computing resources to enhance the scalability and eliminate the single points of failure that affect availability.
- *Load-Balanced Cluster*. Load-balanced clusters can increase application performance for the current number of users by sharing workload across multiple servers.
- *Tiered Distribution*. *Tiered Distribution* organizes the system infrastructure into a set of physical tiers to optimize server environments for specific operational requirements and system resource usage.

Appendix

A

Pattlets

Pattlets are actual patterns to which this guide refers, but which it does not discuss in detail. For more information about why pattlets are used, see Chapter 2, "Organizing Patterns." The following table lists each pattlet mentioned in this guide and, where applicable, a reference to the original work that identified it.

Table A: Pattlets

Pattlet	Solution	Reference
Four-Tiered Distribution	Refines *Three-Tiered Distribution* by separating the Web servers into their own tier.	Microsoft PAG (TBD)
Abstract Factory	Provides an interface for creating families of dependent objects without specifying their concrete classes.	Gamma95
Adapter	Converts the interface of a class into another interface clients expect.	Gamma95
Application Controller	Is a centralized point for handing screen navigation and the flow of an application.	Fowler03
Application Server	An execution environment for enterprise applications. For developers, application servers provide an integrated set of core technical services and high-level frameworks. For administrators, application servers provide integrated management, operations, and deployment services and tools.	Microsoft PAG (TBD)

(continued)

Pattlet	Solution	Reference
Assembler	An instance of the Mapper [Fowler03] pattern Fowler's discussion of the Data Transfer Object (DTO) pattern talks about using an assembler object to populate the DTO with data.	Fowler03
Bound Data Control	Dynamically binds a presentation or view component directly to the data it is presenting.	Microsoft PAG (TBD)
Bridge	Decouples an abstraction from its implementation so that the two can vary independently.	Gamma95
Command(s)	Encapsulates a request as an object, thereby letting you parameterize clients with different requests, queue or log requests, and support undoable operations.	Gamma95
Decorator	Attaches additional responsibilities to an object dynamically. Decorators provide a flexible alternative to subclassing for extending functionality.	Gamma95
Facade	Provides a unified interface to a set of interfaces in a subsystem. Facade defines a higher-level interface that makes the subsystem easier to use.	Gamma95
Gateway	An object that encapsulates access to an external system or resource.	Fowler03
Implementing Data Transfer Object in .NET with Serialized Objects	Discusses implementation of Data Transfer Object using a .NET serialized object.	Microsoft PAG (TBD)
Layer Supertype	A type that acts as the supertype for all types in its layer.	Fowler03
Layers	Structures applications that can be decomposed into groups of subtasks in which each group of subtasks is at a particular level of abstraction.	Buschmann96
Mapper	An object that sets up a communication between two independent objects.	Fowler03

Pattlet	Solution	Reference
Mediator	Defines an object that encapsulates how a set of objects interact. Mediator promotes loose coupling by keeping objects from referring to each other explicitly, and lets you vary their interaction independently.	Gamma95
MonoState	Similar to *Singleton* but focuses on state rather than identity. Instead of controlling the instances of an object, *MonoState* ensures that there is only one shared state for all instances by declaring all data members static.	Martin02
Observer	Defines a one-to-many dependency between objects so that when one objects changes state, all its dependents are notified and updated automatically.	Gamma95
Naming Service	A well-known repository that maps external names to specific objects.	Mowbray97
Page Data Caching	An alternative to page caching that caches the data on which a page depends instead of caching the whole page (data plus content).	Microsoft PAG (TBD)
Page Fragment Caching	A refinement of *Page Cache*, where each page is composed of fragments and caching is controlled at the fragment level.	Microsoft PAG (TBD)
Presentation-Abstraction-Controller	Defines a structure for interactive software systems in the form of a hierarchy of cooperating agents. Every agent is responsible for a specific aspect of the application's functionality and consists of three components: presentation, abstraction, and control. This subdivision separates the human-computer interaction aspects of the agent from its functional core and its communications with other agents.	Buschmann96
Proxy	Provides a surrogate or placeholder for another object to control access to it.	Gamma95

(continued)

Pattlet	Solution	Reference
Remote Facade	Provides a coarse-grained facade on fine-grained objects to improve efficiency over a network.	Fowler03
Server Farm	A set of servers that are fed requests from a load balancer.	Microsoft PAG/CIS (TBD)
Special Case	A subclass that provides special behavior for particular cases.	Fowler03
Strategy	Defines a family of algorithms, encapsulates each one, and makes them interchangeable. *Strategy* lets the algorithm vary independently from clients that use it.	Gamma95
Table Data Gateway	An object that acts as a *Gateway* to a database table. One instance handles all the rows in the table.	Fowler03
Table Module	A single instance that handles the business logic for all rows in a database table or view.	Fowler03
Template Method	Defines the skeleton of an algorithm in an operation, deferring some steps to subclasses. Template Method lets subclasses redefine certain steps of an algorithm without changing the algorithm's structure.	Gamma95
Utility Component	A component that provides a commonly used low-level service such as persistence, logging, or lookup.	Microsoft PAG (TBD)

Bibliography

[Alexander79] Alexander, Christopher. *The Timeless Way of Building*. Oxford University Press, 1979.

[Alur01] Alur, Crupi, and Malks. *Core J2EE Patterns: Best Practices and Design Strategies*. Prentice Hall, 2001.

[Beau02] Beauchemin, Bob. *Essential ADO.NET*. Addison-Wesley, 2002.

[Bertrand00] Meyer, Bertrand. *Object-Oriented Software Construction, 2nd Edition*. Prentice-Hall, 2000.

[Burbeck92] Burbeck, Steve. "Application Programming in Smalltalk-80: How to use Model-View-Controller (MVC)." *University of Illinois in Urbana-Champaign (UIUC) Smalltalk Archive*. Available at *http://st-www.cs.uiuc.edu/users/smarch/st-docs/mvc.html*.

[Buschmann96] Buschmann, Frank, et al. *Pattern-Oriented Software Architecture*. John Wiley & Sons Ltd, 1996.

[Crocker02] Crocker, Olsen, and Jezierski. "Designing Data Tier Components and Passing Data Through Tiers." *MSDN Library*, August 2002. Available at: *http://msdn.microsoft.com/library/default.asp?url=/library/en-us/dnbda/html/boagag.asp*.

[Dhawan02] Dhawan, Priya. "Performance Comparison: .NET Remoting vs. ASP.NET Web Services." *MSDN Library*, September 2002. Available at: *http://msdn.microsoft.com/library/default.asp?url=/library/en-us/dnbda/html/bdadotnetarch14.asp*.

[Fowler01] Fowler, Martin. "To Be Explicit." *IEEE Software*, November/December 2001.

[Fowler03] Fowler, Martin. *Patterns of Enterprise Application Architecture*. Addison-Wesley, 2003.

[Gamma95] Gamma, Helm, Johnson, and Vlissides. *Design Patterns: Elements of Reusable Object-Oriented Software*. Addison-Wesley, 1995.

[Herzum00] Herzum, Peter and Sims, Oliver. *Business Component Factory*. John Wiley & Sons, Inc., 2000.

[Ingo02] Rammer, Ingo. *Advanced .NET Remoting*. Apress, 2002.

[Larman02] Larman, Craig. *Applying UML and Patterns*. Prentice-Hall PTR, 2002.

[Lea99] Lea, Doug. *Concurrent Programming in Java*, Second Edition. Addison-Wesley, 1999.

[Mackinnon00] Mackinnon, Tim, et al. "Endo-Testing: Unit Testing with Mock Objects." *eXtreme Programming and Flexible Processes in Software Engineering — XP2000* conference.

[Marcus00] Marcus, Evan, and Hal Stern. *Blueprints for High Availability: Designing Resilient Distributed Systems*. John Wiley & Sons, 2000.

[Martin02] Martin, Robert. *Agile Software Development: Principles, Patterns, and Practices.* Prentice-Hall, 2002.

[Mowbray97] Mowbray, Thomas, J., PhD. *Corba Design Patterns.* John Wiley & Sons, 1997.

[Microsoft02] Microsoft Corporation. "Working with a Typed DataSet," *.NET Developers Guide.* Available from the MSDN Library at: *http://msdn.microsoft.com /library/default.asp?url=/library/en-us/cpguide/html/cpconworkingwithtypeddataset.asp.*

[Microsoft02-1] Microsoft Corporation. "XML Web Services Overview." *.NET Framework Developer's Guide.* Available from the MSDN Library at: *http:// msdn.microsoft.com/library/default.asp?url=/library/en-us/cpguide/html /cpconwebservicesoverview.asp.*

[Microsoft02-2] Microsoft Corporation. "Application Architecture: Conceptual View." *.NET Architecture Center.* Available from MSDN at: *http://msdn.microsoft.com /architecture/default.aspx?pull=/library/en-us/dnea/html/eaappconland.asp.*

[Microsoft03] Microsoft Corporation. "Technical Overview of Windows Server 2003 Clustering Services." Available on the Microsoft Windows Server 2003 Web site at: *http://www.microsoft.com/windowsserver2003/techinfo/overview/clustering.mspx.*

[PnP02] *patterns & practices*, Microsoft Corporation. "Application Architecture for .NET: Designing Applications and Services." *MSDN Library.* Available at: *http:// msdn.microsoft.com/library/default.asp?url=/library/en-us/dnbda/html/distapp.asp.*

[Powell03] Powell, Matt. "DataSets, Web Services, DiffGrams, Arrays, and Interoperability." *MSDN Library*, February, 2003. Available at: *http:// www.msdn.microsoft.com/library/default.asp?url=/library/en-us/dnservice/html /service02112003.asp.*

[Purdy02] Purdy, Doug; Richter, Jeffrey. "Exploring the Observer Design Pattern." *MSDN Library*, January 2002. Available at: *http://msdn.microsoft.com/library /default.asp?url=/library/en-us/dnbda/html/observerpattern.asp.*

[Reilly02] Reilly, Douglas J. *Designing Microsoft ASP.NET Applications.* Microsoft Press, 2002.

[Schmidt00] Schmidt, et al. *Pattern-Oriented Software Architecture, Vol 2.* John Wiley & Sons, 2000.

[Sells03] Sells, Chris. "Sealed Sucks." *sellsbrothers.com News.* Available at: *http:// www.sellsbrothers.com/news/showTopic.aspx?ixTopic=411.*

Note: Despite its title, the "Sealed Sucks" article is actually a balanced discussion of the pros and cons of marking a class **sealed**.

[Sundblad00] Sundblad, Sten and Per. *Designing for Scalability with Microsoft Windows DNA.* Microsoft Press, 2000.

[Wildermuth01] Wildermuth, Shawn. "Typed DataSets in ADO.NET." *.NET Developer.* May 2001.

Index

Symbols

Microsoft®
patterns & practices

Proven practices for predictable results

Patterns & practices are Microsoft's recommendations for architects, software developers, and IT professionals responsible for delivering and managing enterprise systems on the Microsoft platform. Patterns & practices are available for both IT infrastructure and software development topics.

Patterns & practices are based on real-world experiences that go far beyond white papers to help enterprise IT pros and developers quickly deliver sound solutions. This technical guidance is reviewed and approved by Microsoft engineering teams, consultants, Product Support Services, and by partners and customers. Organizations around the world have used patterns & practices to:

Reduce project cost

- Exploit Microsoft's engineering efforts to save time and money on projects
- Follow Microsoft's recommendations to lower project risks and achieve predictable outcomes

Increase confidence in solutions

- Build solutions on Microsoft's proven recommendations for total confidence and predictable results
- Provide guidance that is thoroughly tested and supported by PSS, not just samples, but production quality recommendations and code

Deliver strategic IT advantage

- Gain practical advice for solving business and IT problems today, while preparing companies to take full advantage of future Microsoft technologies.

To learn more about *patterns & practices* visit: *msdn.microsoft.com/practices*

To purchase *patterns & practices* guides visit: *shop.microsoft.com/practices*

patterns & practices
Proven practices for predictable results

patterns & practices current titles

December 2002

Reference Architectures

Microsoft Systems Architecture—Enterprise Data Center   *2007 pages*
Microsoft Systems Architecture—Internet Data Center   *397 pages*
Application Architecture for .NET: Designing Applications and Services   *127 pages*
Microsoft SQL Server 2000 High Availability Series: Volume 1: Planning   *92 pages*
Microsoft SQL Server 2000 High Availability Series: Volume 2: Deployment   *128 pages*
Enterprise Notification Reference Architecture for Exchange 2000 Server   *224 pages*
Microsoft Content Integration Pack for Content Management Server 2001
      and SharePoint Portal Server 2001   *124 pages*
UNIX Application Migration Guide   *694 pages*
Microsoft Active Directory Branch Office Guide: Volume 1: Planning   *88 pages*
Microsoft Active Directory Branch Office Series Volume 2: Deployment and
      Operations   *195 pages*
Microsoft Exchange 2000 Server Hosting Series Volume 1: Planning   *227 pages*
Microsoft Exchange 2000 Server Hosting Series Volume 2: Deployment   *135 pages*
Microsoft Exchange 2000 Server Upgrade Series Volume 1: Planning   *306 pages*
Microsoft Exchange 2000 Server Upgrade Series Volume 2: Deployment   *166 pages*

Reference Building Blocks

Data Access Application Block for .NET   *279 pages*
.NET Data Access Architecture Guide *60 pages*
Designing Data Tier Components and Passing Data Through Tiers   *70 pages*
Exception Management Application Block for .NET   *307 pages*
Exception Management in .NET   *35 pages*
Monitoring in .NET Distributed Application Design   *40 pages*
Microsoft .NET/COM Migration and Interoperability   *35 pages*
Production Debugging for .NET-Connected Applications   *176 pages*
Authentication in ASP.NET: .NET Security Guidance   *58 pages*
Building Secure ASP.NET Applications: Authentication, Authorization, and
      Secure Communication   *608 pages*

Operational Practices

Security Operations Guide for Exchange 2000 Server   *136 pages*
Security Operations for Microsoft Windows 2000 Server   *188 pages*
Microsoft Exchange 2000 Server Operations Guide   *113 pages*
Microsoft SQL Server 2000 Operations Guide   *170 pages*
Deploying .NET Applications: Lifecycle Guide   *142 pages*
Team Development with Visual Studio .NET and Visual SourceSafe   *74 pages*
Backup and Restore for Internet Data Center   *294 pages*

For current list of titles visit: *msdn.microsoft.com/practices*

To purchase *patterns & practices* guides visit: *shop.microsoft.com/practices*

patterns & practices

Proven practices for predictable results